The Uprooted

Americans almost instinctively know we have a tradition and an obligation to shelter the oppressed. *The Uprooted* finally gives us a way to explain where that instinct comes from and why it represents a vital responsibility for us and for all countries."

NICHOLAS RIZZA, *Refugee Coordinator*
AMNESTY INTERNATIONAL

This exciting new book is a welcome addition to the field of youth education. It comes at a time when refugees are daily in the news and when anti-immigrant sentiment is fueled by misinformation and myth. The book is an easy-to-use set of curriculum materials providing an historical and current treatment of refugee issues.

Real-life experiences of refugees are interwoven with the complexities of immigration policy. The problem-solving exercises challenge students' analytical skills in interpreting statistics and news reports. Other concrete activities such as interviews and mock trials put students in the roles of refugees and decision-makers, enabling them to experience first-hand the importance and impact of refugee policies on the lives of individuals and on our identity as a society.

We look forward to using these materials. No other single resource is as comprehensive."

NANCY D. ARNISON, *Director*, THE B.I.A.S. PROJECT
(BUILDING IMMIGRANT AWARENESS AND SUPPORT)

Around the world the tide of refugees is rising, and with it a wave of fear and prejudice against those seeking refuge in other lands. What is it like to be uprooted, suddenly and forever, by civil war or ethnic cleansing, man-made famine or brutal human rights abuses? Just how difficult is it to win asylum in another country? Is there a difference between immigrants and refugees? What are this country's policies toward each? And how can we, as Americans and members of our own communities, best respond to the needs of the newcomers in our midst?

This imaginative resource not only addresses these questions but provides ways for students and others to experience and participate in some of the issues involved. Through a wealth of information and hands-on activities, **The Uprooted** makes a compelling bridge between the classroom and the newsroom, the pages of history and the policies shaping many lives today."

ANN ARMSTRONG CRAIG
WOMEN'S COMMISSION FOR REFUGEE WOMEN AND CHILDREN

Amnesty International is a worldwide human rights organization that works impartially for the release of prisoners of conscience; fair and prompt trials for political prisoners; and an end to torture, executions, "disappearances," and political killings.

David Donahue and Nancy Flowers are part of the Educator's Network of Amnesty International, a group committed to making human rights part of every American's basic education. The network strives to teach students and teachers at every level about their responsibility to respect, protect, and promote the rights of all people. The network provides materials, workshops and speakers for integrating human rights into the curriculum and publishes *The Fourth R,* a journal of curriculum and resource materials for teachers.

Information on the Educator's Network of Amnesty International or its educational resources can be obtained by writing to

Amnesty International
53 Jackson Street, Room 1162
Chicago IL 60604
phone: (312) 544-0200
fax: (312) 427-2060

The Uprooted

REFUGEES
AND THE
UNITED STATES

A Multidisciplinary Teaching Guide

✦

David M. Donahue and Nancy Flowers

with the Human Rights Education Steering Committee
Amnesty International USA

FOR FURTHER INFORMATION CONTACT:
Hunter House Inc., Publishers
P.O. Box 2914 • Alameda CA 94501-0914

THE AUTHORS ARE GRATEFUL FOR PERMISSION TO REPRINT THE FOLLOWING:
Jewish Grandmothers by Sydelle Kramer and Jenny Masur. Copyright © 1977 by Sydelle Kramer and Jenny Masur. Reprinted by permission of Beacon Press; *The Far East Comes Near: Autobiographical Accounts of Asian Students in America,* Lucy Nguyen-Hong-Nhiem and Joel Martin Halpern, eds. (Amherst: University of Massachusetts Press, 1989), copyright © 1989 by The University of Massachusetts Press; "The Case of Florvil Samedi," Helsinki Watch, 485 Fifth Avenue, New York NY 10017-6104; "Growth of a Nation," Copyright 1985, Time Inc. Reprinted with permission; *American Mosaic: The Immigrant Experience in the Words of Those Who Lived It,* by Joan Morrison and Charlotte Fox Zabusky, by permission of the University of Pittsburgh Press. © 1980, © 1993 by Joan Morrison and Charlotte Fox Zabusky; "Crossing the Schoolhouse Border," by Laurie Olsen, California Tomorrow Policy Research Report, 1988.

Photographs pages 32, 38, 60 © Underwood Archives; "Spoiling the Broth," page 72, © Historical Pictures/Stock Montage; The cartoon on page 73, © 1992 by *The Miami Herald;* reprinted with permission; The cartoon on page 73 © Don Wright.

Photographs pages 3, 33, 85 courtesy of UNHCR; photographs pages 7, 24 courtesy of UNHCR/A. Hollman; photograph page 26 courtesy of UNHCR/N. van Praag; photograph page 34 courtesy of UNHCR/Celig, Freiburg; photograph page 57 courtesy of UNHCR/R. Manin; photograph page 91 courtesy of UNHCR/M. Vanappelghem; photograph page 151 courtesy of UNHCR/J. Mohr; photograph page 162 courtesy of UNHCR/Coloegven; cartoons pages 6, 110 courtesy of *The Washington Post;* photographs pages 80, 82, 115, 122, 135, 141 courtesy of Eric Avery; photograph page 116 courtesy of U.S. Committee for Refugees; photograph page 164 courtesy International Institute of the East Bay.

Library of Congress Cataloging-in-Publication Data
Donahue, David M.
The uprooted : refugees and the United States : a resource curriculum /
by David M. Donahue and Nancy Flowers. — 1st ed.
p.   cm.
Includes bibliographical references (p. 174) and index.
ISBN 0-89793-122-X (pbk.) : $15.95. — ISBN 0-89793-179-3 (spiral) : $22.95
1. Refugees—Study and teaching—United States. 2. refugees—Unites States.
3. Refugees—Government policy—United States. I. Flowers, Nancy. 1940–   . II. Title.
JV66601.R4D66   1995
325' 21'0973—dc 20   95–5134
CIP

ORDERING INFORMATION

Trade bookstores and wholesalers in the U.S. and Canada, please contact

PUBLISHERS GROUP WEST
4065 Hollis, Box 8843
Emeryville CA 94608
Telephone 1-800-788-3123 or (510) 658-3453
Fax (510) 658-1834

◆

COLLEGE TEXTBOOKS/ COURSE ADOPTION ORDERS

Hunter House books are available at discounts
when purchased in bulk by schools and colleges.
For details, please contact

Special Sales Department
HUNTER HOUSE INC.
P.O. Box 2914
Alameda CA 94501–0914
Telephone (510) 865-5282
Fax (510) 865-4295

◆

SPECIAL SALES

Please contact Hunter House at the address and phone number above.

◆

ORDERS BY INDIVIDUALS OR ORGANIZATIONS

Hunter House books are available through most bookstores
or can be ordered directly from the publisher by calling toll-free:

1-800-266-5592

. . . .

PROJECT CREDITS

Project Editor: Lisa E. Lee   *Production Manager:* Paul J. Frindt
Cover Design: Jil Weil   *Book Design:* Dian-Aziza Ooka
Copy Editor: Rachel Farber   *Proofreader:* Theodora Crawford   *Index:* Kathy Talley-Jones
Sales & Marketing: Corrine M. Sahli   *Publicity & Promotion:* Darcy Cohan
Customer Support: Sharon R. A. Olson, Sam Brewer
Administration & Rights: María Jesús Aguiló
Order Fulfillment: A&A Quality Shipping Services
Publisher: Kiran S. Rana

Set in Adobe Garamond and Franklin Gothic by 847 Communications, Alameda CA

9 8 7 6 5 4 3 2 1   First edition

ACKNOWLEDGMENTS

The project has received generous help from many sources, especially from the members of Amnesty International's Human Rights Education Steering Committee and staff of Amnesty International USA. The following individuals and organizations have also made significant contributions to this work:

The Aurora Foundation
AUSTCARE
Eric Avery
Carolyn Bishop
Mabel C. McKinney-Browning, American Bar Association
The Church World Service
Suzy Comerford, Jesuit Refugee Service
Bill Fernekes
Lorna Gentry, Teacher's Network Amnesty International Canada
Anneliese Hollman, UN High Commissioner for Refugees
International Catholic Child Bureau Incorporated
International Institute of the East Bay
Melissa Jameson
The Lutheran Immigration and Refugee Service
Peter Martorella
James McManus, Castilleja School
Deborah Menkart, Network of Educators on Central America
Frank Moan, S.J., *Refugee Voices*
Terry Mullen
Dian-Aziza Ooka
Koula Papanicolas, U.S. Committee for Refugees
David Shiman
The Smithsonian Institute
Keith Suter, Trinity Peace Research Institute
United Nations High Commissioner for Refugees
U.S. Catholic Conference Migration and Refugee Service
U.S. Committee for Refugees
University of Minnesota Human Rights Center
Dava Jo Walker, U.S. Catholic Conference
Barbara Welch
Laurie Wiseberg, Human Rights Internet
Women's Commission for Refugee Women and Children

CONTENTS

PART I: INTRODUCTION

PART II: REFUGEES AND U.S. HISTORY

Contents, continued

PART III: REFUGEES AND THE UNITED STATES TODAY

Contents, continued

PART IV: REFUGEES AND YOUR COMMUNITY

Contents, continued

PART V: APPENDICES

LIST OF ACTIVITIES

This resource curriculum represents the volunteer efforts of many dedicated educators within Amnesty International USA and its Human Rights Education Steering Committee.

Project Coordinators: David M. Donahue and Nancy Flowers

Contributors: David M. Donahue, James Flannery, Nancy Flowers, Sean Fottrell, Rick Halperin, Ed Markarian, Jeanne Paterson.

AMNESTY INTERNATIONAL AND REFUGEES

Amnesty International is a worldwide movement that works to protect human rights. It seeks the release of prisoners of conscience, people detained for their beliefs, color, sex, ethnic origin, language, or religion who have not used or advocated violence. It works for fair and prompt trials for all political prisoners and opposes the death penalty and all other forms of torture. Amnesty does not support or oppose any government or political system but is concerned only with the protection of rights guaranteed to all peoples of the world by the United Nation's *Universal Declaration of Human Rights* (UDHR).

Amnesty International opposes the forcible return of anyone to a country where he or she is likely to become a prisoner of conscience, to "disappear," or to be tortured or executed. To help these refugees Amnesty provides information to governments of asylum countries about the risks refugees might face if they are forced to return home. It also seeks to protect the rights of people claiming to be refugees, asking governments to give them a fair hearing When asylum seekers are detained, Amnesty works to see that they receive a prompt, fair, individual hearing.

Believing that educating about human rights is an important way to protect human rights, Amnesty International also makes an effort to inform people about the protection that they are entitled to under international law. This curriculum is an example of that effort.

PART I

INTRODUCTION

✦

WHY LEARN ABOUT REFUGEES?

Today more than 20 million people on the face of the globe have been forced to leave their homes. Yet most other people know little or nothing about who these refugees are, where they came from, where they are, or why they have fled. In fact, most Americans cannot distinguish between refugees and immigrants, even among people who enter their own communities to create new lives.

Since the colonial period the United States has been a place of refuge for people fleeing persecution, and today the United States admits more refugees than any other nation. In 1992, for example, this country admitted over 137 thousand refugees, while the next most receptive countries were Canada (36.4 thousand), United Kingdom (16.4 thousand), Sweden (12.8 thousand), and France (10.9 thousand). Although these figures suggest a generous refugee policy, the United States government rejects many requests for asylum here. All refugees are not equal before U.S. law, and complex political and social factors determine who is granted safe haven in the United States and who is excluded.

The heartfelt wish of almost all refugees, however, is not to settle in the United States or any other country but to go back to their own homes. People usually flee across the border into the nearest neighboring nation and wait, often for years, for conditions to improve so they can safely return home. Most of the world's refugees are from poor countries too distant from the United States to make travel here even a possibility. Furthermore, differences of climate, culture, language, and custom make resettlement in the United States far from desirable for most refugees.

No one wants to become a refugee. Refugees are people uprooted by events so terrible that they must flee to survive. Except in cases of natural disaster, most people would never choose to give up everything and everyone they know to live among strangers if their human rights were being respected. Thus an essential way to address refugee problems is to address the forces that violate people's rights: armed conflict, economic and social injustice, and political persecution. In the final analysis, the basic solution to the refugee problem lies in achieving greater respect for human rights in all nations.

"War is the ugliest thing I have ever seen! There is nothing like going back to one's homeland. It is a hundred times better to be living under a tree in one's own country than to be in a comfortable house in a foreign land."

—Dona Transito, a Salvadoran refugee about to return home

GOALS OF THIS CURRICULUM

TO PROVIDE INFORMATION

■ To examine a complex social problem that is both a historical and current phenomenon around the world and in the United States

■ To explore the interrelation of political, economic, and cultural systems that create refugee problems

■ To relate the impact of global events, cross-cultural values, and national politics and legislation to the student's individual life and community

TO BUILD EMPATHY

■ To put a human face on factual information about political and economic instability

■ To recognize the importance of community

■ To realize the emotional trauma of flight, loss, displacement, exclusion, and assimilation

TO STIMULATE SOCIAL ACTION

■ To promote informed, critical thinking as a function of U.S. and world citizenship

■ To affirm a humane conception of justice that asserts the student's responsibility to respect, protect, and promote the rights of others

TO ESTABLISH STANDARDS FOR INQUIRY AND EXPRESSION IN A VARIETY OF SUBJECT AREAS

■ To accept conflict as a factor of all cultures and to explore how and if resolution is possible

■ To express oneself with verbal precision, factual accuracy, and creative imagination

Photo courtesy UNHCR

Most refugees want to return to their homeland, but cannot because of persecution there. When persecution no longer exists, the UNHCR helps refugees return to their native country.

USING THIS CURRICULUM

Believing that people of all ages need to learn about refugees, the authors of this resource curriculum hope it will be used both within and beyond the school setting. These activities are adaptable to adult civic groups, youth organizations, English as a Second Language classes, religious education classes, and any other place where people are trying to learn about the world around them today.

Here are a few guidelines for using the curriculum:

1. **Every activity can be used independently.** Few groups will have the time to work through the whole curriculum from start to finish. Each activity is a self-contained unit and does not presuppose information contained in previous activities. Suggestions for appropriate subject areas and age level are listed with each activity.

2. **Every activity is accompanied by a full description.** Suggestions for effective use, necessary handouts, and maps are included with each activity.

3. **All necessary background material is provided in the text.** Some may be used by the teacher or leader and others photocopied for the group.

4. **Most activities offer suggestions for further action or inquiry.** These include activities that encourage participants to take appropriate actions in their home communities.

The New Colussus
Emma Lazurus, 1883
Inscribed on the base of the Statue of Liberty

Not like the brazen giant of Greek fame,
With conquering limbs astride from land to land;
Here at our sea-washed sunset gates shall stand
A mighty woman with a torch, whose flame
Is the imprisoned lightning, and her name
Mother of Exiles. From her beacon-hand
Glows world-wide welcome; her mild eyes command
The air-bridged harbor that twin cities frame.
"Keep, ancient lands, your storied pomp," cries she
With silent lips. "Give me your tired, your poor,
Your huddled masses yearning to breathe free,
The wretched refuse of your teeming shore.
Send these, the homeless, tempest-tost to me.
I lift my lamp beside the golden door!"

LEARNING ABOUT REFUGEES: AN OVERVIEW

WHO IS A REFUGEE?

The moment people flee across the borders of their home country because they fear persecution for reasons of race, religion, or membership in a particular national, social, or political group, they become refugees. They are forced to leave their homes, usually against their will, and they cannot return unless conditions change.

HOW MANY REFUGEES ARE THERE?

The United Nations High Commission for Refugees (UNHCR) estimates more than 20 million refugees throughout the world, the majority from Africa, Central America, the Middle East, Asia, and Europe. More than 80% of these refugees are women and children, a vulnerable population who often need assistance. Although the first choice of refugees is to return to their homelands, many have sought asylum in the United States. Between 1975 and 1992 more than 1.7 million refugees were resettled in the United States

DO REFUGEES HAVE RIGHTS?

The international protection of refugees is incorporated in the Convention Relating to the Status of Refugees, adopted at Geneva in 1951. The convention stipulates that refugees shall not be returned

"One day, a day just like any other, my younger brother died. In a very confusing investigation, all we could find out was that the vehicle in which he was driving with a friend was hit by a heavy truck.

"One day, a day just like any other, my niece Carminda disappeared. She was captured by men in plain clothes. Her father was never to see her again.

"One day, a day just like any other, Jaime, a poet, was arrested in town. Later on, we saw his body, savagely tortured and mutilated . . . .

"Another day, another day like any other, I got off the bus at the university and was told that a death threat had been received by our newspaper. . . . Someone working with the Archbishop said to me, 'the country needs you here, but the people need you alive. Wherever you get to, wherever you happen to be, continue to write.' After our conversation I presented myself to the Mexican embassy and asked for a visa so that I could leave the country. . . .

"But will I ever be back walking through the valleys and hills of my small Central American country? I don't know. I only hope that life continues to nourish me with an understanding of the citizens of the world. Because I have learned that when you have only one breath left, when you have only one last penny in your packet, your solitude and the love you have inside you are enough to enable you to start again."

—Julio Henriquez, 46-year-old poet, refugee in Canada

Photo courtesy The Washington Post

*Asylum seeker being consoled at a
detention center.*

against their will to a country where their lives would be endangered. The convention also describes the basic rights a refugee can claim in the country of asylum, including the right to work, the right to social and other benefits, and the right to identity papers and travel documents. The United States is a signatory to this convention.

WHO HAS THE RESPONSIBILITY TO CARE FOR REFUGEES?

Protecting and caring for refugees is the special charge of the United Nations High Commission for Refugees, which assists the country of asylum in coping with the needs of refugees. In the United States refugees are the responsibility of many federal agencies ranging from the Immigration and Naturalization Service, which makes all decisions about asylum claims and processes all applications for resettlement by refugees, to other agencies that oversee health and social service programs for refugees. In addition, many local, national, and international humanitarian organizations offer assistance to refugees. Private individuals acting independently also make important contributions to the welfare of refugees, especially in their own communities.

> "If a stranger lives with you in your land, do not molest him. You must count him as one of your own countrymen and love him as yourself—for you were once strangers yourselves in Egypt."
>
> —Leviticus 19:33–34

> If one amongst the Pagans
> Asks thee for asylum,
> Grant it to him
> So that he may hear the word
> Of God; and then escort him
> To where he can be secure.
>
> —The Koran 8.72

HOW ARE REFUGEE PROBLEMS RESOLVED?

There are five main options:

- **Voluntary Repatriation:** The refugee chooses to return to the country of origin. This is usually the first choice of most refugees.
- **Involuntary Repatriation:** The refugee is denied asylum in a country and is forced to return to the country of origin.
- **Asylum/Refugee Status:** The refugee is granted asylum or refugee status in the first country to which he or she flees.
- **Resettlement:** The refugee flees to one country and then resettles permanently in a third country, often one with a different culture. Many refugees in the United States were resettled here because returning to their home countries was impossible.
- **Local Integration:** The refugee settles permanently in the country that offers first asylum. This solution is possible only when that country has the land, resources, and desire to settle refugees.

Photo courtesy UNHCR/A. Hollman

At this center in Hong Kong refugees wait to be resettled.

WHAT ARE THE GLOBAL AND DOMESTIC
ISSUES RELATED TO REFUGEES?

Refugees present a number of problems to the world community and the United States. The U.S. is currently debating its financial ability and environmental capacity to handle large numbers of refugees, while the public complains of "compassion fatigue" and questions its psychic resources for responding to the multitude of refugee crises across the globe. U.S. courts are deciding the legality of providing sanctuary and listening to appeals for asylum. In addition the government is asking whether asylum seekers coming to the U.S. are "political refugees" escaping persecution or whether they are "economic refugees" seeking a better standard of living. Meanwhile many humanitarian organizations fight the deportation of thousands of asylum seekers who may meet with violence when they return home.

A complex problem like refugees must be examined through the lenses of many disciplines: geography, history, law, economics, political science, psychology. No simple explanations or simple solutions exist. Studying the interrelatedness of factors in this one aspect of human life challenges us to examine conflicting rights and opinions and to explore how and if resolution is possible. Studying refugees thus becomes a model for approaching other complex global and national issues.

"I felt I could not be honest at the asylum hearing, and I did not feel at liberty to say so. All questions the judge asked me had a double meaning: the answers could have been both 'Yes' and 'No.' Everything in the courtroom was meant to frighten me, to intimidate me, to humiliate me, to throw me out of the country. It seems to me that with these kinds of proceedings, it doesn't matter whether one goes with or without a lawyer."

—Guatemalan detained in Boston

FACT OR FICTION?
An Introductory Activity

OVERVIEW: Students compare facts with some of their own prejudices and preconceived notions about refugees. In the process, they become acquainted with the enormity of the refugee situation in the United States and world today, as well as with some basic facts about who refugees are, and why and to where they flee.

AGE LEVEL: Middle school–adults

TIME: About 30 minutes

MATERIALS:
- Handout 1: Fact or Fiction? cards
- Handout 2: Information cards

SUBJECT AREAS: Current events, geography, U.S. history, world studies

OBJECTIVES:
- To assess the validity of personal prejudices and preconceived notions about refugees
- To understand some of the 5 *W*'s (who, what, why, where, and when) about refugees in the United States

PART 1

Ask students to find a partner for this activity. Duplicate enough **Fact or Fiction? cards** for each pair in two separate envelopes marked **Fact or Fiction?** and **Information.** Have students read the **Fact or Fiction? cards** first without looking at the **Information cards.** Ask pairs to decide whether the statements on the cards are true or false and to keep a tally on a separate sheet of paper.

PART 2

After pairs have made their initial decisions, have them look at the **Information cards** and match each one with a **Fact or Fiction? card** to determine whether they correctly identified the statement as true or false.

FURTHER ACTIVITY

Assign students to make their own sets of **Fact or Fiction?** and **Information cards.** Suggest they look in encyclopedias, history books, or newspaper and magazine articles for more facts about refugees.

FACT OR FICTION? CARDS

FACT OR FICTION?

Since the end of World War II, more refugees have come to the United States from Vietnam than from any other country.

FACT OR FICTION?

When they come to the United States most refugees arrive in New York.

FACT OR FICTION?

Most of the world's refugees are fleeing to the United States.

FACT OR FICTION?

About 100,000 refugees apply for asylum in the United States every year.

FACT OR FICTION?

Most refugees arrive in the United States without help from any organization either by sneaking across the border or landing in boats they sail from their homelands.

FACT OR FICTION?

Because of war and guerrilla fighting in Central America, the United States usually grants asylum to people from that region.

From *The Uprooted: Refugees and the United States* ©1995 Nancy Flowers and David M. Donahue, published by Hunter House Inc., Publishers, 1-800-266-5592.

FACT OR FICTION?

The President decides how many refugees will be admitted to the United States.

FACT OR FICTION?

Formal government policy towards those fleeing to the United States to escape persecution was first developed during the administration of George Washington.

FACT OR FICTION?

The largest number of refugees entering the United States during the 1980s were from Mexico and Central America.

FACT OR FICTION?

The United States considers a refugee to be anyone fleeing persecution based on race, religion, nationality, membership in a group, or political opinion as well as anyone fleeing poverty and the lack of economic opportunity.

FACT OR FICTION?

The United States grants asylum to more refugees than any other country in the world.

FACT OR FICTION?

The quota for persons granted asylum in the United States is 10,000 annually, with most of those slots reserved for persons fleeing communist regimes.

INFORMATION CARDS

INFORMATION

In the years since World War II, more refugees have come to the United States from Cuba than from any other country. The Vietnamese are the second biggest refugee group during that period, followed by refugees from Poland, Laos, the former U.S.S.R., and Cambodia.

INFORMATION

In April, 1989, (a typical month) 1,830 refugees arrived in California, more than any other state. New York ranked as the second most popular point of arrival with 878 refugees arriving. Florida, Texas, Massachusetts, and Illinois (in that order) were the other most popular points of arrival for refugees to the United States.

INFORMATION

Most of the world's refugees live too far away from the United States to afford travel here. In addition, many refugees are from nations with cultural and social backgrounds very different from the U.S., making resettlement here less than desirable. More than 80% of the world's refugees live in poor countries, often next to the nations from which they flee. The first choice of most refugees is to return home when conditions become safe.

INFORMATION

During the 1980s, applications for asylum fluctuated (for example, 193,000 applications in 1981) but generally about 100,000 refugees applied for asylum each year during the 1980s.

INFORMATION

Only about 10 percent of refugees arrive in the United States without help from any organization. Most are sponsored by voluntary agencies, such as the United States Catholic Conference, the Hebrew Immigrant Aid Society, or the Lutheran Immigration and Refugee Service.

INFORMATION

Cases of people seeking asylum in the United States from El Salvador, Guatemala, and Honduras have some of the lowest approval rates. By contrast people from the former U.S.S.R., China, and Romania have had some of the highest approval rates in the recent past.

From *The Uprooted: Refugees and the United States* ©1995 Nancy Flowers and David M. Donahue, published by Hunter House Inc., Publishers, 1-800-266-5592.

INFORMATION

The number of refugees admitted to the United States during a particular year is determined by the President after consultation with the Judiciary Committees of the House of Representatives and Senate. After conferring with these committees, the President can adjust the number of refugees to be admitted if a world emergency occurs that requires such a change. For fiscal year 1992, the president set a ceiling of 142,000 refugees.

INFORMATION

Although the United States has been a place of refuge for persons fleeing persecution since the colonial era, refugees were not considered separately from immigrants until after the end of World War II.

INFORMATION

Tremendous legal and illegal immigration to the United States from Mexico and Central America occurred during the 1980s. The largest number of refugees, however, was from Southeast Asia. Other large refugee groups during the 1980s included Soviets, Poles, Afghans, Ethiopians, and Romanians.

INFORMATION

The United States definition of a refugee includes persons fleeing persecution based on race, religion, nationality, membership in a group, or political opinion. In addition, anyone fleeing a well-founded fear of persecution on account of the previous reasons is also a refugee. Persons who are deemed solely to be fleeing poverty and the lack of economic opportunity are *not* considered refugees. While immigration to the United States may be an option for such people, seeking refugee status or asylum is not.

INFORMATION

The United States admits far more refugees than any other nation. For example, in 1992 the U.S. admitted 137,395 refugees. Next were Canada (36,409), United Kingdom (16,435), Sweden (12,791), and France (10,943).

INFORMATION

There is no annual quota for people granted asylum in the United States. Each request for asylum is determined on an individual basis. Ceilings exist only for the number of refugees who will be resettled in the United States from overseas.

From *The Uprooted: Refugees and the United States* ©1995 Nancy Flowers and David M. Donahue, published by Hunter House Inc., Publishers, 1-800-266-5592.

WHAT'S THE NEWS?
A Current-Events and Geography Activity

OVERVIEW: Using recent newspapers and news magazines, students recognize the extent and global nature of the refugee situation today. In addition they learn that refugees are forced to flee for a variety of reasons ranging from wars to persecution to natural disasters. By looking through local newspapers, students realize that refugees are a concern not only in distant corners of the world but in their own country and perhaps their own community as well.

AGE LEVEL: All levels

TIME: 30–45 minutes

MATERIALS:

- National and local newspapers and news magazines

- A world map

- A copy of the Universal Declaration of Human Rights (see Appendix E)

SUBJECT AREAS: current events, geography, language arts, U.S. history, world studies

OBJECTIVES:

- To describe current refugee stories in the news and explain some of the causes of refugee problems such as wars, natural disasters, and persecution

- To understand how refugees' human rights are often not respected

- To appreciate the complexity and global nature of the refugee problem

- To become aware of refugees in the United States and the local community

PART 1

Divide the class into groups of four.

One student in each group will be the facilitator, making sure the group accomplishes its task.

Another student will be the recorder, writing down the group's work.

Another student will be the reporter, reporting the group's findings back to the class.

The other student will be the timekeeper, making sure the group accomplishes its task in the allotted time.

All students will read newspaper articles and contribute their ideas to the group discussion.

Give each group of students several recent newspapers and magazines. Ask them to search for articles about refugees and cut them out.

Ask each group to do the following:

1. Summarize each article in three to four sentences.

2. Determine why the refugees had to leave their home (e.g., war, natural disaster, persecution, economic crisis).

3. Use the Universal Declaration of Human Rights to identify any abuses of these peoples' human rights.

4. Suggest what you and other students can do to help refugees.

5. *Optional:* you may ask students to paste their articles and suggestions about how to help on poster or mural paper and display these in the room.

PART 2

Have each group of students report its findings to the rest of the class. If a bulletin board is available, display a world map and pin the articles or poster displays to the board and connect each article with a piece of colored string or yarn to the country from where the story originates. This will help reinforce the idea that refugees are both a local and global concern.

FURTHER ACTIVITIES

1. Ask students to watch several newspapers for continuing coverage of one particular refugee story. Pose the following questions for students to answer in discussion or writing:

   ■ For how long did coverage of this story continue?

   ■ Did the articles get longer or shorter?

   ■ What are some possible reasons for the story disappearing or becoming more important?

   ■ Did one particular newspaper do a better job than others of covering a refugee story? If so, what made the quality of its coverage better?

   ■ What questions do you have about the issue after reading a particular paper's coverage?

   ■ What additional information would you like to know about the subject?

   ■ Were any particular issues neglected in the coverage of these refugee stories?

2. If students were struck by a particular newspaper's coverage of refugee issues, encourage them to write to the editor either praising or criticizing the paper. See the activity **The Power of the Pen,** page 165, for suggestions on organizing letter writing.

"THREE STRIKES—YOU'RE OUT"
An Introduction to Refugee Studies

OVERVIEW: By placing the student in situations of disorientation, arbitrary rulings, and pressured decision-making, this exercise simulates some of the emotional factors of refugee reality and also conveys factual information about global refugee problems.

AGE LEVEL: Middle school–adult

TIME: 2–3 hours

MATERIALS:
- Handout 3: Creole Asylum Application
- Handout 4: Where Do They Come from? Where Do They Go?
- Handout 5: U.S. Admissions Statistics
- Handout 6: Resettlement and Asylum Statistics
- World map, pencils, scratch paper

SUBJECT AREAS: Current events, geography, religious studies, U.S. history, world studies

OBJECTIVES:
- To foster empathy for those involved in the stressful and arbitrary asylum-seeking process
- To increase information about and interest in global refugee problems, the factors that create refugees, and how the U.S. government makes distinctions among different refugee groups
- To help students identify areas in which they lack information and understand how and where to find it

NOTE: The teacher's ability to "act the part" in this activity contributes to students' sense of appropriate disorientation and their realization of the vulnerability of refugees to factors of chance.

The exercise is adaptable to different ages and contexts, but all require opportunities to express their responses at every phase.

Arousing students' awareness of areas in which they lack information is an important goal of this lesson. Avoid the temptation to provide the missing information. Encourage them instead to consider how they can find out for themselves.

PART 1. STRIKE ONE: THE APPLICATION FOR ASYLUM

Wait a few minutes before entering the room. Let the group gather and anticipate your arrival. When you enter, do not greet or acknowledge anyone. Instead, begin passing out the Creole applications for asylum, **Handout 3: Asylum Application.** Ignore questions, Say only, "Complete this form. You must answer all the questions. You have three minutes." If anyone comes in late, give them the forms with the comment: "You're late. Now you have only ____ minutes left to complete this form." Ignore protests that they cannot read the form.

After less than three minutes, announce, "The time is up. Put your pencils or pens down." Some people will begin to "get the point" right away. Others will protest vehemently and others will give up quickly. Some won't have any idea what is going on. Ignore all responses.

Collect the forms again without any personal exchanges with the group. Then explain that students have just filled out an application for asylum as a refugee. A positive or "WI" answer to any question under number 15 is grounds for denial of asylum. Go through the forms reading the names of individuals, such as "I see, _____, you have answered yes to question number 15a. Asylum denied." If students ask why a *yes* answer means exclusion, reply, "It's the rule."

Ask the group what they think the point of the preceding exercise was. Explain that this is an application for asylum in Spanish Creole and that time pressures, a language they could barely decipher, unfriendly treatment, and uncertainty about the "rules" were intended to give a sense of some of the feelings asylum applicants experience.

Discuss with the group how they feel during this experience. Ask:

■ How did you feel when you were expected to fill out an unintelligible form? How did you feel to be hurried?

■ How did you feel when you could not get any help with your questions?

PART 2. DEFINING TERMS

Ask students to suggest definitions for *refugee* and *asylum,* and write their suggested definitions on the board under each term. After a number of definitions have been offered, explain that the formal definitions used by the United Nations are helpful. Write these definitions on the board or display them from an overhead projector.

REFUGEE: A person who leaves his or her country of origin because of a "well-founded fear of persecution for reasons of race, religion, nationality, membership in a particular social group, or political opinion." (Definition used by U.S. Refugee Act of 1980 and the United Nations.)

POLITICAL ASYLUM: Legal permission to live in a country given by its government to people fleeing danger or persecution in their country of origin.

Help the group identify which of their own definitions conform to those of the United Nations. Clarify the distinction between a *refugee* and an *immigrant,* "a person who chooses voluntarily to come to a country to settle permanently and obtain citizenship."

PART 3. STRIKE TWO: WHERE DO THEY COME FROM? WHERE DO THEY GO?

Introduce some refugee statistics by asking the group to name the countries and/or regions of the world where they think the 20 million refugees are to be found. As an area is mentioned, first ask someone to locate that area on the map. Then write on the board the name of the country, its continent, and the name of the person who mentioned that country. The name of the person who suggested the country will seem irrelevant at this point in the activity, but will be used later.

Once the group has covered most of the major regions, pass out or display from an overhead projector **Handout 4: Where Do They Come from? Where Do They Go?** Ask students to add to the written list and locate on the map any areas omitted in their discussion. Then ask them to survey the whole list and speculate on the reasons for refugees in each major region; e.g., famine, war, natural disaster, etc. The group will have information about some regions while they may know nothing about other areas. Resist the temptation to fill in additional information. Instead ask the group, "What further information do you need to explain these statistics?" Make a list of their suggestions.

PART 4. INTRODUCING UNITED STATES REFUGEE POLICIES

Review the definition of *refugee*. Ask the group to evaluate whether, on the basis of what they know about why people fled each of these major regions, they think these different groups would fit the definitions based on "reasonable fear." Then distribute or display from an overhead projector **Handout 5: U.S. Admissions Statistics.** Referring to the person whose name was written on the board as suggesting a country with a low admission rate, say something like "Sorry, Jean, you're from _____. According to these statistics, you have only a ____% chance of admission to the United States." The purpose of this part of the activity is to simulate the frustration and uncertainty refugees experience when faced with seemingly arbitrary rules and regulations.

Ask the group, "Why do you think the approval rate is high for some countries and low for others?" Again resist the temptation to offer an opinion or information. Write students' responses on the board.

Again ask the group, "What further information do you need?" and add suggestions to the previous list.

Conclude this part by asking the group, "How would you go about finding the information you need?" Assign individuals or small groups to investigate listed areas to discover why they have high concentrations of refugees. Older participants who wish to investigate U.S. policy will need guidance in finding sources such as encyclopedias and reference books like those listed in **Appendix B: Refugees and the United States—A Teaching Bibliography.** Invite students to report their findings at the next meeting.

PART 5. STRIKE THREE: YOU'RE OUT

Work through **Activity 4: Packing Your Suitcase,** on page 24 with the class.

PART 6. CONCLUSION

1. Review the main points of this lesson:
- definition of *refugee*
- reasons people flee
- definition of *political asylum*
- bases for granting asylum
- frustration and uncertainty felt by refugees as they leave their homes

2. Ask students to recall what they felt uninformed about, such as why certain areas have high concentrations of refugees and why different groups have high or low rates of approval for refugee status. Ask them to discuss useful resources and ways to find information about refugees and refugee policy.

FURTHER ACTIVITIES:

Offer the group opportunities to assimilate and express what they have learned. Try to conclude by leaving them with unanswered questions and new interest in and concern about refugees. The following are appropriate closing activities.

1. Ask students to identify a current world event that might cause people to flee their homes and become refugees. Suggest they take the part of a refugee from such a situation and make an argument to the Immigration and Naturalization Service (INS) for why they should be admitted as a refugee.

2. Have students imagine they are lawyers representing a refugee from one of the countries listed in **Handout 5: U.S. Admissions Statistics** as having a very low rate of admission. Ask them to write arguments in favor of their clients being granted asylum. As an alternative, they might imagine they are lawyers for the government and write arguments showing why the refugee should not be granted asylum.

3. Encourage students to think of an historical event that created many refugees. Assign them to write an account of what their experiences might have been if they had been refugees in that time and place.

ASYLUM APPLICATION

1. APELLIDO:_____ A#_____

2. PRIMER NOMBRE: _____

3. FECHA DE NACIMIENTO:_____

4. PAIS, CIUDAD DE RESIDENCIA: _____

5. OU GENYEN FANMI NA ETAZINI? _____

6. KISA YO YE POU WOU:_____

_____

_____

7. KI PAPYE IMIGRASYON FANMI OU YO GENYEN ISIT: _____

_____

8. KI LAJ OU? _____ KI SEX OU?   FI   GASON

9. ESKE OU ANSENT?   WI   NON

10. ESKE OU GEN AVOKA?   WI   NON

11. NON AVOKA-W? _____

12. HA RECIBIBO ALGUNOS PAPELES DE LA MIGRA? CUALES SON?

_____

13. OU JAM AL NAHOKEN JYMAN? WI NON

14. CANTIDAD DE FIANZA: _____

15. ESKE YO FANM PESEKITE-W EN AYITI POU OKEN NAN REZON SA YO? WI NON

a. ou te fe pati nan you group politik?	WI	NON
b. senpatize ak group politik ki kont gouvenman-an?	WI	NON
c. fe pati de group elev aktivis?	WI	NON
d. pwoblem ak Tonton Makout?	WI	NON
e. fe pati de yon oganizasyon relijye?	WI	NON
f. paske ou tap bay opinyon politik-ou?	WI	NON
g. paske ou genyen ganmi ki nan aktivite politik?	WI	NON
h. paske ou te manb nan yon group sosyal?	WI	NON

From *The Uprooted: Refugees and the United States* ©1995 Nancy Flowers and David M. Donahue, published by Hunter House Inc., Publishers, 1-800-266-5592.

WHERE DO THEY COME FROM? WHERE DO THEY GO?

PRINCIPAL SOURCES OF THE WORLD'S REFUGEES AND ASYLUM SEEKERS
(AS OF DECEMBER 31, 1993)*

Afghanistan**	3,429,800	Mali	87,000
Palestinians	2,801,300	Western Sahara**	80,000
Mozambique**	1,332,000	Zaire	79,000
Former Yugoslavia**	1,319,650	Mauritania	79,000
Burundi	780,000	Bangladesh	53,500
Liberia**	701,000	Uzbekistan	51,000
Somalia**	491,200	Guatemala	47,200
Eritrea**	421,500	Iran	39,000
Sudan	373,000	Cambodia	35,500
Angola	335,000	Chad	33,400
Vietnam	303,500	Laos	26,500
Azerbaijan**	290,000	Nicaragua	23,050
Burma**	289,500	El Salvador	21,900
Rwanda**	275,000	Uganda	20,000
Sierra Leone**	260,000	Senegal	18,000
Togo	240,000	South Africa	10,600
Ethiopia	232,200		
Armenia**	200,000		
Tajikistan**	153,000		
Georgia**	143,000		
Iraq	134,700		
China (Tibet)	133,000		
Sri Lanka**	106,650		
Bhutan**	105,100		

*Source: *World Refugee Survey,* 1994

**Indicates that sources vary widely in number reported

U.S. ADMISSIONS STATISTICS

ASYLUM CASES FILED WITH U.S.
IMMIGRATION AND NATURALIZATION SERVICE DIRECTORS
JUNE 1983–SEPTEMBER 1989 (CUMULATIVE)

Country	Approval rate for cases decided	Cases granted	Cases denied
Total	25.1%	35,358	105,300
U.S.S.R.	72.6%	306	115
Romania	70.3%	1,470	619
Iran	61.5%	13,061	8,173
Czechoslovakia	47.4%	170	188
Ethiopia	43.5%	1,796	2,325
China	41.8%	265	368
Syria	40.8%	207	300
South Africa	40.1%	57	85
Poland	37.0%	2,971	5,053
Afghanistan	36.6%	421	729
Somalia	33.8%	262	512
Vietnam	32.8%	75	153
Hungary	29.8%	206	485
Nicaragua	27.1%	10,872	29,154
Uganda	26.2%	98	276
Philippines	16.6%	87	435
Pakistan	15.0%	77	433
Cuba	14.9%	397	2,266
Yugoslavia	11.9%	57	421
Lebanon	9.5%	171	1,623
El Salvador	2.5%	1,004	37,666
Honduras	2.2%	32	1,407
Sri Lanka	2.1%	3	141
Haiti	2.1%	39	1,795
Guatemala	2.0%	112	5,411

Source: *Reasonable Fear: Human Rights and Refugee Policy*, Amnesty International, 1990

RESETTLEMENT AND ASYLUM STATISTICS

REFUGEES RESETTLED AND PERSONS GRANTED ASYLUM IN RELATION TO LOCAL POPULATION

(IN ORDER OF REFUGEES TO POPULATION RATIO)*

Resettlement country	Number of refugees resettled and persons granted asylum 1975–1992 cumulative	Number of refugees resettled and persons granted asylum 1992 only	Population of resettlement country (millions)	Ration of resettled refugees to total population
Sweden	152,608	12,791	8.7	1:57
Canada	407,379	36,409	28.1	1:69
Australia	205,862	9,758	17.8	1:86
United States	1,731,090	137,395	258.3	1:149
Denmark	34,089	4,100	5.2	1:153
Norway**	27,410	2,830	4.3	1:157
Switzerland	32,297	8,839	7.0	1:217
France	227,085	10,943	57.7	1:254
New Zealand	13,028	800	3.4	1:261
Austria	29,007	2,289	7.9	1:272
Netherlands	30,300	4,553	15.2	1:502
Germany***	112,264	9,189	81.1	1:722
Spain	39,166	296	39.1	1:998
United Kingdom**	35,032	16,453	58.0	1:1,656

  * Source: *World Refugee Survey,* 1994
  ** Statistics unavailable for 1975–81
  *** Does not include ethnic Germans from the former Soviet Union, Poland, and Romania

ACTIVITY 4

PACKING YOUR SUITCASE
A Simulation Activity

OVERVIEW: This exercise simulates the kind of practical and emotional choices a refugee must make when leaving home, as well as the unforeseen consequences these choices can have.

AGE LEVEL: Early childhood–adult

TIME: ½ hour

MATERIALS:
■ Pencils and scratch paper

SUBJECT AREAS: Current events, religious studies, social studies

OBJECTIVES:
■ To foster empathy for the emotions and problems refugees face in leaving their homes
■ To further understand the anxiety of the asylum-seeking process and the potential for arbitrariness in the asylum determination process

NOTE: This exercise is adaptable to a variety of ability levels, from adults who make and discuss a written list to young children who can be asked to pack a real bag and bring it to class.

Photo courtesy UNHCR/A. Hollman

The suitcases of refugees ready to begin a new life in the United States.

PART 1

Read or explain the following scenario:

"You are a teacher in _____ (insert any country on which you would like to focus). Your spouse disappears and is later found murdered. Your name appears in a newspaper article listing suspected subversives. Later you receive a letter threatening your life because of your alleged political activity. You decide to flee. Pack your bag: you can only take five categories of things (e.g., toiletries, clothing, photographs, books) and only what you can carry in one bag by yourself. You have five minutes to make this list."

While students are deciding, you might knock on a desk or table and say something like, "Hurry, they're coming."

PART 2

Tell the group you will be role-playing a government official in charge of determining asylum for refugees. Ask some of the participants to read their lists. After each list (usually 95%) that does not include evidence of "reasonable fear of persecution" (i.e., the newspaper article or the letter), say, "Asylum denied," explaining that there is insufficient evidence to prove a threat existed.

Read aloud the definition of *refugee* used by the U.S. Refugee Act of 1980 and the United Nations: *"A person who leaves his or her country of origin because of a well-founded fear of persecution for reasons of race, religion, nationality, membership in a particular social group or political opinion."* Explain that when a government acknowledges the existence of this "well-founded fear," it grants *political asylum* or *refugee status* and allows the person to remain in the country. Those who enter the country but cannot prove "well-founded fear of persecution" are expelled and usually returned to their country of origin.

PART 3

Encourage participants to discuss the experience. Ask:

- How did you feel making these choices under pressure of time?
- What practical considerations entered into your choices, such as packing personal identification and professional certificates or diplomas?
- What were the emotional reasons for your choices?

Ask students next to evaluate the United Nations' definition of *refugee*. Ask:

- Why does the world community need a shared definition? What would happen if no common definition of *refugee* existed?
- What considerations do you think went into making this shared definition? Political? Economic? Religious? Other?

Conclude by explaining the purpose of this exercise: to help participants experience the panic and loss of a sudden forced departure, the vulnerability of those who flee to accident, and the potential for arbitrary application of rules and definitions. Invite students to discuss what they learned by participating in such a scenario.

ADAPTATION FOR YOUNG CHILDREN

PART 1

Read children the following version of the scenario, which simplifies the details and stresses the perspective of a refugee child:

"A war is going on in your country. Your parents feel your family is in danger living at home. They decide to escape to another country where you could be safer. At supper one night they tell you that your whole family will leave first thing tomorrow morning. After supper you are to pack what you will take with you in a backpack or suitcase that you will carry yourself. You can only take five kinds of things. Pack your bag with the things you would want to take with you."

Ask children to go home and actually pack a bag with the things they would want to take or to make a list of those things.

A large percentage of refugees are children.

PART 2

Have children share their lists or bags and discuss how they made their choices. Ask:

■ What did you take and why? What item(s) seemed most important to include?

■ What did you have to leave behind and why?

■ What was hardest to leave behind?

PART 3

Encourage children to express how they might feel if they really had to pack and leave home. Explain the purpose of this experience to the children: to help them understand the feelings of refugees who must really face this experience.

"Mother, I think we should go to a hotel now. I really need a bath and some clean clothes."

—Malika, eight-year-old Afghani refugee in Pakistan

"When I saw my mother putting clothes in a sack, I asked where we were going. She said we were going to visit our aunt for the weekend. After we got to this camp—I was just little then—I kept asking when we would get to her house. I asked for a long time, but no one paid any attention, and then I forgot about it . . . . I don't dream a lot, but twice it has happened that I have dreamed of my aunty's house. Only when I go inside, it is our house. We had a pretty house. I wish I could have said goodbye to our animals."

—Yousaf, Afghani refugee in Pakistan

REFUGEES AND U.S. HISTORY

HISTORICAL OVERVIEW OF GLOBAL REFUGEE MOVEMENTS

THE CONSISTENT CAUSES OF FLIGHT

There have always been refugees. Myths and traditional stories from cultures across the world recount instances of forced flight, situations in which families, clans, tribes, and even whole nations have had to leave their homes in order to survive. Recorded history documents these desperate movements of people in search of a safe place to live. From century to century, continent to continent, the reasons for flight remain remarkably consistent.

Violent natural disasters, such as volcanic eruptions, earthquakes, floods, storms, or fires and more gradual natural causes such as drought, change of climate, or depletion of soil fertility, have always caused people to flee their homes. Prehistoric remains suggest a continuum of violence created by human beings: invasions, civil wars, and attacks on one group by another precede written history. Human response to danger from nature and other people also remains the same: people try to remove themselves and their loved ones as far from danger as possible.

THE CONSISTENT CONSEQUENCES OF FLIGHT

Whatever the cause of flight, people always suffer when they are forced to leave home. Foremost are physical dangers and hardships. No one is assured of food, shelter, or safety. The weakest people, the very young, the elderly, and the sick, become the least likely to survive. Refugees also experience grave emotional pain: fear, grief, loss, disorientation. Many who manage to stay alive never forget the psychological trauma of flight.

REFUGEE MOVEMENTS BEFORE THE TWENTIETH CENTURY

Before the modern era, national borders were vaguely defined, and a person could move from one country to another without passport or visa. The right to asylum, which can mean a refugee's right to survival, was recognized as a matter of custom and common law. Buddhism, Islam, and Judaism all have scripture and traditions that respect the needs of the fugitive. Many cultures have had longstanding traditions of *sanctuary,* a designated place where fugitives could claim safe haven for a period. In medieval Europe, for example, church law allowed a fugitive to take refuge in a church building for 40 days. So long as the person remained inside the building, no one could do him or her harm. After 40 days the fugitive could choose to be turned over for prosecution or swear to leave the country forever. The custom of sanctuary gradually declined after the Renaissance as civil law became strong enough to protect citizens from arbitrary punishment. The French Constitution of 1793 was the first written code of law to set down that victims of persecution have a right to asylum.

Although the basic causes and conditions of flight have remained consistent throughout history, great changes have occurred in the world's understanding of what a refugee is. The United Nations' definition of a refugee as a person who leaves his or her country of origin because of a "well-founded fear of persecution" would have had a different meaning before the nineteenth century, for few people would have understood "country of origin" to mean a legally defined area. Until the rise of central governments, most of the globe had no clear-cut countries with precise borders; instead regions were comprised of people who shared a culture. Most people thought of themselves as members of a cultural "nation"—the Ibo, Mayan, or Basque peoples, for example, not residents of a place defined by law. The Cherokee Nation, for example, identified themselves by their religion, language, customs, and dress, as well as by the home territory they occupied in the southern Appalachians.

REFUGEES IN THE TWENTIETH CENTURY

The tumultuous events of the early 20th century caused the numbers of refugees around the world to escalate. During the Balkan Wars of 1912–13, Greeks, Bulgarians, and Turks fled from their homes. Later ethnic Hungarians were ousted from Bulgaria, ethnic Germans were forced to leave Poland, and Armenians and Assyrians were driven from their homes in the Middle East. The ravages of World War I sent thousands from their homes in Germany, France, Belgium, Austria, and Poland. The 1917 Soviet Revolution and subsequent counter-revolutions created nearly two million refugees. In the 1930s, Jews and others began to flee Nazi persecution in Germany, the Spanish Civil War forced refugees from Spain, and the newly created nation of Iraq began slaughtering its Assyrian population.

It was this rising wave of refugees that led the League of Nations, an international organization that functioned between World Wars I and II much like the United Nations does today, to establish a **High Commissioner for Refugees** in 1921. The first High Commissioner was Fridtjof Nansen, a Norwegian explorer and humanitarian who served from 1921 to 1930. Nansen worked to help Greek, Turkish, and many other refugee groups. However, World War II created a refugee crisis too immense to be managed within the structures of the old League of Nations.

Among its first actions after being founded in 1946, the United Nations proclaimed in 1948 the **Universal Declaration of Human Rights (UDHR)**, which sets standards for the treatment of every person on earth. Article 14 of this historic document specifically addresses refugees, declaring that "everyone has the right to seek and to enjoy in other countries asylum from persecution." As a further result of the events of 1933–45, the U.N. General Assembly passed the **Convention Relating to the Status of Refugees** in 1951. This document defined who was a refugee and gave specific rights to all refugees. It also gave power to the U.N. **High Commissioner for Refugees (UNHCR)** to aid and protect refugees.

Since World War II, wars, revolutions, and natural disasters have continued to create refugee movements. The Chinese Revolution and the division of colonial India into the separate states of India and Pakistan caused millions to leave their homes. The rise of new nations on the continent of Africa and wars in the Middle East, Southeast Asia, and Europe have created millions more refugees. The Horn of Africa has experienced years of drought, famine, and civil wars that have killed millions and forced millions more from their homes. No country on earth has been unaffected by these massive movements of people.

BEYOND THE TWENTIETH CENTURY

The condition of refugees in the twentieth century is unlike all previous eras. As Charles Dickens said of the French Revolution, "It was the best of times. It was the worst of times." On the one hand, more people have been displaced by disasters, both natural and human-made, than in any other period of history. On the other hand, for the first time in history refugees are recognized by international law as having rights and guarantees to safety, and an internationally supported organization exists for the sole purpose of protecting and assisting refugees.

What may the twenty-first century hold for refugees? Certainly there will be refugees. Certainly they will experience the suffering of anyone forced to leave home. Voices are already calling, however, for further support and protection for refugees, both to safeguard the human rights already legally granted them under the United Nations and also to extend those rights. For example, many human rights organizations wish to create a U.N. court that would determine whether a person is a legitimate refugee, rather than leaving this decision to individual countries who may or may not treat refugees fairly.

REFUGEES IN U.S. HISTORY

THE COLONIAL PERIOD

Although the term "refugee" is seldom used to describe them, every school child learns how Mayflower Pilgrims came to a new land to find the religious freedom denied them in their native country. Americans remember with pride the many different peoples who came to find a haven from persecution: Quakers, Mennonites, Moravians, Anabaptists, Catholics, Stuart supporters, and many more.

George Washington urged that the United States should forever be "an asylum to the oppressed and needy of the earth," and refugees have continued for centuries to find sanctuary here. However, attitudes toward refugees, both in official government policy and in popular opinion, have shifted continually, even toward people coming from the same areas. The well-known words of Emma Lazarus' poem inscribed on the base of the Statue of Liberty proclaim, "give me your tired, your poor, your huddled masses yearning to be free . . . I lift my lamp beside the golden door." Not everyone has found that door to be open.

OPPOSITION TO CONTINUED IMMIGRATION

During every period, immigration and refugee policies reflect competing values and political forces; those who support the ideal of the "golden door" disagree with those who wish to be selective about who is permitted inside. Race and ethnicity have much to do with whether someone is welcome. Resistance to newcomers arises not only from those who fear change or who distrust people of a different background or race, but also from those who support labor unions, population control, and environmental concerns. Since the eighteenth century, restrictionists or "nativists" have spoken against admitting some foreigners. In the first half of the nineteenth century some people opposed the increasing number of Roman Catholics from Ireland who were refugees of the famine that resulted from the successive failure of potato harvests, and others feared the radicalism of political refugees from Germany's 1848 revolution.

During the 1880s the demographics of U.S. immigration changed, as immigrants increasingly came from Southern and Eastern Europe, rather than Northern and Western. The new immigrants were Italians, Hungarians, Greeks, Armenians, Poles, Slovaks, Croatians, Ukrainians, Russians, and Serbs. Many of these new immigrants were not Christians. They were poor and did not speak English. Their complexion was described as "swarthy." Their sheer numbers and "foreign" ways of life seemed threatening to many Americans, even to those whose families had been foreigners themselves in recent generations.

In response to growing concerns, in 1907 Congress formed the Dillingham Committee to make a joint Congressional investigation into what was now perceived as an immigration problem: the "new" immigrants from southeast Europe outnumbered the "old" from northwest Europe by four to one.

Operating under "scientific" assumptions that Anglo-Saxon values and racial characteristics were superior, this committee concluded that restricting immigration was "demanded by economic, moral, and social considerations" and advocated a literacy test and admission quotas for each country.

RESTRICTIVE LEGISLATION

The report of the Dillingham Committee resulted in the **Immigration Law of 1917** which, despite President Wilson's veto, passed into law the first serious restrictions on immigrants. The law shut out illiterates and anyone from an "Asiatic barred zone" that covered almost all of Asia except the Philippines. Though extremely restrictive, this law was also the first to recognize refugees as different from other immigrants; it made an exception to these restrictions for all people who could prove they were fleeing religious persecution.

During World War I (1914–1918) immigration all but halted, but a growing conservatism and isolationism kept alive racial and ethnic prejudices and "nativist" fears that foreigners would "pollute" the U.S. population. The Russian Revolution, which created thousands of refugees, raised fears of infiltration by Bolsheviks. A postwar economic depression caused an influx of cheap labor that many people feared would threaten Americans' jobs, and postwar immigration began to rise in a flood tide, with 5,000 immigrants a day entering Ellis Island in 1920. Congressman Albert Johnson summed up the restrictionist response to these conditions: "America is our land . . . the day of unalloyed welcome to all peoples, the day of indiscriminate acceptance of all races, has definitely ended."

The result of this growing resistance to open immigration was the nation's first law generally restricting immigration, the **Quota Act of 1921**, also known as the Johnson Act. The following were its most significant restraints:

Photo © Underwood Archives

Immigrants from four countries, Poland, Norway, Germany, and Russia, looking toward the promised land from Ellis Island.

1. European immigration was limited to 355,000 people, with 55% coming from countries in the northwest and 45% coming from the southeast.

2. Quotas were set for most countries, except those of the Western Hemisphere.

These restrictions were followed by the even more severe **Immigration Act of 1924**, which reduced the annual admissions limit to 164,667 and set quotas for each nation based at 2% of the number of persons from that country already in the United States in 1890, a date chosen because it preceded the great influx of immigrants from Southern and Eastern Europe. In the unapologetic words of J. M. Tincher, a Kansas Congressman, this act successfully shut the door on "Bolsheviks, Wops, Dagoes, Kikes, and Hunkies." Because these restrictive laws remained unchanged until well after World War II and made a distinction only of those fleeing religious persecution, it effectively shut out legitimate refugees, lumping all applicants into what one nativist termed the "wild motley throng," and another our "alien indigestion."

WORLD WAR II

During the years between the two world wars the United States kept its doors tightly shut against immigrants and refugees. Although the Immigration Act of 1924 had recognized the right of those fleeing religious persecution to resettle in this country, Congress defeated several bills which would have allowed refugees from Nazism to enter the United States. The State Department actually tightened the requirements for refugee admission after the outbreak of World War II in 1939, claiming that German spies were posing as refugees. When the SS *St. Louis* attempted to dock at an American port in 1939, it was denied permission because its Jewish refugee passengers did not have the proper visas. The ship was forced to return to Europe where some of its passengers died in

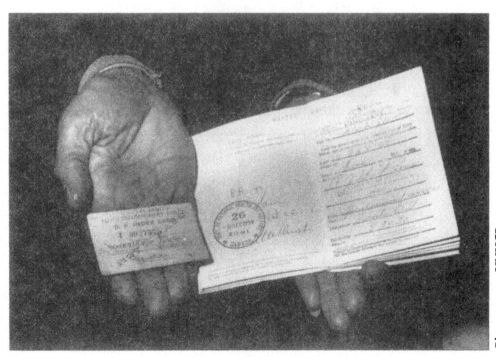

Photo courtesy UNHCR

These documents meant the beginning of a new life for refugees following World War II.

33

concentration camps. In addition, the government created "paper walls" of bureaucracy that effectively prevented refugees from entering the United States. For example, by 1943 the visa application form was more than four feet long (double-sided) and had to be filled out in sextuplicate. Unsuccessful applicants for admission were not allowed to reapply until six months later, and they were not told the reasons for their denial.

Not until after the Second World War did the United States start to open its doors to refugees. President Truman then issued a presidential directive stating that this was "not the time to close or narrow our gates." In 1948 Congress passed the **Displaced Persons Act**, which provided for the admission of 100,000 (later amended to 400,000) displaced persons from the war. The original act gave priority for admission to Balts and agricultural workers, but not Holocaust survivors. Many of these persons were ineligible for admission because the act stated a refugee had to be in Germany by December 22, 1945, and many Polish Jews did not flee to the west until 1946. National origins quotas were not dropped for these refugee admissions but were instead "mortgaged" against subsequent years. The mortgages meant that some nations' quotas were filled well into the twenty-first century and, in the case of Estonia, into the twenty-second century.

Despite the number of displaced persons entering the United States, official policy toward immigrants and refugees remained restrictionist. In 1952 Congress passed the **McCarran-Walter**

Photo courtesy UNHCR / Calig, Freiburg

A refugee camp for displaced persons at the end of World War II

Immigration and Nationality Act, which reaffirmed the national origins quota systems while allowing Asian nations small quotas for the first time. In addition, the act barred the admission of "radicals, communists, and subversives." The act was passed by two votes over the veto of President Truman. In his veto speech, the President gave a forceful argument against the quota system, saying it was "based upon assumptions at variance with our American ideals" and calling it "long since out of date and more than ever unrealistic in the face of world conditions." The President also claimed the law was insulting to the United States' allies in southern and eastern Europe, saying, "Through this bill we say to their people: You are less worthy to come to this country than Englishmen or Irishmen . . . you Turks, you are brave defenders of the eastern flank, but you shall have a quota of only 225!"

THE LESSENING OF RESTRICTION
AND THE END OF NATIONAL QUOTAS: 1952–1980

During the 1950s the United States began its first real definition of refugee policy apart from immigration policy. Increasingly, during that decade, the *de facto* definition of a refugee came to be someone fleeing a communist regime. Through various acts of Congress, the United States admitted hundreds of thousands of refugees from communist nations and provided them with financial assistance and resettlement. President Eisenhower also became the first to use his executive powers to admit large numbers of refugees, usually fleeing communism, outside any established quota.

In 1965 the United States finally abolished the system of national origins quotas for immigrants and refugees. Tipping the balance of immigration from Europe toward Asia and Latin America, the **Immigration Act of 1965** replaced national quotas with a ceiling of 120,000 immigrants and refugees for the western hemisphere and 170,000 for the eastern hemisphere, with those from the east being admitted according to a system giving priority to those with special occupational skills or family in the United States. Refugees were given the lowest priority. Though later amended to create a single ceiling of 270,000 and including western applicants in the priority system, the 1965 act is still the basis for immigration law today.

During the 1960s and 1970s, the United States continued to give priority to refugees from communist nations. In the period from 1965 to 1972, the U.S. admitted 340,000 Cuban refugees, and in the last half of the 1970s, 90,000 Soviet Jews were admitted. In addition, the United States recognized its responsibility to assist refugees fleeing Vietnam at the end of the war in 1975. That year Congress passed the **Indochina Refugee Act** to evacuate 200,000 refugees who were former employees or supporters of the U.S. government and whose lives were in danger after communist takeover, and the **Migration and Refugee Assistance Act** to resettle 135,000 Indochinese refugees in the United States. Legislation alone did not solve Indochina's refugee crisis. Starting in 1978 refugees attempted escape in unseaworthy boats to escape communist takeovers in Laos and Cambodia and the invasion of Cambodia by Vietnam. These "boat people" were turned away by neighboring countries and left at sea by vessels unwilling to pick them up. President Carter finally ordered all U.S.-registered ships to rescue the boat people, and he promised the refugees resettlement in the United States.

DEFINING A REFUGEE: 1980–THE PRESENT

Remembering pictures of boat people clinging to life in leaky ships in the South China Sea, Congress passed legislation bringing the U.S. definition of a refugee in conformity with the definition by the United Nations. **The Refugee Act of 1980** defines a refugee as:

. . . any person who is outside any country of such person's nationality or, in the case of a person having no nationality, is outside any country in which such a person last habitually resided, and who is unable or unwilling to return to, and is unable or unwilling to avail himself or herself of the protection of that country because of persecution or a well-founded fear of persecution on account of race, religion, nationality, membership in a particular social group, or political opinion.

Refugee issues are far from resolved in the 1990s, however. The major refugee issue facing the United States today is determining who is a refugee according to the 1980 law and who is an "economic refugee," fleeing poor economic conditions and seeking better opportunities in this country, a category of refugees not recognized by the U.S. government as eligible for asylum. The U.S. State Department believes that many asylum seekers from Central America and Haiti are economic refugees looking for better living and working conditions. On the other hand, many human rights groups believe these refugees have legitimate claims for asylum based on well-founded fears of persecution. Resolving this issue is the challenge of the 1990s for those charged with protecting refugees.

QUESTIONS FOR DISCUSSION

The history of U.S. attitudes and policy toward immigrants and refugees has been condensed into a timeline and graph, in **Handout 7: U.S. Immigration and Refugee Timeline** and **Handout 8: Growth of a Nation.** These handouts are intended as references in later discussion and activities. You may want to make overheads of them for use in discussions.

The following questions are designed for discussion after students have examined both handouts.

1. How would you characterize immigration and refugee policy:
- from 1875 to 1924?
- from 1924 to 1945?
- from 1945 to 1985?

2. What changes in policy toward immigrants and refugees took place between these three periods?

3. What factors might account for the changes in U.S. immigration and refugee policy?

3. What information in the graph **Growth of a Nation** might be useful in explaining the changes in policy?

4. What kinds of attitudes towards immigrants and refugees are reflected in the policies of each era?

Photo © Underwood Archives

An applicant for American citizenship being examined with two witnesses by a federal officer.

UNITED STATES IMMIGRATION
AND REFUGEE POLICY TIMELINE

NOTE: Until the end of World War II, U.S. policy made no distinction between immigrants and refugees.

1875   **The Immigration Act of 1875,** the first federal regulation of immigration, excludes prostitutes and convicts from entry into the U.S.

1882   **The Chinese Exclusion Act,** forbidding the Chinese from immigrating to the U.S. for a period of 10 years, marks the beginning of explicitly racist immigration policy in U.S. history.

1892   The Chinese Exclusion Act is renewed for another 10 years.

1902   The Chinese Exclusion Act is renewed indefinitely.

1903   **The Immigration Act of 1903** forbids entry into the U.S. of anarchists, beggars, and white-slave traders.

1907   Congress appoints the **Dillingham Committee,** a joint House-Senate commission named after its chairman Senator Dillingham, to investigate immigration from southern and eastern Europe.

1907   President Theodore Roosevelt negotiates the **"Gentlemen's Agreement"** with Japan which informally excludes Japanese from immigrating to the U.S.

1911   The Dillingham Commission issues a 42-volume report that regards immigrants from northern and western Europe as more desirable than immigrants from southern and eastern Europe who were, it was believed, prone to crime, ignorance, and poverty. The commission advocates a literacy test for all immigrants.

1917   Passed over President Wilson's veto, the **Immigration Act of 1917** sets new restrictions on immigration. All immigrants are required to pass literacy tests. The only exceptions are family members of another admissible immigrant and refugees fleeing religious persecution; refugees fleeing political persecution are not granted an exemption. The act also excludes all Asian peoples not already excluded by U.S. law or policy and allows for the deportation of aliens advocating revolution, subversion, or sabotage.

1921   **The Quota Act of 1921** limits immigration to 3% of each national origin group living in the U.S. according to the 1910 census. The overall ceiling for immigration is set at 355,000 European immigrants annually. No quotas are established for immigration from the western hemisphere.

1924   **The Immigration Act of 1924** restricts immigration beyond the 1921 law, setting the annual quota at 2% of each national origin group living in the U.S.

From *The Uprooted: Refugees and the United States* ©1995 Nancy Flowers and David M. Donahue, published by Hunter House Inc., Publishers, 1-800-266-5592.

according to the 1890 census when fewer southern and eastern Europeans were in the U.S. The total ceiling for immigration is reduced to 164,667 annually. The western hemisphere is still exempt from quotas. The act also bars from immigration all persons not eligible for citizenship, making the Japanese, whom the Supreme Court deemed ineligible for citizenship, unable to enter the U.S.

1929 The annual ceiling for immigration is reduced again to 153,714.

1930s The State Department tightens the standards of admission for Mexicans, blocking immigration from Mexico.

1933–38 Various bills in Congress allowing refugees from Nazism to enter the U.S. are defeated. The executive branch also erects "paper walls" of bureaucracy preventing refugees from entering the U.S.

1939 The State Department imposes stricter requirements for refugee admission after the outbreak of war, claiming Nazi infiltrators were posing as refugees.

1943 In a token gesture to its wartime ally, the U.S. grants China a quota of 100 immigrants annually.

1945 In response to the plight of DPs (displaced persons) from the war in Europe, President Truman issues a presidential directive stating, this "is not the time to close or narrow our gates." The directive eases the entrance of DPs.

1948 **The Displaced Persons Act** provides that 100,000 displaced persons be admitted to the U.S. and that national origins quotas be "mortgaged" against quotas for subsequent years if the number of allowable visas for one year is filled. Priority is given to Balts and agricultural workers. Many Jewish Holocaust survivors are ineligible by virtue of a clause limiting the act only to DPs living in Germany by December 22, 1945.

1950–51 The Displaced Persons Act is amended to allow over 400,000 DPs entrance to the U.S. Baltic and agricultural worker priorities are rescinded.

1952 **The McCarran-Walter Immigration and Nationality Act** reaffirms restrictionist approaches to immigrant and refugee admission. The act retains the national origins quota system and bars radicals, communists, and subversives. Japanese exclusion is repealed and Asian nations are allowed small quotas.

1952 President Eisenhower's **Escapee Program** provides financial assistance and resettlement help to refugees escaping communist nations.

1953 **The Refugee Relief Act** ignores national origins quotas and quota mortgaging for refugees. Visas for 200,000 refugees from communist nations are granted.

1956 Using an obscure clause of the Immigration and Nationality Act, President Eisenhower exercises the first mass parole of refugees into the U.S. after the failed revolution against the communist government in Hungary.

1957 **The Refugee-Escapee Act** defines a refugee-escapee as a victim of racial, religious, or political persecution fleeing communist or communist-occupied

From *The Uprooted: Refugees and the United States* ©1995 Nancy Flowers and David M. Donahue, published by Hunter House Inc., Publishers, 1-800-266-5592.

countries or a country in the Middle East. Anti-communists from Hungary and mixed race Dutch-Indonesians fleeing persecution from newly independent Indonesia are the act's first beneficiaries.

1959 The United States offers a welcome home to refugees from Cuba after the overthrow of Fulgencio Batista by Fidel Castro.

1960 **The Refugee Fair Share Law** is passed as a measure to provide for the ongoing admission of refugees. The law authorizes the admission of 25% of the total number of refugees from Europe and the Middle East who have not been permanently resettled under the Attorney General's parole authority.

1962 **The Migration and Refugee Assistance Act** is the first comprehensive refugee assistance law in U.S. history. Giving the president wide latitude to address the refugee situation, the law provides assistance to refugees, annual contributions to the United Nations High Commissioner for Refugees and other international agencies, and money allowing the president to meet pressing refugee needs.

1962 President Kennedy uses his parole authority to admit Chinese refugees, waiting in Hong Kong for resettlement. Though large numbers were not admitted, the admission of Chinese refugees presages a change in attitude toward Asian refugees.

1965 **The Immigration Act of 1965** liberalizes immigration policy and tips the balance of new immigrants away from Europe and toward Asia and Latin America. The act abolishes national origins quotas and sets a ceiling of 120,000 for western hemisphere immigrants and 170,000 for eastern hemisphere immigrants. Eastern immigrants are admitted according to a preference scale giving priority to those with needed occupational skills and family ties in the U.S. Refugees are assigned the lowest priority.

1965–72 Under the **Freedom Flight Program**, the United States accepts 340,000 Cuban refugees.

1974 **The Jackson-Vanik amendment** to the **Trade Reform Act** seeks to block the extension of economic advantages to those countries which restrict or tax emigration of their citizens. The amendment is aimed at the Soviet Union and is an attempt to force the liberalization of its emigration policy for Jews wanting to leave the country.

1975–80 The United States admits 90,000 Soviet Jewish emigres. Soviet allowances for Jewish emigration swing unpredictably up and down.

1975 With the fall of Saigon and the end of the Vietnam War the United States prepares for the evacuation of 200,000 refugees under the **Indochina Refugee Act**. Evacuations are to be limited only to employees of the U.S. government and those whose lives would be in danger after the communist takeover.

1975 Under the **Migration and Refugee Assistance Act of 1975**, 135,000 Indochinese refugees are resettled in the United States.

From *The Uprooted: Refugees and the United States* ©1995 Nancy Flowers and David M. Donahue, published by Hunter House Inc., Publishers, 1-800-266-5592.

1976 The **Immigration Act of 1965** is amended, assigning priority to immigrants from the western hemisphere according to the same scale used for the eastern hemisphere.

1978 The Immigration Act of 1965 is amended to combine both hemispheres and set a single worldwide ceiling for immigrants at 290,000 (reduced to 270,000 two years later).

1978 Refugees continue to leave Southeast Asia following the communist takeovers in Laos and Cambodia and the invasion of Cambodia by Vietnam. Turned away by neighboring countries, the refugees or "boat people" are left at sea. President Carter orders all ships under U.S. registry to pick up "boat people" and promises them resettlement in the U.S.

1980 The U.S. admits 125,000 refugees from Cuba as part of the "Mariel Boatlift Operation."

1980 Congress passes the **Refugee Act of 1980**. The act brings the definition of a refugee in conformity with the definition by the U.N. Convention on the Status of Refugees.

1981 The Reagan Task Force on Immigration and Refugee Policy recommends legislation to "establish an emergency mass migration fund for domestic crises" and development of permanent "detention centers."

1981–90 Over 21,000 Haitians are intercepted at sea as they flee Haiti. All Haitians arriving in the United States, including those applying for political asylum, are detained in prison.

1990 The **Immigration Act of 1990** provides for "temporary protective status," preventing for 18 months the deportation of individuals fleeing emergency situations.

1991–94 Following the coup against President Jean-Bertrand Aristide of Haiti, thousands of Haitians attempt to leave the island, fearing terrorism and murder for their support of the ousted president. Many are turned back to Haiti by the Coast Guard; others are kept in detention at the U.S. naval base at Guantanamo. A small percentage are allowed to make their case for refugee status.

1994 The Immigration and Naturalization Service recognizes that gays and lesbians may belong to a persecuted social group that deserves asylum under the Refugee Act of 1980.

1994 To reduce the backlog of asylum cases and to cut down the number of future cases, the Clinton administration proposes doubling the number of asylum hearing officers, denying work permits for up to six months to asylum seekers, and charging $130 for an asylum application (which would make the U.S. the only nation charging for asylum).

Growth of a Nation
A Historical Perspective on Immigrants and Refugees in the United States

The following reprint from *Time* magazine provides background information on immigrants and refugees to the United States from 1820–1984 including who they were and how many came as well as where they originated and why they left.

Sometimes it was their own national disasters that sent immigrants flocking to America, sometimes it was wars or revolutions, and sometimes it was simply the lure of the New World. The influx, which the Government began to record in 1820, roughly follows the ups and downs of the U.S. economy, although improvements in transportation also fueled the urge to move. Overwhelmingly Northern and Western European at the beginning of the 19th century, the ethnic mix has become steadily more varied, a trend that is accelerating today.

1820–40

Europe's population doubled in the century after 1750, and the Industrial Revolution caused widespread unemployment for artisans and gave only periodic work to others.

These pie-charts track the changing percentages of immigrants from Europe, Asia and the Western Hemisphere. Major countries within these broad slices are noted.

80%
Ireland 34.8
Germany 21.4
Britain 13.6
6.1%
13.9%

EUROPE
ASIA
WESTERN HEMISPHERE
OTHERS

The rapidly expanding country that awaited the newcomers looked like this:

British & U.S.
U.S. Territories
Original 13 States
Spanish
New States As of 1820

While the government was acquiring adjoining land from colonial powers, most of the Indians were pushed west of the Mississippi.

1840–60

In 1843 the first iron-hulled steamship, the *Great Britain*, crossed the Atlantic. Most of the immigration was from Northern and Western Europe to the Northern U.S. The Irish came to the cities as a result of the potato famine of 1845–49. They were followed by Germans and Scandinavians who opted for the farmlands of the Midwest.

93.9%
Ireland 39.3
Germany 32.2
Britain 16
1%
3.2%
1.9%

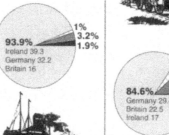

Ocean transport became safer, faster, and cheaper.

1860–80

Nearly 200,000 Chinese laborers came to the West, largely to build the railroads. The Central and Union Pacific linked the two coasts in 1869.

84.6%
Germany 29.4
Britain 22.5
Ireland 17
3.7%
11.1%
0.6%

1860–80

Italians, Poles, and Czechs, as well as Jews from throughout Europe, came in large numbers. The Chinese Exclusion Act of 1882 was the first federal attempt to limit immigration by nationality.

Ellis Island was established as the primary immigrant processing center in New York.

Concentrations of foreign-born population (% of total).

0–10%
10–30%
30% and over

92.8%
Germany 21.9
Britain 12.1
Ireland 11.7
Italy 10.7
Austria-Hungary 10.6
Russia 8
1.6%
5.2%
0.4%

Number of immigrants admitted

800,000
700,000
600,000
500,000
400,000
300,000
200,000
100,000

POGROMS IN RUSSIA AGAINST JEWS

IRISH POTATO FAMINE
FINANCIAL PANIC
CALIFORNIA GOLD RUSH
CASTLE GARDEN, N.Y. IMMIGRANT DEPOT
CIVIL WAR
HOMESTEAD ACT
ECONOMIC DEPRESSION
POST-WAR DEPRESSION
CHINESE EXCLUSION ACT
STATUE OF LIBERTY
ELLIS ISLAND OPENED

Fiscal years 1820 1825 1830 1835 1840 1845 1850 1855 1860 1865 1870 1875 1880 1885 1890 1895 1900

From *The Uprooted: Refugees and the United States* ©1995 Nancy Flowers and David M. Donahue, published by Hunter House Inc., Publishers, 1-800-266-5592.

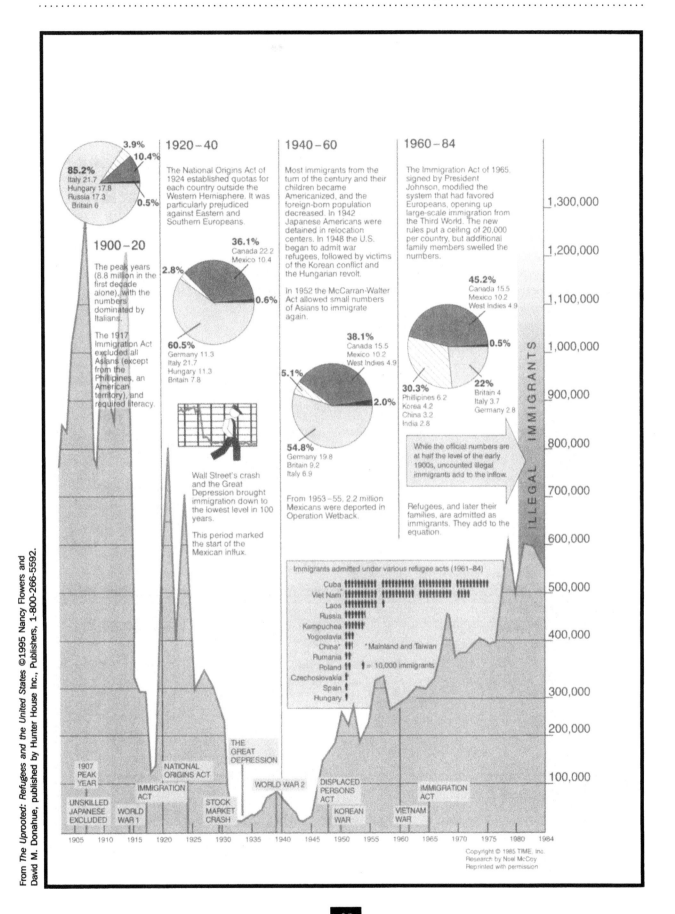

From *The Uprooted: Refugees and the United States* ©1995 Nancy Flowers and David M. Donahue, published by Hunter House Inc., Publishers, 1-800-266-5592.

1920–40

The National Origins Act of 1924 established quotas for each country outside the Western Hemisphere. It was particularly prejudiced against Eastern and Southern Europeans.

1900–20

The peak years (8.8 million in the first decade alone), with the numbers dominated by Italians.

The 1917 Immigration Act excluded all Asians (except from the Philippines, an American territory), and required literacy.

Wall Street's crash and the Great Depression brought immigration down to the lowest level in 100 years.

This period marked the start of the Mexican influx.

1940–60

Most immigrants from the turn of the century and their children became Americanized, and the foreign-born population decreased. In 1942 Japanese Americans were detained in relocation centers. In 1948 the U.S. began to admit war refugees, followed by victims of the Korean conflict and the Hungarian revolt.

In 1952 the McCarran-Walter Act allowed small numbers of Asians to immigrate again.

From 1953–55, 2.2 million Mexicans were deported in Operation Wetback.

1960–84

The Immigration Act of 1965, signed by President Johnson, modified the system that had favored Europeans, opening up large-scale immigration from the Third World. The new rules put a ceiling of 20,000 per country, but additional family members swelled the numbers.

While the official numbers are at half the level of the early 1900s, uncounted illegal immigrants add to the inflow.

Refugees, and later their families, are admitted as immigrants. They add to the equation.

85.2%
Italy 21.7
Hungary 17.8
Russia 17.3
Britain 6

3.9%
10.4%
0.5%

36.1%
Canada 22.2
Mexico 10.4

2.8%
0.6%

60.5%
Germany 11.3
Italy 21.7
Hungary 11.3
Britain 7.8

38.1%
Canada 15.5
Mexico 10.2
West Indies 4.9

5.1%
2.0%

54.8%
Germany 19.8
Britain 9.2
Italy 6.9

45.2%
Canada 15.5
Mexico 10.2
West Indies 4.9

0.5%

30.3%
Phillipines 6.2
Korea 4.2
China 3.2
India 2.8

22%
Britain 4
Italy 3.7
Germany 2.8

ILLEGAL IMMIGRANTS

Immigrants admitted under various refugee acts (1961–84)

Cuba
Viet Nam
Laos
Russia
Kampuchea
Yogoslavia
China*   *Mainland and Taiwan
Rumania
Poland   † = 10,000 immigrants
Czechoslovakia
Spain
Hungary

1,300,000
1,200,000
1,100,000
1,000,000
900,000
800,000
700,000
600,000
500,000
400,000
300,000
200,000
100,000

1907 PEAK YEAR

NATIONAL ORIGINS ACT

THE GREAT DEPRESSION

IMMIGRATION ACT

WORLD WAR 2

DISPLACED PERSONS ACT

IMMIGRATION ACT

UNSKILLED JAPANESE EXCLUDED

WORLD WAR 1

STOCK MARKET CRASH

KOREAN WAR

VIETNAM WAR

1905 1910 1915 1920 1925 1930 1935 1940 1945 1950 1955 1960 1965 1970 1975 1980 1984

JEWISH REFUGEES FROM EASTERN EUROPE: 1890–1990
Case Studies in Changing Policy and Circumstances

OVERVIEW: Using contemporary personal narratives as primary material, students are asked to examine the political and social factors that influenced which refugees were accepted and rejected for admission to the United States.

AGE LEVEL: High school

TIME: 1 hour

MATERIALS:

■ Handout 9: Jewish Refugees from Eastern Europe: 1890–1990, Historical Overview

■ Handout 10: Jewish Refugees from Eastern Europe: 1890–1990, Case Studies

SUBJECT AREAS: Current events, government, U.S. history

OBJECTIVES:

■ To compare the changing factors that influence U.S. policies and attitudes toward refugees

■ To show how the U.S. government responds to similar human problems at different times

PART 1

Assign the class to read **Handout 9: Jewish Refugees from Eastern Europe: 1890–1990, Historical Overview,** either in small groups or as homework. Then have the class read and discuss **Handout 10: Jewish Refugees from Eastern Europe: 1890–1990, Case Studies** and answer the questions that accompany each case.

Discuss with the whole class their responses to the case studies. The epilogues to the case studies can be read along with the cases, but to avoid having discussion influenced by the actual outcomes, it is best reserved until the end of the activity.

PART 2

After reading all the case studies, ask students to consider the following questions either as the basis for a writing assignment or a discussion.

■ Beyond the persecution of each of the four cases, what other factors might influence the U.S. government to admit them or not? Can you classify these factors? Are they political factors? Economic factors? Racial? Ethnic? Conditions existing in a particular period?

■ Three of the four examples suffered violence, oppression, and war. Do you think these persons would have qualified as refugees before their actual suffering? Are there any parallels between the stories of the Eastern European Jews and refugee situations in the world today?

■ Anti-Semitism played a role in the persecution of these women, and it has played a role in the determination of U.S. refugee and immigration policy in the past. Compare the story of the SS *St. Louis* (See World War II, p. 33.) with the story of Tanya Shimiewsky. What factors may have caused the United States to admit after the war persons who could have been denied admission during the war? What role has anti-Semitism played in U.S. immigration and refugee policy? Do you think anti-Semitism affected the admission of any of these four refugees?

■ Conclude this activity by reading the epilogues with the class. Discuss with students what factors helped each woman to gain admission to the United States.

JEWISH REFUGEES FROM EASTERN EUROPE: 1890–1990, HISTORICAL OVERVIEW

During the last century, United States immigration and refugee policy has undergone radical changes. So too have conditions in many parts of the world. In particular the history of Jewish immigration from Eastern Europe during the last century serves to illustrate the way laws and history interact.

JEWS IN EASTERN EUROPE

The history of Jews in Eastern Europe has followed a painfully fluctuating course between periods of promising tolerance and periods of radical oppression. When Russia absorbed a large part of Poland into its territory at the end of the eighteenth century, it incorporated the largest population of Jews in the world. The government of Czarina Catherine the Great (1762–1796) welcomed Jewish merchants in hopes they would stimulate commerce, but Catherine also established the Pale of Settlement, an area from the Baltic Sea to the Black Sea where with few exceptions all Jews were to live and work.

During the reign of Czar Nicholas I (1825–1855), conditions deteriorated with the imposition of new anti-Jewish laws that prohibited Jews from living in villages where they had lived for generations and made Jews subject for the first time to conscription into the Russian army. Although the draft age for Russian soldiers was twenty to thirty-five, under the punitive revised law Jewish boys could be taken into the army as young as twelve. During their military service, which could last up to twenty years, Jews were mistreated and many were forcibly converted to Christianity.

Conditions improved briefly during the reign of Czar Alexander II (1855–1881), who opened school and universities to Jews and liberated more than twenty million people from hereditary servitude on landlords' estates. But the assassination of "The Czar Liberator" by revolutionary terrorists set off a wave of pogroms, attacks on Jews that were tacitly or openly encouraged by the government. Alexander II's repressive successor, Alexander III (1881–1894), enacted severe laws that narrowed the Pale of Settlement and placed limitations on the role Jews could play in professional, economic, and political life.

These repressions, especially the successive pogroms that swept Jewish communities, brought about a great wave of Jewish immigration to the United States from 1881–1921. Jews, primarily from Germany, and Sephardic Jews from the south of Europe, had been immigrating to the United States since the colonial period, but their numbers were small, and they were quickly assimilated into American society. The many Eastern Europeans, however, shared a distinctive culture and language, Yiddish, that set them off from previous Jewish immigrants and other Americans.

WORLD WAR I AND THE RUSSIAN REVOLUTION

The fall of the czarist regime and the Bolshevik Revolution at first seemed to promise Russian Jews hope for equality and freedom in a new Soviet Union. Many Jews, especially of

From *The Uprooted: Refugees and the United States* ©1995 Nancy Flowers and David M. Donahue, published by Hunter House Inc., Publishers, 1-800-266-5592.

the older generation, opposed the overt atheism of Lenin, who opposed all religions as "forms of spiritual oppression"; many young Jewish people, however, became committed Bolsheviks. The communist government abolished the Pale, and Jews flocked to Moscow to take advantage of opportunities for education and work. Many revolutionaries, including some of Lenin's closest advisors, were Jews. For a brief period Jews felt themselves to be on an equal footing with all other citizens, though for some the price of these expanded opportunities was giving up their Jewish heritage. They increasingly identified themselves as part of the Soviet federation rather than as members of a religious minority.

During the same period Jews in Russia were entering a period of expanding possibilities, eastern European Jews outside Russia were experiencing the full force of World War I, from which the Bolsheviks had withdrawn, having made a separate peace with Germany. Old repressions, like anti-Semitism and legal restrictions, were compounded with the chaos and deprivation of warfare.

THE HOLOCAUST

Although during the 1930s many Jews in Germany and other western countries were able to flee Nazi persecution, relatively few Jews in the eastern part of Europe fully realized the danger of Nazi racism or had the means to escape it. Jews from all parts of Europe met their deaths at German hands, either by execution in their hometowns or in the gas chambers of the extermination camps, but the greatest devastation was in the east where whole towns were depopulated.

Most of the Jewish people who survived the Holocaust had neither family nor home to return to when the war was over. These refugees usually chose to emigrate from Europe, and the majority fled to the newly established Jewish homeland, Israel. Others sought admissions to countries around the world.

JEWS BEHIND THE IRON CURTAIN

From World War II until the late 1980s, global politics entered the "Cold War" period when the United States and its western allies were in continual conflict with the Soviet Union and its eastern allies. All the countries of the Eastern bloc were governed by communist regimes that generally maintained both internal and foreign policies in conformity with those of the dominating Soviet Union.

During this period Jews in Eastern Europe experienced continued discrimination. The Soviet government discouraged the free practice of religion, banned the teaching of Hebrew, and not only rejected most applications to emigrate but punished those Jews who had applied, depriving them of their jobs and privileges like housing and higher education. These "*refusniks*," Jews who were denied the right to leave their own country, became the subject of international controversy. Except for a brief period of "detente" during the 1970s, when East and West established cordial relations, the West used the *refusniks* to illustrate the East's human rights abuses. Whenever a group of Jews managed to gain permission to leave, they were welcomed by the United States and other western countries.

Since the breakup of the former Soviet Union, many Jews have emigrated and the number is expected to grow. The State of Israel anticipates that the majority, nearly a million immigrants, will settle there.

From *The Uprooted: Refugees and the United States* ©1995 Nancy Flowers and David M. Donahue, published by Hunter House Inc., Publishers, 1-800-266-5592.

JEWISH REFUGEES FROM EASTERN EUROPE: 1890–1990, CASE STUDIES

THE TESTIMONY OF RUTH KATZ, A RABBI'S DAUGHTER IN RUSSIA

From Jewish Grandmothers *by Sydelle Kramer and Jenny Masur. Copyright © 1977 by Sydelle Kramer and Jenny Masur. Reprinted by permission of Beacon Press.*

"In 1905 there was a Kishinev pogrom [in imitation of the infamous 1903 pogrom in the city of Kishinev]. Well, after that the czar decided that it was good to have pogroms all over. So it came [when I was] about six years old an order to the Russian highest offices to make a pogrom in our town for Sunday. So about one in the morning, that officer himself risked his life. He knocked on the window and told my father to go to synagogue and call all the Jews together and tell them to hide in the cellar for 24 hours—that tomorrow morning, when the soldiers come to kill the Jews, they'll open the doors and they won't see anybody; they'll think the Jews left. Middle of the night, my father called the Jews together. We were a town of maybe 150 families. Never will I forget that experience, that 24 hours in the cellar. There was no water, no toilet services, but we managed . . . .

"Now there is a story about how I came to America [when] I was a little over sixteen years. We had a neighbor in Russia and he paid the soldiers that let boys [draftees escaping the harsh Russian conscription of Jewish males] across the border. So he was caught and he was sent to jail. My father went to the state and vouched for him and told them that he'll never do that business again if they'll free him. So that neighbor had a brother in Baltimore, who brought the whole family to Baltimore. And they wanted to be grateful to my father. . . . So that neighbor wrote, 'Send me the two younger girls first. And by the time you'll sell [your possessions], they'll go to school and get a little English education.' So an older sister and I came to Baltimore. . . . That was in 1913, and in 1914 we had the war. After the war, my parents were too old and too broken up and too sick to come. The rest of the family never came. There were three sisters and two brothers here."

1. On the basis of her testimony, do you think Ruth Katz should have received admission to the United States as a refugee in 1913? If the events she describes had happened in the last few years, do you think she would receive admission today? Should she? Explain the reasons for your answers.

2. On the basis of her testimony, does Ruth Katz qualify as a refugee under the definition used today by international law? Explain the reasons for your answers.

3. Ruth Katz applied for admission to the United States in 1913. What was the likelihood that she would be admitted? What would be the likelihood of her parents' gaining admission if they had tried to enter the United States in 1921 after World War I? Explain the reasons for your answers. (See **Handout 9: Jewish Refugees from Eastern Europe: 1890–1990, Historical Overview,** p. 46 and **Handout 7: United States Immigration and Refugee Policy Timeline,** p. 38 for more information.)

THE TESTIMONY OF ROSE SOSKIN,
A YOUNG GIRL IN POLAND DURING WORLD WAR I

From Jewish Grandmothers *by Sydelle Kramer and Jenny Masur. Copyright © 1977 by Sydelle Kramer and Jenny Masur. Reprinted by permission of Beacon Press.*

"I was born in 1906. We were raised in Semiatycze, Grodnoguberniia. Originally it was Poland. Then it became Russia because the Bolsheviks came in, and then the Germans came in and chased out the Bolsheviks. We had the Germans for four years. They were pretty nasty, but not as bad as in World War II . . . .

"We were five children, and we only had one bedroom. I'll never forget it. We used to sleep on top of the oven . . . . When we used to go to pick wood in the woods or pick berries, they wouldn't let us. Because, you see, we were Jews. The *skutsim* [Polish gentiles] used to throw stones or take a nice long piece of wood and chase us. I still have one mark from a cane that he was chasing me with, and I fell down, I couldn't run anymore. He just beat me so that my foot was split up and I was bleeding like a pig . . . .

"We all spoke Polish and we were all going to school . . . . In the Polish school, we had to stand on our knees on Sunday and sing, and we had to cross ourselves, even if we were Jewish girls; otherwise, they wouldn't let us go to the school . . . . They killed plenty, too. They killed some citizens in the town that were just innocent people. One fellow that used to date my older sister was talking back to the Polacks (that was before the Bolsheviks came in), and they said, 'He's a Bolshevik.' He was trying to hide, and they killed him. His own parents had to take him to the cemetery on a board. It was terrible a tragedy—just martyrs.

"Then the time of war [World War I] was marching on Poland. They had the front right in the town . . . . You couldn't go out, the bullets was always going over, you know.

"Then the Russians came in. They brought in Russian teachers, and we had to learn the Russian language. And they made us sing in Russian the *Internationale* in school. We had to talk Russian in the street when we got out from school.

"We had about three synagogues, but they burned them down. They didn't like the Jewish religion to be kept up. They wanted everybody to go with them, to be Russian. They didn't allow religion in school even.

"When the Germans came, we were forced to learn German. We were learning all kinds of German songs. We were young kids; young kids are easier to learn, and to forget, than grownup's . . . . Here in the United States, we're doing things in American way; there we had to do Polish way, we had to do Russian style, we had to do German style, and were pushed from one school to the other, and from one style to the other. Our education was very hard . . . .

"We used to be hungry in school and hungry when we came home from school. It was tough, it was tough quite a few years. Just smelling bread was enough [to make us hungry] . . . .

"For four years, the Germans stayed, and they cleaned out everything in town. We couldn't get butter, we couldn't get eggs, we couldn't get cheeses, we couldn't get anything, and then they started taking away cows, so it was just impossible to keep alive. Even if there would be anything, we didn't have money to buy . . . .

"During the day, we couldn't go out; the war was in our town. It was like the front, you know; they were shooting all through, so nobody went out. [If] we were sticking our nose even through the window, we were scared. Then we were forced to take things that didn't belong to us, so we can eat. We didn't go steal in joy or anything but we would have to go and take some potatoes or turnips just to keep up, just to keep from dying from hunger. We could eat even grass that time, like cows. We were really hungry, desperate for everything that's food . . . .

"We were right on the front so we were always hiding in the basement, day and night. We didn't know what day it is or what time it is. We just kept saving our lives. Most of the time, we were drinking boiled water . . . . Many times, my mother, she should rest in peace, used to run out at night to the fields for water and potatoes, turnips, carrots, beets. And we were always looking from the basement to the street to see if Mommy's coming because without her, we were just like lost.

"And then we couldn't make a fire. The soldiers would march by and they would see smoke coming out the chimney, they would break the door down and come in. One time, I think it was Friday, my mother got some turnips, but we couldn't eat them—they were too hard. So she says she'll just try to cook them a little bit. We couldn't wait until they got soft, but when she tried to cook the turnips, the smoke was coming. And we hear the Polacks; my mother says: 'Kids, let's all stay together,' and we were all tying up with my mother. All of a sudden, you hear the knock and the door was broken off, and there must have been six or seven [soldiers].

"This picture, I can close my eyes or open my eyes. Many times I lay down and I'm thinking of that: it was such a funny way, how they were so angry, and they were so mean when they were outside; they said when they find any Jewish people, they'll cut their throats like you'll kill in the stockyards. Life made them so aggravated: they didn't sleep enough, their life didn't mean anything. The soldiers were not particularly after anybody, but they were hungry. They'd fight for food. But when they come in, they all started laughing instead of being mean, you see; they saw we were all holding onto my mother all around . . . . So we gave them water, and we gave them the turnips; we were grabbing pieces ourselves. We were all very hungry . . . .

" . . . A war is a funny thing, see; there are so many bad things happening that you just can't imagine that could ever happen in your life. You can live through your whole life, you could never go through the experience that people go through when they live through a war, in a town especially that the war is right on."

1. On the basis of her testimony, do you think Rose Soskin should have received admission to the United States as a refugee in 1919? If the events she describes had happened in the last few years, do you think she would receive admission today? Should she? Explain the reasons for your answers.

2. On the basis of her testimony, does Rose Soskin qualify as a refugee under the definition used today by international law? Explain the reasons for your answers.

3. If Rose Soskin had applied for admission to the United States in 1919, after the conclusion of World War I, what would be the likelihood that she would be admitted? What would be the likelihood if she had tried to enter before the war in 1914? Explain the reasons for your answers. (See **Handout 9: Jewish Refugees from Eastern Europe: 1890–1990, Historical Overview,** p. 46 and **Handout 7: United States Immigration and Refugee Policy Timeline,** p. 38 for more information.)

From *The Uprooted: Refugees and the United States* ©1995 Nancy Flowers and David M. Donahue, published by Hunter House Inc., Publishers, 1-800-266-5592.

THE TESTIMONY OF TANYA SHIMIEWSKY, A POLISH HOLOCAUST SURVIVOR

From Joan Morrison and Charlotte Fox Zabusky, American Mosaic: The Immigrant Experience in the Words of Those Who Lived It. *© 1980, © 1993 by Joan Morrison and Charlotte Fox Zabusky. Reprinted by permission of the University of Pittsburgh Press.*

"When the Germans came to our town, we were scared in our own houses. Then they made the ghetto. In my town! They moved all the Jews from the whole town together, just in a few streets. And they brought in Polish people from someplace and they put them in the houses where the Jews used to live.

"We had to wear the Jewish star. It is still always in my subconscious. When I get dressed, I always look whether I have it on. It never leaves me. It was a yellow star and black—a yellow patch and the Star of David on it, and Jew written there. We had to wear it on all clothes, whenever you went out. If you were caught without it, they put you in jail.

"This was in '39. It was very bad . . . . One Saturday I heard that they took people, whole groups of people, and they send them out to Germany. And I saw that my husband doesn't come home from work. I didn't know what happened to him. I went out and someone told me she saw that they took them out. "I might as well tell you. They took Karl in there with the whole bunch." And they sent him away someplace. They were working putting rails for trains. And then he was in other concentration camps, in Auschwitz, and—I forgot already what concentration camps, Buchenwald, Dachau. He came out, he was like this forty kilos, eighty pounds—this big man.

"I stayed on with my mother and my child—she was then five years old . . . . And one day we heard that they're going to send out the rest of us, the whole town . . . . We were allowed to take a little knapsack and a little food. I put one dress on top of another, and another on top of the other, and a coat. The Polacks were standing inside, just looking. We had a janitor with a daughter, and she was always saying, "This house is going to be mine." And now we could see how it was true. They were just standing on the side and laughing. When we left our house, my mother said, 'I will never come here again.'

"We had to strip, take off all the clothes. There were men and women we knew, and we had to stay in one line, nude. And the doctors marked the people who were able to go to work *A*, and the other people *B* here—on them. I had *A* and my mother got *B*, and I knew right away that we're not going to be together.

"They took us to a big marketplace and they were selecting, saying *A* should go one side and *B* another side. And I left my little girl with my mother, and she was crying. I still have a guilty conscience that I left her. I always say to myself, maybe I should have stayed with my baby and my mother. And the other mothers with little infants, they ripped out the little children from them and threw them over fences . . . .

" . . . It was pouring rain, pouring rain, and we were standing all night in this big rain—everybody. And then in the morning they took us to Lodz, and my mother stayed with my daughter and I never saw them again. They told us that they sent the children and the old people someplace else to help in the fields, pick spinach and do little things. But a few people stayed on to help them, to manage with the people that were left, and a few days later they came in to the Lodz ghetto. These people told us that the Germans opened graves, and alive they put them in there and shot them there.

From *The Uprooted: Refugees and the United States* ©1995 Nancy Flowers and David M. Donahue, published by Hunter House Inc., Publishers, 1-800-266-5592.

" . . . After the holidays, after Rosh Hashanah, they sent us all out. The women and children were sent to Ravensbruck. From this camp some children are still alive—this is the only camp where they kept children alive . . . . We young women—of course, I was still young—were sent out to Wittenberg, and there we used to work in factories. We were making airplanes. I was put to make airplane wings . . . .

"And that's our life. I was there till the end of the war, till April 28 [1945]—and the Germans left. There were a lot of airplanes, and we knew that the war is close. And all of a sudden they walked out. One day we went out and we saw there were no Germans around. We didn't know what to do. There was still bombing going on, so we thought it's safer to stay in the camp. We went in the kitchen, their kitchen, and we got our food. We were happy. It was over. It was over . . . .

"Would you believe it? We walked back to Poland, a group of maybe eight or ten girls. We got hold of a wagon, a little wagon on four wheels, wooden, with a hold-on like a cross, to hold on to and pull on. Daytime we walked. At night we went into a German town, to the mayor, and they gave us money and food and lodging for the night. And we would stay just a night.

"When we came to Poland, the Polacks said, 'So many of you survived?' We were glad we came to our native country after Germany, and this is how they welcomed us. This broke our hearts more than anything else . . . . I looked around for somebody from my family. There was no one . . . ".

1. On the basis of her testimony, do you think Tanya Shimiewsky should have received admission to the United States as a refugee in 1946? If the events she describes had happened in the last few years, do you think she would receive admission today? Should she? Explain the reasons for your answers.

2. On the basis of her testimony, does Tanya Shimiewsky qualify as a refugee under the definition used today by international law? Explain the reasons for your answers.

3. If Tanya Shimiewsky applied for admission to the United States in 1946, just after the end of World War II, what would be the likelihood that she would be admitted? What would be the likelihood if she had tried to enter before the war, for instance in 1938? What would be the likelihood if she had tried to enter during the Cold War, for instance, in 1956? Explain the reasons for your answers. (See **Handout 9: Jewish Refugees from Eastern Europe: 1890–1990, Historical Overview,** p. 46 and **Handout 7: United States Immigration and Refugee Policy Timeline,** p. 38 for more information.)

THE TESTIMONY OF SOFIA RABINOVICH, A RUSSIAN DOCTOR

From Joan Morrison and Charlotte Fox Zabusky, American Mosaic: The Immigrant Experience in the Words of Those Who Lived It. *©1980, ©1993 by Joan Morrison and Charlotte Fox Zabusky. Reprinted by permission of the University of Pittsburgh Press.*

"I knew each minute of my life that I am Jewish. It was my mother—when I was a little child, she *benscht licht* [blessed the candles] on Sabbath evening, Friday evening before Sabbath. Then something changed. You know, it's difficult for a child to understand. I was

From *The Uprooted: Refugees and the United States* ©1995 Nancy Flowers and David M. Donahue, published by Hunter House Inc., Publishers, 1-800-266-5592.

too young to understand, but I know that everybody stop to go to church. Christian people stop and Jewish people stop. With the Revolution, nobody was religious.

"When I was in high school, before World War II, nobody had a problem if he was a Jew or if he was not a Jew, because everybody was equal. But with World War Second, start grow the customs against Jews. It was because of the Nazis.

"I was a student in medical school and I was in the Leningrad blockade. They closed the door to Leningrad. You cannot go out, you cannot go in, and you always under the attack of bombs. And hunger, because you had not food. It was a terrible time . . . . How to stay alive? It is difficult to believe how it was . . . . In the middle of the room, you had a little stove. And what you burn? Your desk, chairs, everything what you had.

"Some people died, students died, teachers died. Some people tried to stay in bed, maybe it will help, and these people died first. But life continued . . . . You lose your weight, you are like a skeleton, but you live. It's a lucky chance. We stayed alive . . . .

"I finished medical school in 1942 . . . . I grew from one position to another, and I received the highest that I can be for a man—not a woman, for a man. For a woman, it was unusual to be chief of a special research department . . . . It didn't matter that I was Jewish . . . .

"[But] for my son it was no future there. You know, he had the gold medal after school . . . . He decided to be a doctor, and he finished medical school in 1972. He was an excellent student . . . He said that he wanted to be in research, and they told him, "No, you will not go in research. You will go as a practitioner in a little town, in the country," Because he was a Jew. It was not another reason—everybody know, everybody knows. It is enough to have a point in your passport that you are a Jew . . . .

"He was disappointed . . . . But I understand it go from bad to worse, and he will never have a position in the hospital. It's impossible. We always thought about our son, and we wanted to do for him the best. I had a very good position, but I was disappointed. So we decided to leave Russia."

1. On the basis of her testimony, do you think Sofia Rabinovich should have received admission to the United States as a refugee in 1974? If the events she describes had happened in the last few years, do you think she would receive admission today? Should she? Explain the reasons for your answers.

2. On the basis of her testimony, does Sofia Rabinovich qualify as a refugee under the definition used today by international law? Explain the reasons for your answers.

3. Sofia Rabinovich applied for admission to the United States in 1974, during the "cold war." What was the likelihood that she would be admitted? Explain the reasons for your answers. (See **Handout 9: Jewish Refugees from Eastern Europe: 1890–1990, Historical Overview,** p. 46 and **Handout 7: United States Immigration and Refugee Policy Timeline,** p. 38 for more information.)

From *The Uprooted: Refugees and the United States* ©1995 Nancy Flowers and David M. Donahue, published by Hunter House Inc., Publishers, 1-800-266-5592.

JEWISH REFUGEES FROM EASTERN EUROPE: 1980–1990
EPILOGUES

1. About "The Testimony of Ruth Katz"

Ruth Katz's recollections capture a young person's view of the harsh early decades of the twentieth century for Russian Jews. Her easy admission to the United States reflects the open-door policy that characterized the early decades of the twentieth century when no distinction was made between refugees and immigrants.

2. About "The Testimony of Rose Soskin"

The experiences of Rose Soskin, recorded when she was 69, reflect some of the conditions of war and persecution that World War I brought on Jews in Eastern Europe outside Russia. Her father had entered the United States before World War I and the imposition of the Immigration Law of 1921, left her mother and five children to support themselves in Poland during the war.

After the war, with the help of the Hebrew Immigration and Aid Society, a nongovernmental organization that helps Jews emigrating from the Soviet Union, the family was reunited in the United States, gaining admission because their father was already in the country. But most refugees fleeing the same conditions found admission already barred by the restrictive new immigration laws.

3. About "The Testimony of Tanya Shimiewsky"

Tanya Shimiewsky's experience of the holocaust is rare—not only was she among the survivors, but miraculously she later found that her husband had also lived through concentration camps. After they were reunited, they like many other survivors decided to emigrate to the newly founded state of Israel. However, the offer of employment and sponsorship by relatives persuaded them to go to the United States instead, where they raised a family.

Looking back Tanya Shimiewsky says, "I've been here twenty-five years, and I still have dreams. When my grandson was born, I reminded myself about when they took the babies. The memories start coming back, and all these things are just alive again. Would you believe that a person can take so much? I still say I'm going back to Poland and look for my daughter . . . .

I never told my children all these things, never told them what I went through, because I didn't want to hurt them. Now I think I was wrong. Maybe they would understand life better. This [story] is for them."

4. About "The Testimony of Sofia Rabinovich"

As Sofia acknowledges, her family's application to emigrate came during a rare period when exit visas were relatively easy to obtain: "It was an excellent time, 1974. The relation between Russia and the United States, it was the best." With the help of the Hebrew Immigration Aid Society, Sofia and her family passed fairly easily out of Russia to the United States. Now her son practices medicine in New Jersey, and she spends her time translating her scientific books and articles into English.

Hers is not a typical story, however. Thousands of Jews were not only refused exit visas but also persecuted as "enemies of the state" for even applying for permission to leave. Many of these "refusniks" waited long years for their exit visas, if they were granted at all. With the dissolution of the former Soviet Union, however, restrictions on emigration were relaxed and many thousands of Russian Jews were able to leave the country, most going to settle in Israel.

From *The Uprooted: Refugees and the United States* ©1995 Nancy Flowers and David M. Donahue, published by Hunter House Inc., Publishers, 1-800-266-5592.

FROM EXCLUSION TO ACCEPTANCE
Restrictions Against Asian Immigrants and Refugees During the Last 150 Years

OVERVIEW: After reading a history of American immigration and refugee policy toward Asians, students are asked to analyze the factors which caused a group of people formerly excluded from admission to the United States to become one of the biggest immigrant and refugee groups today.

AGE LEVEL: High school

TIME: 1 hour

MATERIALS: Handout 6: From Exclusion to Acceptance

SUBJECT AREAS: Current events, U.S. history

OBJECTIVES:
- To analyze the factors, particularly racism that influenced U.S. policy and attitudes toward Asian immigrants and refugees
- To analyze the extent to which racism plays a role today in U.S. immigration and refugee policy

PART 1

Assign the class to read **Handout 11: From Exclusion to Acceptance** either in small groups or as homework. Use the following questions as the basis for a writing assignment or class discussion:

- Give examples of how racism influenced U.S. immigration and refugee policy toward Asia.
- What other factors influenced U.S. immigration and refugee policy toward Asia?
- In what ways, if any, does racism influence immigration and refugee policy today? What other factors influence U.S. immigration and refugee policy today?

PART 2

Ask students to look at the cartoons and other images of the Chinese from the late nineteenth century, on pages 62–63. What stereotypes did "native" Americans have of Asians, particularly the Chinese? How did those stereotypes influence attitudes toward Asian immigrants and refugees?

FURTHER ACTIVITIES

1. Have students draw an editorial cartoon or write a letter to the editor in response to the cartoons included in this section.

2. Ask students to use posterboard to create the front page of a Beijing newspaper reporting the Chinese Exclusion Act or a Tokyo newspaper reporting on the exclusion of Japanese in the Immigration Act of 1924.

3. Invite recent Indochinese refugees to discuss their journeys to the United States as well as the adjustments they have made since arriving.

Photo courtesy UNHCR/R. Manin

Vietnamese refugees or "boat people" being rescued in the South China Sea.

FROM EXCLUSION TO ACCEPTANCE
Restrictions Against Asian Immigrants and Refugees During the Last 150 Years

American policy toward Asian immigrants and refugees has ranged from total exclusion to acceptance during the last 150 years. Initially welcomed as a source of cheap labor, immigrants from Asia were legally excluded from the United States within several decades of their first arrival. This exclusionary policy continued for over 60 years and was liberalized only gradually, often in response to crises like the collapse of South Vietnam or other foreign policy concerns of the U.S. such as opposing communism. By the 1960s, however, when national quotas for immigrant and refugee admissions were dropped, Asian immigrants and refugees started to arrive in the U.S. in large numbers. By 1985 they constituted half of all newcomers to the U.S.

CHINESE IMMIGRATION

According to the American Immigration Commission, the first Chinese arrived in the United States in 1820. Until the 1860s the Chinese Imperial Code forbade expatriation, and even after the code was revoked, emigration was not encouraged. Up until the mid-1850s most of the Chinese immigrants were from the Kwangtung province, the area around Canton in southeast China. They came to work on California's farms, railroads, and gold mines. Employers had a favorable impression of industrious Chinese who worked for low wages. Native white workers, on the other hand, viewed the Chinese as a threat to "free labor" and used physical violence to intimidate them. Because China had no official envoy to the U.S. until 1878, Chinese immigrants had no protection. Threats to native white wages were not the only reason for anti-Chinese sentiment. Deep-seated prejudice against color, which had already warped American attitudes and policies toward blacks and native Americans, also fueled sentiments against the Chinese, who were the first substantial group of nonwhite immigrants to arrive in the U.S.

Responding to these fears and prejudices the California legislature passed laws against the Chinese, such as "An Act to Prevent the Further Immigration of Chinese or Mongolians to This State," as early as 1858. Four years later the legislature passed "An Act to Protect Free White Labor Against Competition With Chinese Coolie Labor and to Discourage the Immigration of the Chinese to the State of California."

On the national level, Congress responded to cries of a "yellow peril" by approving the Exclusion Act of 1882, which barred all Chinese from immigrating to the United States for a period of 10 years. This was subsequently renewed for another 10 years in 1892 and extended indefinitely in 1902. The Chinese Exclusion Act thus began the period in U.S. history during which immigration policy was officially racist.

JAPANESE IMMIGRATION

Japanese immigrants to the United States went through a period of welcome followed by antagonism and finally exclusion similar to the Chinese. When the Japanese first came in the

From *The Uprooted: Refugees and the United States* ©1995 Nancy Flowers and David M. Donahue, published by Hunter House Inc., Publishers, 1-800-266-5592.

nineteenth century, they filled a gap in the labor market working in fields. As their numbers increased and they competed with native farmers, whites developed anti-Japanese organizations to limit the movement and activities of the Japanese as well as prevent their immigration. Opposition to the Japanese reached its height around the turn of the twentieth century, after the Chinese "threat" had already been dealt with. In 1906 the San Francisco school board passed a resolution banning Japanese children from the public schools and in 1907 anti-Asian riots flared along the West Coast as newspapers whipped up xenophobia. Not wanting to affront Japanese pride but wanting also to appease those calling for immigration restrictions against the Japanese, President Theodore Roosevelt negotiated the "Gentlemen's Agreement" with Japan in 1907. With this informal understanding, both the United States and Japan agreed to stop all unwanted immigration.

FURTHER LEGISLATION AGAINST ASIAN IMMIGRATION

Restriction against Asians was even more firmly established in the Immigration Act of 1917, passed by Congress over President Wilson's veto. The Act called for exclusion of all immigrants from the "Asiatic barred zone." With the Chinese and Japanese already excluded, this act closed the door on any other immigrants or refugees from Asia.

During the 1920s, the call to end all immigration became louder. Consequently, Congress approved the Immigration Act of 1924 which, in addition to severely limiting the number of immigrants from southern and eastern Europe by setting national quotas, reaffirmed the exclusion of "Orientals" by banning all aliens who would be ineligible for citizenship. Because the Supreme Court had earlier ruled that Japanese immigrants could not be naturalized, the intent of the law was obvious. Japan, which had been willing to accept informal restrictions, viewed the language of the law as an insult to its pride, and the Japanese government proclaimed a day of national humiliation. The only Asians still allowed into the United States were Filipinos. Under a special provision of the Phillipine Independence Act of 1934, Congress allocated the Phillipines a quota of 50 immigrants annually.

By the Second World War, anti-Asian racism was expressed not only in immigration restriction, but in internment of Japanese-American citizens. Two months after the bombing of Pearl Harbor, President Roosevelt signed Executive Order 9066 ordering the removal of Japanese-Americans on the West Coast from their homes to isolated "relocation camps." By June, 1942, 120,000 Japanese-Americans had been uprooted from their homes, jobs, and lives.

GRADUAL RELAXATION OF RESTRICTIONS AGAINST ASIANS

The first relaxation of the ban on Asian immigrants was made in 1943 when, in a token gesture to a wartime ally, the United States granted China a quota of 100 immigrants per year. A further token liberalization came in 1952 with the passage of the McCarran-Walter Immigration and Nationality Act, which repealed Japanese exclusion, assigned tiny quotas for immigration to Asian nations, and gave Asian immigrants the right to naturalization.

During the 1950s, in response to the refugee crisis resulting from the Second World War, the United States passed legislation to meet the pressing needs of hundreds of thousands of refugees. The Refugee Relief Act of 1953 ignored national quotas for the first time and the Refugee-Escapee Act of 1957 established the first official definition of a refugee as a victim of racial, religious, or political persecution fleeing communist, communist-occupied, or

From *The Uprooted: Refugees and the United States* ©1995 Nancy Flowers and David M. Donahue, published by Hunter House Inc., Publishers, 1-800-266-5592.

Waiting at a Los Angeles train station to be interned at Owens Valley.

Photo © Underwood Archives

communist-dominated countries or a country in the Middle East. Though Hungarians fleeing the Soviet invasion of their country were the first beneficiaries of this law, it also benefitted Asian refugees. Culturally and racially mixed Dutch-Indonesians, displaced after Indonesia's independence from the Netherlands, were allowed refuge in the U.S., though without the public welcome of the Hungarians.

During an era when confronting communism was the centerpiece of all foreign policy, refugees fleeing communism stood the best chance of resettlement in the U.S. In May, 1962, the government of communist China relaxed its border controls, causing a flood of refugees to Hong Kong, which was already deluged with refugees. Using his presidential parole power to admit refugees, President Kennedy admitted several thousand Chinese refugees. Ironically, these were not the people who escaped China in 1962 but those already in Hong Kong who had been cleared for immigration since 1954 but were unable to enter because of the small Chinese quota.

THE IMMIGRATION ACT OF 1965

The Immigration Act of 1965 radically changed the ethnic mix of immigrants and refugees to the United States. Abolishing all national origins quotas, it established two ceilings for immigration—120,000 for the western hemisphere and 170,000 for the eastern hemisphere.

Within the eastern hemisphere, priority was established for persons with family ties and certain occupational skills. In 1978 the hemispheres were combined under a single priority system, and an overall ceiling of 290,000 (decreased by 20,000 two years later) was established. This act more than any other opened new opportunities for immigration from Asian countries that had been excluded or severely limited up until that time.

Refugees, placed last in order of priorities under the Immigration Act, continued to be of secondary importance to immigration policy. Only 6% of all admissions were for refugees. Again, often in response to confrontations with communism, special admissions were allowed. At the end of the Vietnam War, the U.S. made special provisions for the admission of up to 200,000 refugees from Vietnam, to be limited to U.S. employees and those whose lives would be in danger after the communist takeover. Popular sentiment was not in favor of large-scale resettlement of Vietnamese refugees, however. A 1975 Harris Poll found that only 36% of U.S. citizens thought Indochinese refugees should be admitted, while 54% supported exclusion. By the end of 1975 when 135,000 refugees had been evacuated from Indochina and resettled in the United States, the temporary relocation camps on Guam and Wake Island were closed in anticipation of the resettlement program's end. The "boat people" changed those plans.

THE "BOAT PEOPLE"

After the communist Khmer Rouge takeover of Cambodia, the Vietnamese invasion of Cambodia, and the communist Pathet Lao control of Laos, hundreds of thousands of new refugees sought asylum. Neighboring states that were already overburdened with refugee problems, such as Thailand, Singapore, and Malaysia, closed their borders. As a result refugees were forced to flee their homelands in dangerously overcrowded and under-provisioned boats, hoping to be rescued at sea. In violation of maritime law, many ships refused to pick up the refugees. Others that did found they were not allowed to land in port. In 1978 President Carter ordered all U.S.-registered ships to pick up refugee "boat people," promising resettlement in the United States if they so wanted. Many Hmong, the mountain-dwelling Laotians who were wartime allies, and other southeast Asians were resettled in U.S. communities as a result.

THE REFUGEE ACT OF 1980

It was during this time, when Americans were watching pictures of boat people on the news and feeling guilt and responsibility for those fleeing the communist regimes of Indochina, that Congress approved the Refugee Act of 1980, the first formal statement of U.S. refugee policy in history. From exclusion of all Asian refugees and immigrants less than half a century earlier, the United States had moved to official recognition of its responsibility to help refugees, motivated in no small part by the boat people of Indochina.

From *The Uprooted: Refugees and the United States* ©1995 Nancy Flowers and David M. Donahue, published by Hunter House Inc., Publishers, 1-800-266-5592.

GETTING THE WORDS RIGHT
A Vocabulary Activity Using Immigration and Refugee Terms

OVERVIEW: After reviewing **Appendix A: Immigration and Refugee Terms,** students are asked to choose the correct word in a series of historical, religious, and contemporary examples.

AGE LEVEL: High school

TIME: 1 hour

MATERIALS:
- Handout 12: Getting the Words Right
- Appendix A: Immigration and Refugee Terms

SUBJECT AREAS: Language arts, U.S. history, world studies

OBJECTIVES:
- To use immigration and refugee terms accurately
- To relate current refugee situations to analogous religious and historical situations

PART 1

Distribute **Appendix A: Immigration and Refugee Terms.** Go over each term with the class, offering students opportunities to use the words orally and to ask questions. Provide as many opportunities as possible for students to pronounce the words, use them them in sentences, and vary their part of speech (e.g., *emigrate, emigrant* as noun and adjective, *emigration*). Ask students to supply examples from their own experiences and illustrative sentences for the words. You may want to supplement their examples with others, especially from current events.

The etymologies will help some students, especially in differentiating between *emigrate* and *immigrate*. Especially stress the difference between these pairs:

- *immigrant* and *refugee,* which is defined by law and has specific legal implications
- seeking *asylum,* which a person does if she or he is already in the United States, and seeking *refugee status,* which must be done from an office outside the United States

PART 2.

Distribute **Handout 12: Getting the Words Right.** Ask students to complete it using **Appendix A: Immigration and Refugee Terms** as a glossary.

Review the completed handout, asking students to explain their choice of answers. Help the class generate a list of the most frequently confused words from this exercise and discuss why these particular words cause difficulty.

PART 3

Ask the class to make up additional vocabulary exercises based on any period of U.S. history, including contemporary events.

Answer key to GETTING THE WORDS RIGHT

A	B.
1. migrants	1. origin
2. emigrants	2. first asylum
3. been resettled	3. resettlement
4. being repatriated	4. repatriated to
5. immigrants	5. economic refugees
6. found asylum in	6. work
7. refoulement	7. "coyote"
8. naturalized	8. detains
9. repatriated persons	9. refoulement
10. naturalized	10. sanctuary

GETTING THE WORDS RIGHT
A Vocabulary Activity Using Immigration and Refugee Terms

HISTORICAL EXAMPLES

Using **Appendix A: Immigration and Refugee Terms** (page 172) for reference, circle the correct word in the following historical examples.

1. When the Protestant religion was banned in France in 1598, many Huguenots, or French Protestants, escaped persecution by fleeing to England, a Protestant country, or the English colonies in America.

Which of the following terms does NOT describe their situation in England's American colonies?

aliens   exiles   migrants   refugees

2. In the eighteenth century, British citizens imprisoned for debt were allowed to serve out shortened prison sentences if they would settle permanently in the English colony of Georgia. Those who choose this option were _____ from England

displaced persons   emigrants   immigrants   refugees

3. In the nineteenth century the United States government forced Cherokee Indians to leave their homes in the southern Appalachians and live on reservations in Oklahoma. They had _____.

been deported   immigrated   migrated   been resettled

4. One attempt of the Abolitionist Movement to "help" former slaves was to return them to their home countries in Africa. These returned former slaves were _____.

being deported   emigrating   being exiled   being repatriated

5. As a result of famine caused by a disease that destroyed potato crops, many Irish farmers came to seek new lives in the United States. Which term describes their situation in America?

asylum seekers   deportees   emigres   immigrants

6. Thousands of Armenians fled Turkey after an estimated two million of their fellow Armenians were massacred in 1916. They _____ many countries, especially the United States, to build new lives.

were deported to   emigrated to   took asylum in   were repatriated to

From *The Uprooted: Refugees and the United States* ©1995 Nancy Flowers and David M. Donahue, published by Hunter House Inc., Publishers, 1-800-266-5592.

7. In the 1950s, Soviet troops violently put down an uprising against the communist government of Hungary. Forced to flee, many Hungarians were received by the United States, which especially welcomed people escaping communism. Which word does NOT describe what these refugees were offered by the United States?

    asylum   haven   refoulement   refuge

8. Because conditions in Hungary did not change for many years, most of these Hungarians eventually were _____, becoming U.S. citizens with full rights (except the right to run for President).

    naturalized   detained   displaced   resettled

9. After the American Revolution, many Tories, or supporters of the British government, left the new United States for Canada, which was still British territory at that time, or returned to to Britain. These Tories were _____.

    repatriated persons   immigrants   exiles   naturalized persons

10. The Immigration Act of 1924 banned all aliens who were ineligible for citizenship. Because the Supreme Court had previously ruled that Japanese could not be _____, the Japanese were effectively prevented from immigrating to the United States.

    naturalized   expelled   repatriated   deported

CONTEMPORARY EXAMPLES

Fill in the blank with an appropriate word from **Appendix A: Immigration and Refugee Terms.** More than one term may be used correctly in a single blank.

A. During the late 1970s civil war racked Cambodia. The Pol Pot regime drove thousands of city dwellers into the countryside where they starved while raising crops for the army. Then the Vietnamese army invaded and further warfare erupted. Thousands of Cambodians fled into Thailand where they lived in camps waiting for conditions to allow them to return home. After many years of waiting, some of these Cambodians have given up hope of returning to their country, and with the help of relief agencies like the U.N. High Commission for Refugees, they have have found new, permanent homes in other countries, including the United States.

    1. For these refugees Cambodia was their country of _____.

        resettlement   origin   repatriation   first asylum

    2. Few Cambodians settled permanently in Thailand; it was these refugees' country of _____.

        resettlement   origin   repatriation   first asylum

    3. For many of these refugees, the United States is their country of _____.

        resettlement   origin   repatriation   first asylum

From *The Uprooted: Refugees and the United States* ©1995 Nancy Flowers and David M. Donahue, published by Hunter House Inc., Publishers, 1-800-266-5592.

4. In the early 1990s warring factions in Cambodia made a peace settlement, and the new coalition government invited Cambodian refugees in Thailand to return home. Cambodians who decided conditions were safe enough and returned were _____ Cambodia.

   resettled in   given asylum in   repatriated to

B. Unable to find work in their native Mexican village, the two Villas brothers decide to go the United States, hoping to earn enough there to help their wives, parents, and children at home. They sneak across the border and eventually find jobs harvesting crops in California's Central Valley.

   5. They are _____ in the United States.

   economic refugees   asylum seekers   political refugees   religious refugees

   6. Without a "green card" the Villas brothers will not legally be able to _____ in the United States.

   go to school   marry   work   use social services

   7. Because sneaking across the border is dangerous as well as illegal, the Villas brothers needed help. They paid for the services of _____ to get across the U.S. border

   the Immigration and Naturalization Service   a "coyote"
   the U.N. High Commissioner for Refugees   Amnesty International

   8. The Immigration and Naturalization Service _____ all persons who are illegally in the United States until it can determine the validity of their claims for asylum.

   deports   detains   naturalizes   repatriates

C. After the 1991 coup against President Aristide in Haiti, thousands of Haitians, including some of Aristide's supporters, attempted to leave the country for the United States. The Coast Guard stopped Haitian boats off the coast of Florida, refusing most claims for asylum.

   9. The Haitians who were not granted asylum faced _____ to their homeland.

   resettlement   voluntary repatriation   refoulement

D. Some religious communities in the United States provide shelter and assistance to persons seeking asylum.

   10. These churches, mosques, and synagogues are part of the _____ movement.

   immigration   refoulement   sanctuary   emigration

From *The Uprooted: Refugees and the United States* ©1995 Nancy Flowers and David M. Donahue, published by Hunter House Inc., Publishers, 1-800-266-5592.

INTERPRETING CARTOONS
Refugees in the United States as Seen Through Editorial Cartoons

OVERVIEW: Using editorial cartoons as a primary resource, students analyze the differences and similarities over time of the response to immigrants and refugees. They also develop the interpretive skills necessary to understand editorial cartoons.

AGE LEVEL: High school–adult

TIME: About 45 minutes

MATERIALS: Overhead transparencies created from the cartoons on pages 71–73; an overhead projector

SUBJECT AREA: U.S. history

OBJECTIVES:

- To describe the differences and similarities over time of the United States response to immigrants and refugees
- To interpret editorial cartoons and understand the cartoonist's point of view

PART 1

Using an overhead projector, show students the six cartoons reproduced here in rough chronological order. Ask students the following questions about each cartoon:

- How are immigrants and refugees depicted?
- What was the reaction of Americans to these immigrant groups as reflected in each cartoon? (Some cartoons describe the official response of the U.S. government while others depict the attitude of American citizens.)
- Does the cartoon argue for restrictions against immigrants and refugees or does it argue for welcoming immigrants and refugees?
- Describe the reasons immigrants and refugees are welcomed or not welcomed in the cartoon.

PART 2

After showing all the cartoons, ask:

- In general, how are immigrants and refugees depicted?
- Judging from these cartoons how has the response of Americans (both the government and the public) changed over time? In what ways has it stayed the same?

■ Irony is the difference between expected results and the actual outcome. What is ironic about some Americans NOT wanting to let in immigrants and refugees?

■ Can you find examples of racial and ethnic stereotypes in these cartoons? Try to define the stereotypes used to depict particular immigrant groups.

PART 3

One of the cartoons uses the metaphor of a wave to describe the refugees and immigrants coming into the United States. Ask students what other metaphors they can think of or ask them to complete the following statement:

Immigrants and refugees coming to the United States today are like _____.

Have students draw cartoons that illustrates their metaphors. Post the cartoons around the classroom. Ask the following questions after students have completed their cartoons:

■ Do the metaphors and cartoons present a positive or negative view of immigrants and refugees?

■ What explanations are there for the way immigrants and refugees are depicted?

■ Can you find examples of racial and ethnic stereotypes in these cartoons? Try to define the stereotypes used to depict particular immigrant groups?

REFUGEES IN POLITICAL CARTOONS

"They Would Close to the New-Comer the Bridge that Carried Them and Their Fathers Over." The descendants of the old immigrants faced the dilemma caricatured here.

A popular notion was that special-interest groups supported the flow of poor immigrants to the United States.

From *The Uprooted: Refugees and the United States* ©1995 Nancy Flowers and David M. Donahue, published by Hunter House Inc., Publishers, 1-800-266-5592.

The "new" immigrants were attacked as illiterate paupers, criminals, and advocates of anarchy and socialism.

From *The Uprooted: Refugees and the United States* ©1995 Nancy Flowers and David M. Donahue, published by Hunter House Inc., Publishers, 1-800-266-5592.

Illustration © Historical Pictures/Stock Montage, Inc.

"Spoiling the Broth"

From The Uprooted: Refugees and the United States ©1995 Nancy Flowers and
David M. Donahue, published by Hunter House Inc., Publishers, 1-800-266-5592.

Illustration © Don Wright

Illustration © 1992 Moran, The Miami Herald

THE NUMBERS TELL THE STORY
Interpreting Timelines and Charts

OVERVIEW: Using **Handout 7: U.S. Immigration and Refugee Policy Timeline** and **Handout 8: Growth of a Nation,** students learn the history of immigration and refugee flight to the United States and formulate hypotheses to explain why the U.S. response to immigration changed over time. They also learn how numbers can be manipulated to support different points of view.

AGE LEVEL: High school

TIME: About 45–60 minutes

MATERIALS:

- Handout 14: The Numbers Tell the Story

- An overhead transparency or copies prepared from Growth of a Nation (pages 42–43), an overhead projector

SUBJECT AREA: current events, geography, U.S. history, world studies

OBJECTIVES:

- To learn immigration trends in the United States since 1820 and the reasons behind them

- To interpret information from different kinds of graphs and charts

- To analyze how information can be used selectively to convey different and sometimes opposing points of view

PART 1

Distribute or project the timeline of immigration to students. Ask students to answer the questions on **Handout 14: The Numbers Tell the Story** individually, in pairs, or in groups, or ask the questions in class and have students discuss their answers.

PART 2

Ask students to choose one of the following roles and assign them the accompanying writing assignment:

- **Presidential Speechwriter:** You are writing a speech that the President will deliver at the base of the Statue of Liberty. What statistics or facts will you use to make the point that the United States opens its arms wide to immigrants? Write the opening paragraph to the President's speech.

- **Author:** You are researching a book on Asian immigration to the United States. You believe that Asians have been treated unfairly. What statistics or facts will you use to demonstrate that U.S.

policy has favored Asian immigrants less than others? Write the opening paragraph or jacket flap copy for your new book.

- **U.S. Senator:** You are adamantly against more refugees coming to the United States, and you want to give a speech on the floor of the Senate expressing your opinions. What statistics or facts will you use as support for your opinion? Write the concluding paragraph of your speech in the Senate.

- **Newspaper Editorial Writer:** Your paper is in favor of liberal immigration policies that would allow greater numbers of immigrants into the United States. What statistics or facts will you use to argue that the U.S. should accept large numbers of immigrants? Write the concluding paragraph to your newspaper editorial.

THE NUMBERS TELL THE STORY
Interpreting Timelines and Charts

1. Answer the following questions based on **Handout 7: U.S. Immigration and Refugee Policy Timeline**:

A. What years were the peak years for immigration?

B. Where did most immigrants come from during those years?

C. Before 1960 what part of the world did most immigrants come from?

D. Since 1960 where have most immigrants come from?

2. Answer the following questions referring to the timeline and a U.S. history book:

A. "Push factors" are reasons immigrants have for leaving their home countries. What push factors might have caused immigrants to leave during peak years of immigration?

B. "Pull factors" are reasons immigrants have for choosing their new countries. What pull factors might have caused immigrants to come to the U.S. during peak years of immigration?

C. In a few sentences, describe how the United States' policy of admitting immigrants and refugees has changed since 1820?

D. What are some possible explanations for these changes of attitude?

E. How might these changes in attitude have been linked to where the immigrants were coming from?

F. How might these changes in attitudes have been linked to what was happening in the United States?

3. The following questions are based on the graph, "Growth of a Nation":

A. During the years 1961–84, from which countries did the most immigrants admitted to the U.S. under refugee acts come?

B. What characteristics do these nations share?

C. Why do you think the United States decided to grant asylum to refugees from those countries at that time?

From *The Uprooted: Refugees and the United States* ©1995 Nancy Flowers and David M. Donahue, published by Hunter House Inc., Publishers, 1-800-266-5592.

PART III

REFUGEES AND THE UNITED STATES TODAY

UNITED STATES REFUGEE AND ASYLUM POLICY

WHO IS A REFUGEE?

While refugees have looked to the United States as a haven for hundreds of years, refugee policy in the United States was not established until recently. The Refugee Act of 1980 defines who is a refugee and establishes policy for determining which refugees and how many of them shall be admitted. The act defines a refugee as:

> . . . any person who is outside any country of such person's nationality or, in the case of a person having no nationality, is outside any country in which such a person last habitually resided, and who is unable or unwilling to return to, and is unable or unwilling to avail himself or herself of the protection of that country because of persecution or a well-founded fear of persecution on account of race, religion, nationality, membership in a particular social group, or political opinion.

This definition is similar to the one found in the United Nations Convention on the Status of Refugees, and it applies to refugees resettling in the United States as well as those seeking political asylum. The United States grants refuge or asylum only to those who are persecuted on account of race, religion, nationality, membership in a social group, or political opinion. It does not grant asylum or refugee status to those who are suffering from economic hardships shared by an entire country as a result of government policy.

DETERMINING THE NUMBER OF REFUGEES TO BE ADMITTED

Every year the President, in consultation with the Judiciary Committees of both the House of Representatives and the Senate, determines the number of refugees that will be admitted during the following year, as well as how that number will be divided among various regions in the world. The administration uses several criteria to determine the number of refugees who will be allowed admission to the United States. These criteria include the need for resettlement by refugees throughout the world, the anticipated level of support for asylum that will be provided by other countries, the impact of refugees on U.S. foreign policy, and the social and economic impact of the refugees once they are resettled. The total number of refugees admitted from year to year varies, the average being around 60,000. In recent years at least half of the annual number of admissions has gone to refugees from Southeast Asia. Applications are considered on a first-come-first-served basis, and every year more people apply for refugee status than there are places. Typically, persons who qualify as refugees are placed on waiting lists. In an emergency, such as a natural disaster or war, the President can consult with the Judiciary Committees and revise the number of allowable refugees. Also, the Immigration Act of 1990 provides for "temporary protective status," which prevents for 18 months the deportation of individuals fleeing emergency situations. Although there is a quota for refugees (people applying from abroad for resettlement), the United States has no annual quota for political asylum-seekers (persons already on U.S. soil applying for refugee status). In all other respects, however, the law states that qualifications for those seeking asylum and refugees are the same.

RECENT DEVELOPMENTS

Although the Refugee Act of 1980 defines a "refugee", applying that definition in a post-Cold War world is the challenge for refugee policy in the future. Persons who at one time would have had no trouble receiving asylum must now go through a long, uncertain process, while others who would never have dreamed of asylum a few years ago may stand a better chance.

Until recently, asylum seekers from the Eastern bloc nations stood a very good chance of receiving asylum. Now they are processed for asylum according to the same procedures as other asylum seekers, and they must prove persecution individually. Even Jews from the former Soviet Union have been denied refuge by the United States, which now claims anti-Semitism is no longer institutionalized in the nations that once comprised the U.S.S.R. Nonetheless, change comes slowly; more than 50,000 former Soviets, mostly high-level dissidents, Jews, evangelical Christians, and those with close ties to the United States, qualified for refugee status in 1992, more than from any other region.

The Immigration and Naturalization Service (INS) and the federal courts have continued to define what constitutes persecution of a well-founded fear of persecution. In 1994, a federal judge ruled that China's "one child" birth control policy amounted to persecution on account of political opinion. Also in 1994, the INS granted asylum for the first time to someone claiming persecution based on sexual orientation. In that case, the INS ruled that Jose Garcia from Mexico was persecuted because of his membership in a social group.

Determining who is a refugee and who is not a refugee takes time. Nonetheless, in 1994 the Clinton administration proposed changes in the asylum system that would "streamline" the process. Under the

Photo courtesy Eric Avery

Illegal immigrants being released from leg cuffs at the Laredo, Texas, bridge. They will be escorted over the bridge to Mexico for deportation.

proposed new regulations, the United States would become the first nation in the world to charge refugees a fee—$130—to apply for asylum. Applicants for asylum would also be denied work permits for up to six months. The intent of the legislation is to cut down on "frivolous" asylum applications. At the same time, many legitimate applicants for asylum come from some of the poorest countries in the world, where $130 is a tremendous sum of money. Clinton also proposed doubling the number of asylum hearing officers from 150 to 300 to handle the backlog of 364,000 applications. The backlog grows at a rate of 10,000 cases a month. In 1993, 150,386 people from 154 nations applied for asylum in the United States. Of those, 18,110 were denied and 5,105 were approved. The rest are pending.

GOVERNMENT AGENCIES RESPONSIBLE FOR REFUGEES

Several government agencies have responsibility for refugees. The **Immigration and Naturalization Service (INS)**, an agency of the U.S. Department of Justice, makes all decisions about asylum claims and processes all applications by refugees for resettlement. The INS is responsible for determining whether a person meets the legal definition of a refugee. The agency also has enforcement powers to apprehend, detain, and deport.

The **Office of the U.S. Coordinator for Refugee Affairs** coordinates efforts on behalf of refugees between public and private agencies and between different levels of government. The **Bureau for Refugee Programs**, located in the State Department, develops and implements policies related to refugee relief and assistance overseas and U.S. contributions to international refugee organizations. It sets priorities for admission of refugees to the U.S. and provides resources for the processing and training of refugees. When refugees arrive in the U.S., the Bureau oversees their reception and placement in communities through cooperative agreements and contracts with voluntary agencies.

The **Office of Refugee Resettlement**, part of the Department of Health and Human Services, is responsible for U.S. programs to help refugees who have settled here. Usually administered by state governments, these programs include cash assistance, medical assistance, and social services. The **Office of Refugee Health** coordinates the activities of Public Health Service agencies involved in refugee health programs. In addition, it oversees medical screening of refugees. Agencies in individual states also assist refugees, sometimes in cooperation with voluntary agencies. They offer help such as language and job training as well as cash assistance.

Unlike immigrants, who are not allowed to use most welfare programs, refugees are eligible for government programs to help them make the transition to life in the United States. This government assistance is designed to be transitional only as refugees settle in their new homes. Since most refugees had no time to plan their flight and few resources to establish new homes in another country, these programs are especially important for them. Unlike many immigrants, refugees usually do not have families in the United States to whom they can turn for help. Most refugees become self-supporting, and their reliance on government support decreases over time.

APPLYING FOR REFUGEE STATUS AND ASYLUM IN THE UNITED STATES

Refugees enter the United States in one of two ways: by applying for **refugee status** in this country after fleeing from their home country to another country, or by directly entering the United States and asking for **asylum**. The application processes for both are similar, but there are some differences, each presenting advantages and disadvantages for the refugee. Both processes are described here.

PROCEDURES FOR APPLYING FOR REFUGEE STATUS

Anyone who is an object of persecution or who is fleeing a well-founded fear of persecution on the basis of race, religion, nationality, or membership in an organization or political party is eligible to file for refugee status in the United States. This is different from **asylum** (described on page 17), which is available only to persons who have already entered the United States. A person who is not living in the United States must file for refugee status at one of the 14 Immigration and Naturalization Service (INS) offices located overseas in Frankfurt, Vienna, Athens, Rome, New Delhi, Seoul, Bangkok, Hong Kong, Singapore, Manila, Mexico City, Guadalajara, Monterrey, and Panama City. Refugees can walk into these offices and usually begin the application process immediately. However, the application must be made in person and cannot be completed by mail. Because refugees often do not have passports, getting into a country where an INS office is located is not easy.

Qualifying for Refugee Status   Refugees must prove to the INS that they are or will be objects of persecution. Generally persecution is defined as a threat to life or physical safety. Discrimination based on race, religion, or nationality could also be examples of persecution if those persecuted are unable to find jobs, get apartments, or worship. The loss of civil rights such as

Photo courtesy Eric Avery

Detained women await processing at an INS Detention Center near Harlington, Texas.

freedom of speech or press is not considered persecution by the INS. The persecution must also be greater than the general persecution suffered by everyone in the applicants' home country. For example, persons from a nation where political violence is widespread cannot claim refugee status unless the violence directed at them is greater than what most people in their country experience. In addition, the persecution must be specifically aimed at the person applying for refugee status. For instance, persons fleeing a country because they belong to an ethnic group which is discriminated against cannot claim refugee status unless they can prove that they personally have suffered from the discrimination targeted at that group.

Refugees must also prove that they have no safe haven in any country other than the United States. The INS does not consider a refugee's preference for living in the United States as a factor in determining admission. Refugees offered resettlement in another country will not be allowed refuge in the U.S. In addition, refugees are required to prove that they can pay for their transportation to the U.S. and have some means of support after they arrive. Usually these are provided for by private agencies such as churches and refugee assistance organizations. A refugee's spouse and children under 21 years of age are automatically granted refugee status if they can document their relationship to the refugee.

Applicants for refugee status are responsible for filling out a form requesting refugee status in the United States. They must also produce documents such as birth certificates and proof that they are being persecuted, and all these documents must be originals or government-certified copies. Because many refugees flee their homes in haste, they often do not have time to collect the necessary documents. Sometimes the INS office accepts other kinds of documents in lieu of birth and marriage certificates and permits refugees to prove their persecution by writing a sworn statement describing their experiences. In addition, documents such as newspaper articles, statements from reliable people familiar with the situation in that country, or human rights reports from organizations like Amnesty International can be used to support the applicants' claims.

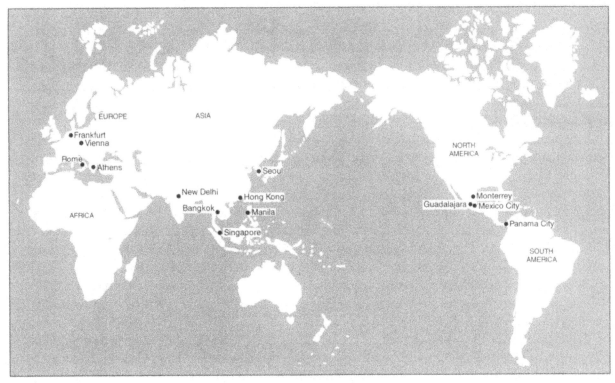

INS offices outside the United States

The final stage of the application requires a medical examination and a personal interview with an INS official. Refugees are expected to pay from $20 to $100 for an exam by a private physician, who makes sure they do not have conditions such as tuberculosis, venereal diseases, AIDS, or insanity that would make them ineligible. After the exam the INS official looks over the application and asks questions in great detail about the applicant's persecution at home.

Granting or Denying Refugee Status If all the papers are in order and the INS determines that the applicant is fleeing a well-founded fear of persecution, then the refugee is granted a travel document. This allows the successful applicant to enter the United States as a refugee. If refugees do not enter the U.S. within four months after approval, then they lose this refugee status.

If the INS turns down a person's application for refugee status for some reason, no formal appeal process exists. The only recourse is to make another application. When the INS refuses an application, they explain the reasons behind their denial. The most common reason is that the applicant failed to prove sufficiently that he or she is an object of persecution or has a well-founded fear of persecution. Some applicants also fall into the "excludable" category that includes people who have health problems or criminal backgrounds or who have lied to the INS or an INS officer. When these people are denied, they may then apply for a waiver of excludability. If reapplication or a waver of excludability is unsuccessful, refugees have no recourse to the U.S. court system or appeal through any government or international agency.

All refugees who enter the United States are eligible for "green cards," official work permits issued by the government, one year after their arrival. They may live, travel, and work at any job for any company wherever they want within the U.S. However, they cannot travel in and out of the U.S. without special documents.

PROCEDURES FOR APPLYING FOR ASYLUM

Like applicants for refugee status, those seeking asylum must also be the objects of persecution or have a well-founded fear of persecution. The application for asylum status is similar to that for refugee status. Unlike refugees, however, persons seeking asylum must already be on U.S. soil, which includes any state, territory, or embassy of the United States. There is no annual quota for people granted asylum, nor do people seeking asylum need sponsors. People seeking asylum may enter the U.S. legally or illegally.

Qualifying for Asylum Status Also like refugees, applicants for asylum must demonstrate that they have not been offered refuge in another country. They must also demonstrate "continuous flight," meaning that at no time in the journey from home country to the United States did the applicant for asylum have any choice but to continue to the United States. An applicant who came to the U.S. by a direct plane or boat usually has no problem meeting this requirement. However, the INS will check to see if an applicant passed through other countries along the way and applied for asylum in those countries. Applicants must demonstrate that the United States was the first opportunity for them to seek asylum. If the applicant cannot, the INS may for that reason refuse asylum. Again, an applicant's preference for living in the United States is not taken into consideration by the INS.

The application for asylum is made at a local INS office in the United States. After filing the paperwork, which is almost identical to that required for refugee status, the applicant is required to appear for an interview with an INS official. Then the entire application is sent to the State

Department, which may make an advisory opinion before the INS can make a final decision. Sometimes this process can take months. In the meantime, those applying for political asylum are granted permission to work if their claim has some initial merit.

Granting or Denying Asylum   A person who succeeds in gaining asylum can apply for a "green card." Unlike refugees, the person granted asylum faces a special problem here. While there is no quota for asylum, there is a quota for green cards that can go to persons who have been granted asylum. Only 5,000 green cards can be granted annually to persons with asylum. Many wait years for a green card. In addition, asylum status must be renewed every year. If the INS determines that the fear of persecution no longer exists in the home country, the person who had asylum may have to leave the U.S.

Should the application for asylum be denied, an applicant for asylum has more avenues of appeal than a person applying for refugee status. The INS must give the reasons for turning down an application. If there is insufficient evidence of persecution, the applicant can submit more evidence and have the case reopened. A "motion to reopen" costs $110. Even applicants who face deportation hearings may renew their asylum status while the hearings continue. If a reopened application is turned down then an appeal can be made to the Board of Immigration Appeals in Washington. The final avenue of appeal if that is unsuccessful is a review in one of the U.S. Circuit Courts of Appeals.

Those who are denied asylum may also be eligible for "extended voluntary departure" (EVD). The U.S. government has extended EVD to Ugandans, Poles, Afghans, Ethiopians, and most recently Chinese after the Tienanmen massacre. EVD allows foreign nationals to stay in the United States temporarily because of general conditions of violence and instability, as well as concerns about human rights abuses in the home country.

Photo courtesy UNHCR

Illegal aliens being arrested in El Paso, Texas.

REFUGEE OR NOT?

Maria is 25 years old and crossed into the United States near San Diego, California, in late 1989. She walked from El Salvador through Guatemala and Mexico on her way to the United States. For years she has thought of the U.S. as a safe haven from the fighting going on in her own country between government soldiers and the rebel army, and now she is applying for asylum. Although she has never been a target of the violence going on in her country, many others in her village have been, and she fears that she will be singled out as a target if she is forced to return.

Kol-Som is not sure about her age, but she believes she is about 70 years old. She left Cambodia for Thailand in 1979 after the Vietnamese invaded her country. Her children are still in Cambodia. Her husband died during the flight to Thailand. She has no family outside Cambodia and has lived in a refugee camp since leaving her homeland. She works as a traditional midwife, helping other women in the camp.

Jorge, 33 years old, left Cuba during the "Mariel Boatlift" of 1980 during which over 125,000 Cubans sailed for American shores. He was unhappy with the communist government in Cuba and wanted to join his cousins in Miami, who had opened a successful grocery store since arriving two decades earlier.

Jan is an 18-year-old sailor on a Polish freighter. He had never been active in politics. When his ship arrived in Houston in 1985, Jan jumped overboard in a dramatic escape and asked for political asylum.

Ivan is a 19-year-old sailor on a Russian freighter docked in Baltimore in 1993. He has never been active in politics, nor has he been in trouble with the government. He is worried about his future, however, now that the Soviet Union has collapsed. One night he left the ship and applied for asylum.

Kambar, in his early twenties, survived three attacks on his village in central Afghanistan by government forces attempting to rout Soviet troops. During the third attack more than half the village's population was killed. Kambar feared for his safety but was also reluctant to leave his family's land, which they have farmed for generations. Finally, after a family meeting he left Afghanistan for a refugee camp in Pakistan, where he has lived for the past year.

Blanche is a young mother with two small children. She and her children left Haiti with about 40 others in early 1990 in a leaky boat headed for southern Florida. She was escaping the unemployment, malnutrition, illiteracy, high infant mortality, and low life expectancy that have resulted from the years of dictatorship and political turmoil in Haiti.

Dennis, an Irish citizen trained as a school teacher, arrived in the United States on a tourist visa in 1988 shortly after graduating from college. Because there are few jobs in Ireland, Dennis stayed in the United States after his visa expired, and although it is illegal for any company to hire a foreign citizen without the proper working papers, he has been employed at various construction sites in the Boston area. The work is menial, and the salary is paid "under the table."

Maria's chances for asylum are poor. She must demonstrate that she was in "continuous flight" and that she herself was the target of persecution. Her fears of persecution if she returns are not grounds for asylum.

Kol-Som may be admitted to the United States if she has a sponsor. Because of its involvement in the Vietnam War, the U.S. has felt a special responsibility to accept refugees from Southeast Asia.

Jorge is like 125,000 refugees from Cuba during the "Mariel Boatlift," who were admitted to the United States.

Jan had a good chance of receiving asylum in 1985, even if he was not a direct victim of persecution, because he was fleeing Poland at a time when it was ruled by a communist government.

Ivan, like many people trying to leave Russia and other parts of the former Soviet Union would not be granted asylum by the United States today.

Kambar's chances for resettlement in the U.S. are good. Refugees from Afghanistan make up one of the largest refugee communities in the U.S. today.

Blanche's chances for asylum are poor. Most likely her boat would have been intercepted by the Coast Guard and she would have been returned to Haiti. Because she is not fleeing persecution, she would be considered an "economic refugee."

Dennis would be considered an illegal alien because he overstayed his visa. His reasons for leaving Ireland are economic and do not qualify him for asylum were he to apply.

UNITED STATES REFUGEE LAW:
CASE STUDIES OF REFUGEES IN THE UNITED STATES

OVERVIEW: These case studies of actual refugees acquaint students with the kinds of reasons refugees have for fleeing from their home countries and how those reasons among other factors influence decisions about granting asylum in this country. The case studies also give students an idea of the physical and emotional hardships that are a part of the refugees' plight.

AGE LEVEL: High school–adult

TIME: About 45–60 minutes for each case study

MATERIALS:
- Handout 15: Interpreting U.S. Refugee Law (Part 1)
- Handout 16: Interpreting U.S. Refugee Law (Part 2)
- Handout 17: A Well-founded Fear of Persecution

SUBJECT AREAS: Current events, government

OBJECTIVES:
- To learn why refugees seek asylum in the United States
- To critically examine U.S. laws and procedures for admitting refugees
- To develop greater empathy and understanding for the hardships of refugees

PART 1

Distribute **Handout 15: Interpreting U.S. Refugee Law (Part 1).** Ask students to read the case study and use the questions following the reading as the basis for a class discussion or writing assignment. Then distribute **Handout 16: Interpreting U.S. Refugee Law (Part 2)** and have students read the decision and respond to the questions.

PART 2

Distribute **Handout 17: A Well-founded Fear of Persecution.** Have students read and respond to the case of Florvil Samedi.

FURTHER ACTIVITIES

1. Tell students that individuals and organizations with a interest in the outcome of a court case submit "friend of the court" briefs in order to persuade the judges to rule in their favor. Have students write a "friend of the court" brief from the perspective of the Jehovah's Witnesses, an anti-immigration lobbying group, or their own perspectives.

2. Ask students to assume the perspective of José or Oscar Canas and write a diary entry on the day they heard the opinion from the immigration judge or the Board of Immigration Appeals. Remind them to include details about their feelings and thoughts.

3. These case studies may also be used as the basis for mock trials. (For instructions on conducting mock trials, see **You Be the Judge,** page 98.)

4. Ask students to assume the perspective of José or Oscar Canas and write a diary entry for the day they heard the opinion from the Ninth Circuit Court of Appeals. Remind them to include details about their feelings and the thoughts of the moment. Ask students to compare these entries with the diary entries from the day they heard the earlier opinions.

INTERPRETING U.S. REFUGEE LAW (PART 1)
The Case of Canas-Segovia v. INS (1990)

José and Oscar Canas-Segovia (the Canases) were brothers and natives of El Salvador whose religious beliefs barred them from participating in military service. Both were introduced to the Jehovah's Witnesses faith as children and reared in a family in which most members were already Jehovah's Witnesses or studying to be baptized. The Canases had studied the faith since their mid-teens with the goal of becoming baptized, and they considered themselves to be Jehovah's Witnesses. The tenets of their faith prohibited them from participating in military service of any kind.

El Salvador has a policy of mandatory military service for all males between the ages of 18 and 30. The Salvadoran policy does not exempt conscientious objectors on religious or any other grounds and offers no alternatives to military service. The legal penalties for resisting conscription range from six months to 15 years' imprisonment depending on individual circumstances. Fear of this policy caused the Canases to flee El Salvador at the respective ages of 16 and 17.

The brothers entered the United States illegally on January 26, 1985, and two days later they received orders to show why their illegal entry should not subject them to deportation. At their deportation hearing in San Francisco on December 16, 1989, they submitted petitions for asylum on three grounds:

1. Forcible conscription in violation of their religious beliefs amounted to religious persecution.

2. Refusal to serve in the military for any reason would expose them to torture and death.

3. Refusal to serve in the military could cause them to be viewed as political enemies of the government and again expose them to torture and death.

In support of their petition, the Canases presented extensive evidence about the Salvadoran conscription policy and the consequences of refusing to submit to it. José Canas testified that a friend who had fled from the military and returned to his neighborhood was taken away and not seen again. An affidavit was presented from an eyewitness to the torture of an army deserter. A conscript himself, the eyewitness first heard army officials accuse the deserter of being an anti-government guerrilla and then watched as both of the deserter's arms were chopped off.

Affidavits and declarations were also presented by former Salvadoran military officers, a Red Cross physician working in the country, and members of the clergy working there. An affidavit from George McHugh, an expert on the human rights situation in El Salvador, stated that "the government routinely rounds up youths at gunpoint. Those who refuse to join the armed forces for reasons of conscience are tortured and killed."

The immigration judge denied the petitions for asylum, reasoning that the Canases could not establish either a clear probability of persecution or a well-founded fear of persecution

From *The Uprooted: Refugees and the United States* ©1995 Nancy Flowers and David M. Donahue, published by Hunter House Inc., Publishers, 1-800-266-5592.

because they had failed to show that Jehovah's Witnesses were singled out by the Salvadoran government for persecution because of their religious beliefs. The judge concluded that the Salvadoran policy of mandatory conscription could not amount to persecution because it applied equally to all Salvadorans without regard to religious beliefs. The judge also dismissed the United Nations Handbook on Procedures and Criteria for Determining Refugee Status which accords refusal to perform military service on account of genuine reasons of conscience as a basis for refugee status.

The Canases then appealed to the Board of Immigration Appeals, which affirmed the denial of asylum. It emphasized that the Canases had failed to prove intent on the part of the Salvadoran government to single out Jehovah's Witnesses for persecution. It also rejected the Canases' argument that refusing to serve in the military would impute to them a political opinion hostile to the government, thereby exposing them to governmental reprisals including torture and death. Rejection of this argument was based on a prior Board of Immigration Appeals decision in which a petitioner had failed to establish that mere failure to serve in the military would subject him to the attention of Salvadoran death squads. The Canases then appealed to the Ninth U.S. Circuit Court of Appeals.

QUESTIONS FOR DISCUSSION

1. Many refugees leave their countries of origin because of natural disasters or for political, economic, or religious reasons. How would you characterize the Canases' reasons for leaving?

Photo courtesy UNHCR/M. Vanappelghem

Life in refugee camps presents many hardships. Here, a Salvadoran refugee is collecting the ration for his family at a camp in Honduras.

2. The Refugee Act of 1980 formally defined a refugee as someone who flees a country because of persecution "on account of race, religion, nationality, membership in a particular social group, or political opinion." How might this be interpreted in a way favorable to the Canases' asylum petition? How might this be interpreted in a way unfavorable to the Canases' asylum petition?

3. A conscientious objector is someone who refuses to participate in military service because of religious or deeply held beliefs against war. Do conscientious objectors qualify for refugee status according to your interpretation of the Refugee Act of 1980? Should conscientious objectors whose opposition to war is not based on religious principles be allowed to gain asylum in the United States? Why? Should they be granted asylum if their country of origin provides alternatives to military service? Why?

4. Should the Canases have to demonstrate that the Salvadoran government intended to persecute Jehovah's Witnesses in order to receive asylum? Why?

5. The Canases believed that their refusal to perform military service because of their religious beliefs also put them in a position of political neutrality in the Salvadoran conflict. In previous rulings U.S. courts had ruled that political neutrality is no less an expression of political opinion than is the decision to affiliate with an organized faction. Do you agree with this reasoning? Why? How might the previous court rulings affect the Canases' case?

6. Assume you are a judge on the Ninth U.S. Circuit Court of Appeals. How would you rule in the case of Canas-Segovia v. INS (1990)? Explain your decision.

From *The Uprooted: Refugees and the United States* ©1995 Nancy Flowers and David M. Donahue, published by Hunter House Inc., Publishers, 1-800-266-5592.

INTERPRETING U.S. REFUGEE LAW (PART 2)
The Decision of the Ninth Circuit Court of Appeals in the Case of Canas-Segovia v. INS (1990)

In its conclusion, the Ninth Circuit Court of Appeals stated:

> We hold on the record established that the Canases qualify for asylum and withholding of deportation relief because their refusal to serve in the military is based on genuine reasons of conscience and because such refusal will more likely than not subject them to imprisonment, and possibly torture and death on account of their religious beliefs and imputed political opinion. We base this holding in large part upon relevant provisions of the U.N. Handbook that urge the granting of refugee status to conscientious objectors when their country's conscription policy allows no exemptions or alternatives to military service and when the refusal to perform military service is based upon genuine reasons of conscience.

QUESTIONS FOR DISCUSSION

1. What reasons did the Ninth Circuit Court of Appeals have for granting asylum to the Canases?

2. How was the reasoning of the Ninth Circuit Court of Appeals different from the reasoning of lower courts? How did it differ from or agree with your own reasoning in this case?

A WELL-FOUNDED FEAR OF PERSECUTION?
The Case of Florvil Samedi

The following is a first-person account by Florvil Samedi of his reasons for leaving Haiti, his journey to the United States, and his reception here as an asylum seeker.

From Mother of Exiles. *New York: Lawyers' Committee for Human Rights, Helsinki Watch, 1986, pp. 36–42. Reprinted with the permission of Helsinki Watch.*

"I was working as a bus driver in Haiti. I've been doing that since 1977. I have three kids. Two of them are going to private school in Port-au-Prince; the third one is only seven months old. They always had enough to eat. I did not have any economic problems in Haiti; I was never out of work. If it were not for the problems I had with the *macoutes*,* I would still be living in my country.

"In March 1969, my father, Hubert Samedi, was killed by a *macoute*. My father was uncle and godfather to this *macoute* .... When my cousin became a *macoute*, my father was always preaching to him to quit. He told him that he was too young, that he had a future in front of him. Why should he become a member of such an organization like the macoutes? My cousin resented this advice. Then in March, 1969, my cousin's goat wandered onto my father's farm and was eating his crops. When my father saw that, he threw a rock after the goat so it would leave the farm. I don't know how my cousin learned that my father had thrown a rock at his goat, but when he came back from his services that day, he went to my father's house and arrested him and brought him back to the *macoute* headquarters.

"When they arrived there, he beat my father with the butt of his rifle all over his head; then he locked him up ....

"When I arrived in Jacmel, I went to the house of another cousin of mine who was a sergeant in the army, to see what he could do for my father. He told me there was nothing he could do. Finally, my father's brother—who was also my *macoute* cousin's uncle—talked him into releasing my father after six days of harsh imprisonment. I saw my father after he got out of prison and could not believe my eyes. He was in such bad shape he could not even stand up by himself. His face and neck were swollen to twice their normal size and he had wounds on his head and neck. I cannot describe how I felt when I saw my own father in such condition. Sixteen days after he got out of jail, he died as a result of the mistreatment and torture that he was subjected to at the hands of his own nephew. The worst is that we could not bring any complaint against my cousin, for our lives would have been in danger if we tried to do that ....

"On May 20, 1984, my bus was stopped by the macoutes again. They asked me to park my bus and come the next morning to transport people outside the capital to the palace .... I did not park my bus as I was told; I drove away very fast instead.

"Three days later, on May 23, three *macoutes* came and asked my landlord for me. He told them I was not home because he saw that they were dressed in blue uniforms and were

---

*Abbreviation for *tonton macoutes*, the Haitian security forces established by Francois Duvalier, the former president of Haiti. Literally translated, the term *macoute* means "bogeyman" in Creole.

armed. He became more suspicious when the *macoutes* told him not to inform me about the fact that they had come and asked for me . . . . The *macoutes* came back the same night to arrest me. I had the time to jump across a wall and run away.

" . . . I went into hiding at another cousin's house. I don't know how the *macoutes* learned I was in Musseau, but they went to look for me at my cousin's house. My cousin told them I was not present at the house. Not believing her, they shot at the house and one bullet hit my cousin in the leg. When I learned about the incident, I finally believed that my life would be in great danger if I stayed in Haiti . . . .

"I am still afraid to go back to Haiti, even with Duvalier gone. Duvalier is one man, but all his people and the *macoutes* are still there. The head of the government is a *macoute* [Samedi used the term in this context to include any agent of government oppression] and in Haiti, all people who are not *macoutes* are suspected and can be harmed. My situation is especially hard because my family and I have a history of conflict with the *macoutes*.

"I would like to go back to Haiti someday, but not until the structure of the government and the people in power change completely. It is very difficult now, but I can't believe that God will forget about us Haitians or our brothers in South Africa.

"I left Haiti and arrived at the Miami airport on August 9, 1984. I had paid $520 for a visa to come to the United States, but when I arrived in Miami, the immigration authorities said my documents were fake. I told them that I had to leave Haiti because it was not safe for me there and they told me they would take me to a hotel called Krome. I asked them why, if I was going to a hotel, did they have to handcuff me and take my fingerprints. They said that was how they do things in the United States.

"I was in detention for 17 months and 9 days at the Krome jail. When I first came here, I never thought they would put me in jail. I was thinking all the time on why they were keeping me there. What had I done? I didn't think that just for a bad visa I could get one and a half years in jail.

"I think Haitians stay in there longer than anyone else. They are treated worse than people from other countries. People of other nationalities in Krome are told by family and friends on the outside not to socialize with Haitians. We are also discriminated against by the guards and immigration authorities. If people from other countries do things, nothing happens; but the same activity can put a Haitian in solitary confinement. I remember one time a Haitian thought the food looked so funny that he said he wasn't going to eat it. A Cuban who felt the same way took the plate with the food on it and broke it. The officer laughed at the Cuban, but the Haitian was put in solitary confinement for the night. It was terrible to be discriminated against so much. That and being confined for so long made me very depressed. Haitians are good people and don't deserve to be treated like that."

QUESTIONS FOR DISCUSSION

1. How would you describe Florvil Samedi's reasons for fleeing to the United States? Would you call him an economic or a political refugee? Explain.

2. Do you think his reasons for leaving Haiti were valid? Do you believe that his life was in danger in Haiti? What evidence supports your belief?

From *The Uprooted: Refugees and the United States* ©1995 Nancy Flowers and David M. Donahue, published by Hunter House Inc., Publishers, 1-800-266-5592.

3. Do you believe that the Haitian government was justified or unjustified in seeking to arrest Samedi? Why?

4. How would you describe Samedi's reception in the United States?

5. Why is Samedi suffering from psychological problems?

6. Refer to the Refugee Act of 1980 (see U.S. Policy, page 41). Do you think Florvil Samedi qualifies as a refugee according to your interpretation of the law? Explain your reasoning. Do you believe Samedi should be given refugee status in the United States? Why?

7. During the time Samedi was detained, Haitians being deported from the Krome Detention Center in Florida were arrested on arrival in Port-au-Prince, Haiti, and taken by Haitian police to the National Penitentiary. Even though the Haitian constitution says anyone arrested should be brought before a magistrate within 48 hours, the majority of the more than 500 prisoners at the National Penitentiary have been there for at least a year without being tried and many have never even been formally charged. Does this information change your opinion about whether Samedi should be given refugee status in the United States? How?

From *The Uprooted: Refugees and the United States* ©1995 Nancy Flowers and David M. Donahue, published by Hunter House Inc., Publishers, 1-800-266-5592.

The following is excerpted from a letter written by psychiatrist Henri Hall on September 15, 1985, at the request of Florvil Samedi's lawyer, Ira J. Kurzban. The Haitian Refugee Center in Miami believes this letter was instrumental in securing Samedi's release after 17 months.

Dear Mr. Kurzban:

In accordance with your request, appointing me as a disinterested qualified expert, the above-named detainee was examined for psychiatric evaluation on July 1st, 1985, at the Krome North SPC, Miami, Florida, to determine his present mental condition and formulate recommendations. His medical records were made available for review.

First of all, Mr. Samedi was very apprehensive and suspicious about my presence at Krome, since he was not informed of the purpose of my examination. After he was granted the privilege to contact the Refugee Center, he agreed to be interviewed. Immediately, he started to apologize for his mistrust and stated that at Krome, the detainees (and especially Haitians) had suffered so much that everyone became very defensive when being investigated. Finally he was able to open up and revealed most of his troubles since his detention.

Mr. Samedi stated that he was arrested by the INS at the Miami International Airport on August 9, 1984. About a month later the detention began to take its toll on his emotional status to the point that he exhibited what was diagnosed as an acute onset of psychotic depressive episodes, characterized by taking off his clothes and screaming and yelling. Basically, he felt hopeless and helpless. He became very preoccupied with the mistreatment of Haitian detainees. Furthermore, he was unable to sleep at night because of constant noises and fear for his life. He claims that at the slightest noise he would jump and experience an anxiety attack characterized by cold sweat, palpitations and feelings of tension, discomfort, and uneasiness. Presently he continues to present manifestations of anxiety, insomnia, despondent feelings and constant suicidal thoughts, despite his present regimen of medications. As a matter of fact, the psychotropic agents prescribed for him are giving him some unpleasant side effects, such as urinary retention. Consequently he has requested a change of medications, which was not yet granted at the time of the interview.

In addition to all of the above-mentioned frustrations, he is continuously thinking of his family left behind in Haiti. He denies any history of alcohol, drug, or tobacco habits. No family history of mental illness.

It is my expert opinion that Mr. Samedi continues to suffer from a severe depressive condition accompanied by anxiety, which is aggravated by his present environment with further detriment to his mental status. In addition, the paranoid features displayed, even at the time of the interview, are of great concern in terms of potentially serving as a trigger mechanism in the acting out of the frequent suicidal ideations. Thus it is imperative that Mr. Samedi be placed in a more supportive environment, in conjunction with individual psychotherapy to help him return to his premorbid level of functioning.

Very truly yours,
Henri Hall, M.D.

YOU BE THE JUDGE
A Mock Trial to Determine Eligibility for Asylum

OVERVIEW: Students listen to a refugee's story and interpret the law to determine a claim to asylum. In the process they must consider evidence and weigh conflicting claims to make a decision

AGE LEVEL: High school

TIME: About 60 minutes

MATERIALS:
- Handout 15: Interpreting U.S. Refugee Law (Part 1)
- Handout 16: Interpreting U.S. Refugee Law (Part 2)
- Handout 17: A Well-Founded Fear of Persecution?

SUBJECT AREAS: Current events, government, U.S. history

OBJECTIVES:
- To interpret current U.S. refugee law
- To present information in support of an argument
- To balance conflicting values (e.g., allegiance to the law versus helping someone in need)

After students have read one of the case studies, assign them the following roles:
- refugee
- prosecuting lawyer
- defense lawyer
- judge
- experts
- jurors (Although cases in courts of appeal are not decided by jurors, the rest of the class should function as a jury voting on the refugee's claim to asylum.)

The **refugee** is responsible for telling his or her story and answering questions about the case: why he or she left the home country, why and how he or she came to the United States, and what he or she fears will happen if the application for asylum is denied and he or she is deported.

The **prosecuting lawyer** is responsible for presenting evidence, asking questions, and interpreting the law in ways that will weaken the refugee's claim for asylum. The prosecuting lawyer must be familiar with the refugee's story and the law. The prosecution may challenge the relevance of the defense lawyer's questions.

The **defense lawyer** is responsible for presenting evidence, asking questions, and interpreting the law in ways that will strengthen the refugee's claim for asylum. The defense lawyer must be familiar with the refugee's story and the law. The defense may challenge the relevance of the prosecuting lawyer's questions.

The **judge** is responsible for keeping order in the court and determining the relevance of the lawyers' questions. Irrelevant questions will not be allowed in the court.

Experts will be assigned by the lawyers. They might include a psychiatrist who would testify about the refugee's mental health or a political science professor from the local university who would testify on government persecution in the refugee's home country.

The **jurors** are responsible for reaching a decision about whether the refugee should be granted asylum or denied and deported.

The lawyers should begin with opening arguments before questioning witnesses. The refugee should be called as a witness. The lawyers may ask other classmates to prepare testimony as "experts" on such subjects as human rights abuses, the political situation in the refugee's home country, or the refugee's health.

After the lawyers have called all their witnesses, and made a concluding argument, the jurors should reach a verdict and be ready to explain how they made their decision.

HOW FAR SHOULD WE OPEN THE DOOR?
Judging Criteria for Deciding How Many Refugees to Admit

OVERVIEW: Asked to judge what criteria should be used to determine how many refugees are admitted to the United States, students grapple not only with the complexity of determining how to measure certain criteria but with their own biases of what is fair and for whom.

AGE LEVEL: Middle school–adult

TIME: About 45 minutes, including discussion

MATERIALS: Handout 18: How Far Should We Open the Door?

SUBJECT AREAS: Current events, geography, moral education, world studies

OBJECTIVES:
- To understand the many factors that are or might be used to determine how many refugees are admitted to the United States
- To appreciate the complexity of measuring certain criteria that determine refugee admission ceilings
- To view a problem from more than one perspective

PART 1

Distribute **Handout 18: How Far Should We Open the Door?** and have students individually or in groups make decisions about what criteria are important when determining how many refugees to admit to the United States.

PART 2

Use the questions at the end of the handout for a writing assignment or a class discussion.

HOW FAR SHOULD WE OPEN THE DOOR?

Assume you are advising a special government panel examining whether and how limits should be set on the number of refugees allowed into the United States each year. Next to each of the criteria listed below, check whether it is something that can be practically determined, and give your reasons why. Next, check if it is a "fair" criterion or "the right thing" to be concerned about. In the next column state why you believe it is fair or unfair.

CRITERIA	PRACTICAL?	REASONS	FAIR?	REASONS
The number of refugees in the world				
The number of refugees for which the United States feels a special responsibility because it contributed to the refugee problem (e.g., Vietnam War)				
The number of refugees for which the United States feels a special responsibility because of its historical connections to the refugees' home (e.g., the Philippines, which was a former U.S. colony)				
The number of refugees who will be accepted by other countries				

From *The Uprooted: Refugees and the United States* ©1995 Nancy Flowers and David M. Donahue, published by Hunter House Inc., Publishers, 1-800-266-5592.

CRITERIA	PRACTICAL?	REASONS	FAIR?	REASONS
The wealth or poverty of refugees				
The educational background and skills of refugees				
The refugees' ability to speak English				
The overall health of the U.S. economy				
The success of past refugees in adjusting to life in the United States				
The race, religion, or ethnicity of the refugees				
The age and gender of the refugees				

From *The Uprooted: Refugees and the United States* ©1995 Nancy Flowers and David M. Donahue, published by Hunter House Inc., Publishers, 1-800-266-5592.

CRITERIA	PRACTICAL?	REASONS	FAIR?	REASONS
The refugees' family connections to the United States				
The refugees' belief in democracy				
The refugees' belief in capitalism				
The refugees' belief in "un-American" ideology such as anarchism or communism				

QUESTIONS FOR DISCUSSION

1. In general which two or three criteria do you consider most important? Which two or three criteria do you consider least important?

2. How practical are your most important criteria? How fair are your most important criteria?

3. How practical are your least important criteria? How fair are your least important criteria?

4. When determining fairness, did you take the perspective of a refugee? Why or why not? Should these criteria be judged from a refugee's perspective or from someone else's? Explain your belief.

From *The Uprooted: Refugees and the United States* ©1995 Nancy Flowers and David M. Donahue, published by Hunter House Inc., Publishers, 1-800-266-5592.

ARE SOME MORE EQUAL THAN OTHERS?
Evaluating Who Should Be Granted Asylum

OVERVIEW: Forced to take a stand on whether different kinds of refugees should be allowed asylum in the United States, students explore their values about whether some people are more deserving of asylum than others.

AGE LEVEL: Middle school–adult

TIME: About 30 minutes, including discussion

MATERIALS: Handout 19: Are Some More Equal than Others?

SUBJECT AREAS: Current events, geography, moral education, world studies

OBJECTIVES:

- To challenge assumptions about what criteria make a person deserving of asylum
- To begin developing a philosophy of who should be granted asylum

PART 1

Distribute **Handout 19: Are Some More Equal than Others?** to students and have them work individually or in groups to make decisions about where to place certain refugees on the continuum.

PART 2

Use the questions at the end of the handout for a writing assignment or a class discussion.

ARE SOME MORE EQUAL THAN OTHERS?
Evaluating Who Should Be Granted Asylum

Do you think all people who meet the definition of a refugee and apply for asylum in the United States should be equally welcome? Or should some people be more welcome than others? The line below represents a continuum of opinion stretching all the way from "should definitely be granted asylum" to "should definitely not be granted asylum." Based on your own opinions and values, place each asylum seeker on the continuum at what you consider the most appropriate spot, indicating the degree to which you think that person should be entitled to asylum.

|___|____|____|____|____|____|____|____|____|____|____|____|____|____|

should
definitely
be granted
asylum

should
definitely
not be granted
asylum

- **a.** Farmer from a poor country that is ruled by a dictator friendly to the United States, wants a better life in the United States

- **b.** Engineer from a communist nation, wants a better life in the United States

- **c.** Journalist and former prisoner, suffered torture while in jail, outspoken opponent of military junta

- **d.** Mother and children, displaced by war in which the United States was a participant

- **e.** Mother and children, displaced by a war in which the United States was not a participant

- **f.** Mother and children, fled country where guerrilla fighters launch periodic attacks against government positions

- **g.** Nomadic shepherd, fled famine in a very poor country

- **h.** Shopkeeper, left home country because forced by government to convert to another religion

- **i.** Lawyer, assaulted by soldiers on street, spouse was abducted by government and "disappeared"

- **j.** Factory worker and family of three, left home because government discriminates against their ethnic minority

- **k.** Ballet dancer, denied artistic freedom at home

From *The Uprooted: Refugees and the United States* ©1995 Nancy Flowers and David M. Donahue, published by Hunter House Inc., Publishers, 1-800-266-5592.

l. Fisherman, sailed to the United States because he hoped to find a better life

m. Subsistence farmer and family, forced from their land by drought and desertification of their fields

n. Secret police officer for a country that was considered unfriendly to the United States, may have violated other peoples' human rights in the line of work, possesses information which may be useful to the U.S.

QUESTIONS FOR DISCUSSION

1. How did you make your decisions? If you worked in a group, did your group have any difficulty reaching a consensus? Which issues proved difficult? Why?

2. Which criteria made someone more worthy of asylum than another? Did you give higher priority to skilled and educated refugees or unskilled and uneducated ones? Did you give more priority to a person's reason for fleeing or to their person's skills or education? What reasons for fleeing were given the highest priority for granting asylum? What reasons were given the lowest priority?

HOW GENEROUS ARE WE?
Statistics About Refugee Assistance and Asylum

OVERVIEW: Using charts about assistance and asylum given to refugees by the United States, students evaluate U.S. refugee policy and practice regarding allocation of funds and its openness to all refugees, and formulate hypotheses about why the U.S. receives refugees from various countries with different degrees of welcome.

AGE LEVEL: High school

TIME: About 30 minutes

MATERIALS: Overhead transparencies prepared from the following tables, and an overhead projector
■ Handout 20: Who's Paying the Bill?
■ Handout 21: Top Donors to Refugee Relief in 1993
■ Handout 22: Asylum Cases Filed with United States Immigration and Naturalization Service Directory

SUBJECT AREAS: Current events, U.S. history

OBJECTIVES:
■ To compare United States' assistance to refugees with other nations' assistance
■ To analyze U.S. asylum decisions made during the last decade
■ To interpret information from different kinds of charts
■ To analyze how information can be manipulated to convey different and sometimes opposing points of view

PART 1

Using an overhead projector show **Handouts 20** and **21** to students. Ask the following questions and encourage students to discuss their various responses.

1. How does the United States' economic assistance to refugees compare with other nations' assistance in terms of total money donated? In terms of per capita money donated?

2. To which table would congressional representatives refer if they were arguing that the United States is already doing enough to help refugees? Why?

3. Which table would the Danish ambassador use to convince the United States to do more to help refugees? Why?

PART 2

After showing **Handout 22** to students, ask the following questions. Have students respond orally or in writing.

1. Which nation had the highest approval rating for all asylum cases filed during 1983–89?

2. Which nation had the lowest approval rating for all asylum cases filed during 1983–89?

3. Which three nations had the greatest number of asylum cases? What accounted for this?

4. Which nation had the greatest number of cases for asylum approved?

5. Which nation had the greatest number of cases for asylum denied?

6. What might explain the difference between the percentage of cases from the Soviet Union and Romania that were granted asylum and the percentage of cases from El Salvador?

7. Sort the nations on this chart into groups according to common characteristics that might explain why such large numbers of citizens from these countries seek asylum in the United States. Defend your categorizations.

8. What statistics might a Soviet leader have used to say the United States was continuing the Cold War during the 1980s?

9. What statistics might the President have used to say the United States was still a haven for refugees from around the world?

10. What statistics might the United Nations have used to argue that the United States was biased in granting asylum to refugees?

11. What statistics might the United States have used to counter the United Nations' contention?

12. What other statistics or information would you want before you decided whether the United States had any biases in its asylum decision-making process?

PART 3

Students will create various charts to present information and compare the visual impact of these various ways of presenting information.

1. Create pie charts showing the percentage of asylum cases granted and denied for each of the following countries: U.S.S.R., Czechoslovakia, Syria, Yugoslavia, Honduras, Guatemala.

2. Create bar graphs showing the percentage of asylum cases granted and denied for the same countries.

PART 4

Ask the following questions after students have completed the charts.

1. Which method of presenting information (table, pie chart, bar graph) most clearly conveys the discrepancy between asylum approval rates for refugees from different nations? Explain.

2. If you were trying to convince someone that Guatemalans were unfairly discriminated against compared to other nationals seeking asylum, how would you present your argument graphically? Why?

WHO'S PAYING THE BILL?
TOP TWENTY DONORS TO REFUGEE RELIEF IN 1993

United States	$451.99 million
Japan	$141.99 million
Sweden	$98.43 million
Netherlands	$98.20 million
United Kingdom	$85.62 million
Norway	$60.71 million
France	$54.55 million
Germany	$53.36 million
Canada	$47.10 million
Denmark	$42.31 million
Switzerland	$38.95 million
Italy	$28.93 million
Finland	$12.72 million
Australia	$12.04 million
Belgium	$9.26 million
Austria	$3.95 million
Kuwait	$1.95 million
Ireland	$1.53 million
Luxembourg	$1.18 million
New Zealand	$0.86 million

Amounts based on estimated 1993 contributions to UNHCR, IOM, and UNRWA
Source: *World Refugee Survey, 1994*

From *The Uprooted: Refugees and the United States* ©1995 Nancy Flowers and
David M. Donahue, published by Hunter House Inc., Publishers, 1-800-266-5592.

TOP DONORS TO REFUGEE RELIEF IN 1993
According to Contribution Per Capita

Norway	$14.12
Sweden	$11.31
Denmark	$8.14
Netherlands	$6.46
Switzerland	$5.56
Luxembourg	$2.95
Finland	$2.50
United States	$1.74
Canada	$1.68
United Kingdom	$1.48
Kuwait	$1.15
Japan	$1.14
France	$0.95
Belgium	$0.92
Australia	$0.68
Germany	$0.66
Austria	$0.50
Italy	$0.50
Ireland	$0.43
New Zealand	$0.25

Amounts based on estimated 1993 contributions to UNHCR, IOM, and UNRWA
Source: *World Refugee Survey*, 1994

From *The Uprooted: Refugees and the United States* ©1995 Nancy Flowers and David M. Donahue, published by Hunter House Inc., Publishers, 1-800-266-5592.

ASYLUM CASES FILED WITH U.S. IMMIGRATION AND NATURALIZATION SERVICE DIRECTORS (JUNE 1983–SEPTEMBER 1989 CUMULATIVE)

Country	Approval rate for cases decided	Cases granted	Cases denied
Total	25.1%	35,358	105,300
U.S.S.R.	72.6%	306	115
Romania	70.3%	1,470	619
Iran	61.5%	13,061	8,173
Czechoslovakia	47.4%	170	188
Ethiopia	43.5%	1,796	2,325
China	41.8%	265	368
Syria	40.8%	207	300
South Africa	40.1%	57	85
Poland	37.0%	2,971	5,053
Afghanistan	36.6%	421	729
Somalia	33.8%	262	512
Vietnam	32.8%	75	153
Hungary	29.8%	206	485
Nicaragua	27.1%	10,872	29,154
Uganda	26.2%	98	276
Philippines	16.6%	87	435
Pakistan	15.0%	77	433
Cuba	14.9%	397	2,266
Yugoslavia	11.9%	57	421
Lebanon	9.5%	171	1,623
El Salvador	2.5%	1,004	37,666
Honduras	2.2%	32	1,407
Sri Lanka	2.1%	3	141
Haiti	2.1%	39	1,795
Guatemala	2.0%	112	5,411

Source: *Reasonable Fear: Human Rights and Refugee Policy*, Amnesty International, 1990.

From *The Uprooted: Refugees and the United States* ©1995 Nancy Flowers and David M. Donahue, published by Hunter House Inc., Publishers, 1-800-266-5592.

LOCKING UP REFUGEES?
Practicing and Analyzing Discussion Skills

OVERVIEW: In the process of discussing a provocative statement about the rights of newly arrived asylum seekers, students confront their own values about how the United States should greet newcomers and analyze their skills at discussing a "hot," value-laden topic.

AGE LEVEL: High school–adult

TIME: 45–60 minutes

MATERIALS: Handout 23: Detention of Persons Seeking Asylum in the United States

SUBJECT AREAS: Current events, moral education, world studies

OBJECTIVES:

- To clarify values about how asylum seekers should be welcomed in the United States
- To develop discussion skills, including clarity, consistency, and sensitivity
- To promote thoughtful discussion as a way of clarifying values

Refugees at an INS detention facility.

Photo courtesy The Washington Post

PART 1

Divide the class into two groups: discussants and analysts. Discussants and analysts should sit mixed together in one big circle. The discussants will consider the following statement:

People seeking asylum in the United States should be locked up until their claims for asylum are found to be valid and they are granted refugee status.

NOTE: Remind students that persons seeking asylum are already in the United States. Asylum seekers may include people considered "illegal aliens."

A student or the teacher can be a facilitator for the discussion, but in general, the teacher should encourage student-to-student dialogue and play as minimal a role in the discussion as possible.

Have students who are analyzing the discussion work in pairs and listen to their classmates' discussion. Each pair should answer ONE of the following questions assigned to them by the teacher:

1. What issues were discussed? (Include here not only the key issue of detaining refugees that began the discussion but also address other issues that were raised—both relevant and irrelevant.)

2. What positions were taken and by whom?

3. What agreement was reached on the key issue? On any other issues?

4. What things helped move the discussion forward? (i.e., definition or request for definition of terms, examples or facts given or asked for, analogies given, inconsistencies in argument challenged, relevance of statement challenged, summary given, qualification in argument, or concession made)

5. What things slowed the discussion or made it unproductive? (i.e., irrelevant, unclear, or insensitive statements; same argument repeated; issue changed abruptly; personal attacks; too few or inaccurate facts given)

6. What issues were unresolved? If the discussion were to continue, where should it head next?

PART 2

After the discussion is over, the analysts should share their information with the discussants. Use the following questions for a discussion about the activity:

1. Which, if any, of the analysts' findings were surprising?

2. How can students use this information in the future to make discussions more productive?

DETENTION OF PERSONS SEEKING ASYLUM IN THE UNITED STATES

In 1954 the United States abandoned its policy of briefly detaining immigrants and closed down the famous immigrant processing center at Ellis Island. At the same time the Immigration and Naturalization Service (INS) decided to detain only those who presented a threat to national security or public safety. A 1958 Supreme Court opinion characterized the new policy as representing "the humane qualities of an enlightened society."

In 1981, however, the INS began detaining all Haitians arriving in southern Florida to seek asylum. In 1982 a U.S. district court ruled the detention illegal because of procedural problems in implementing the policy. A series of appeals followed. To counter charges that the policy was discriminatory because it only applied to Haitians, the INS decided to detain all aliens, including asylum seekers who arrived in the United States without proper papers. In 1984 the Supreme Court refused to overturn the rule.

THE RATIONALE FOR DETENTION

Currently the INS detains people who arrive at U.S. points of entry seeking asylum until it determines whether they are excludable for any reason. When asylum seekers are detained, they are put in facilities, such as prisons or converted army barracks, where they are kept under guard and their freedoms are severely limited. Gene McNary, the head of the INS during the Bush administration, claimed this action countered the "magnet effect" of aliens flocking to the United States and making "frivolous" claims for asylum. This policy has an especially harsh effect on genuine asylum seekers because often they have left home in haste without proper documents to support their claims.

THE REALITY OF DETENTION

While detention may deter some people from making frivolous claims, it no doubt also deters those who have a well-founded fear of persecution. The INS policy of detention is also in conflict with the spirit of the United Nations' 1967 Protocol Relating to the Status of Refugees, which states nations "shall not impose penalties, on account of their illegal entry or presence, on refugees who, coming directly from a territory where their life or freedom was threatened . . . , enter or are present in their territories without authorization." In addition, the Protocol prohibits unnecessary restrictions on refugees' freedom of movement.

The INS holds asylum seekers in its own facilities and in state and local jails, federal prisons, and private centers under contract to the government. Although some detention facilities offer new buildings and education and recreation programs, detained people have reported overcrowding, the mixing of children, adults, and detained asylum seekers with criminals awaiting deportation, mistreatment by guards, poor health care, minimal privacy, and restrictions on access to lawyers, families, and friends. Conditions at some detention centers like the El Centro facility near San Diego have been improved as a result of letter-writing campaigns by groups like Amnesty International.

From *The Uprooted: Refugees and the United States* ©1995 Nancy Flowers and David M. Donahue, published by Hunter House Inc., Publishers, 1-800-266-5592.

Haitians arriving in Florida, the first asylum seekers to be detained by the INS, were kept at Camp Krome, an abandoned missile base west of Miami near the Everglades. Krome has a normal capacity of 525, but at times more than 1,000 people have been squeezed in. Although Krome offers education programs and has new, permanent buildings to house refugees, it is surrounded by barbed wire and there is no mistaking the complex for anything other than a prison. In 1990 the *Miami Herald* carried reports of guards beating detainees until they vomited blood, of one guard breaking a detainee's arms and legs because he refused to pick up a napkin, and of strip searches during which Bibles and cosmetics were confiscated. As a result of such treatment, some of those detained were giving up their asylum cases and allowing themselves to be deported back to Haiti where an uncertain fate awaited them.

CHILDREN IN DETENTION

Not only are adults detained; children are placed in detention centers as well, sometimes with their families, but often alone because they left home by themselves. The thousands of children in detention each year present a special human rights concern. Often unable to speak English or hire a lawyer, and usually traumatized from events that caused or occurred during their flight, they must do their best on their own to apply for political asylum or fight deportation. Human rights groups are concerned because these children are held in remote, rural areas far from agencies that might be able to offer help. Some of the facilities are privately owned and do not meet minimum standards for the detention of minors. Children have reported being beaten, threatened, and harassed, and they have little or no access to education or legal and social services.

Photo courtesy of Eric Avery

Men in "El Corralon" (the corral) at an INS Detention Centeer near Harlington, Texas. Refugees seeking asylum in the United States, particularly those from Central America and Haiti, are kept in detention centers which are very much like prisons.

Like adults, minors are entitled to a hearing before they may be deported, and they may be released on bail while their cases go forward—a process that can take months or years. Prior to the mid-1980s, most INS districts would release children into the custody of close relatives, a legal guardian, or another responsible adult such as a relief worker. Currently, many INS districts no longer permit responsible adults to take custody of these children. Instead they require that close relatives or legal guardians come to a detention facility or INS office to pick them up. This policy places parents who do not have proper documentation in danger of being arrested, placed in detention, and deported as well. In March, 1993, the U.S. Supreme Court upheld this policy by a vote of 7–2. Writing for the majority, Justice Antonin Scalia said nothing in the Constitution requires these detained children to be freed and that the INS has broad discretion over the detention of alleged asylum seekers.

A child behind barbed wire at an INS detention facility.

Photo courtesy U.S. Committee for Refugees

A SANCTUARY STORY

I first heard about sanctuary when I was living in Mexico. For a year and a half I had been looking for help, for *real* help, because I was living underground, always at risk. When I left Guatemala, I left without money, without any idea of where to go. I will never forget that when I left my father and my mother, each gave me one thing. My father told me, "Son, I don't have anything to give you, any money, any thing." So he took off his hat and put it on my head. My mother had a very cheap watch, and she took the watch from her arm and she put it on my arm. Once when I was caught by Mexican immigration, I offered the agent my hat and watch because I didn't have any money. They were the price for my release.

While I was living underground, a Mexican came to me, because he had heard I was looking for help. He told me that in the United States there was a movement of churches concerned about the situation in Central America. They knew many refugees were being sent back to Salvador and Guatemala, who were now dead. These congregations were offering shelter, legal help, and medical help for refugees. Help was possible for me, my wife, and little daughter.

At the time, I was nearer to the border of Mexico and Guatemala, so I had to cross the whole country to get to the United States-Mexican border. It was a long trip. The Mexican gave us money for shelter, bus fare, and things like that. He didn't advise us in political terms, but he told us how to act on the trip and how to talk with a Mexican accent. He advised us to trust him and the other sanctuary workers. Even though he was traveling with us, we were always mistrusting because we didn't know him or his background. In the meantime we were hoping he was good.

Crossing the border was hard because we had to cross alone—sanctuary people told us what to do but they waited for us inside the U.S. On our first attempt we were arrested, and I was in immigration jail in Arizona for a couple of days. Well, I lied to them; I told them I was Mexican. They deported me to Mexico. Once back in Mexico, I got help to cross the border again. I crossed on foot, and a sanctuary worker drove me to Arizona.

In Phoenix we were helped a lot by Sister Darlene. Since she is a nun, we felt good being with her. She knew that the First United Methodist Church in Germantown, Pennsylvania, was offering sanctuary for our family. We left Phoenix and on the way cross-country we met many people. We stayed at many houses and churches—when I say churches I mean congregations—of Jewish people, Quakers, Christians.

Fifteen days after we arrived in Philadelphia, the First United Methodist Church prepared a welcoming service for us. At first we lived in the church for a couple of months, until a Methodist minister and his family offered us an apartment, where we are now living. During that time we were always in public. We had speaking engagements, because they gave us the opportunity to talk about the atrocities my people are suffering. The time passed this way: we met more people, we started English, we went to meetings and reunions with friends. We didn't stay hidden, but we didn't give our phone number to many people, and we didn't say where we were living.

Sanctuary lawyers helped us apply for political asylum. It took more than one year and thousands of hours of work to get the application in order. They tried to help us live in healthier conditions, because when we arrived we were sick, skinny, weak.

Being in the United States is even harder than being in Mexico. You face a new language and strange food. Your eyes suffer seeing the system, the luxury in this country, the easy way things are done. You get an upset stomach and diarrhea, and you vomit thinking of the uncertainty. Besides suffering, there is resistance to accepting the new situation, resistance to learning the new language. Refugees are mostly people from the countryside, and they confront difficulties when they move to American cities. Some of them come from areas where there is no electricity. Even if they come from a city, it's a big change. For Guatemalans, it is extremely hard to come here. Sixty percent of the population is Indian, with their own languages. They don't speak Spanish, their second language, very well. They can't read or write, so they have trouble communicating with North Americans, and this gives them more headaches. Sometimes the headaches and the stomach upset take years to go away. Every single refugee suffers.

—Guatemalan in sanctuary, Philadelphia

Photo courtesy of Eric Avery

View across the Rio Grande to Nuevo Laredo, Mexico, from Laredo, Texas. Many refugees from Central America cross the Rio Grande to enter the United States.

SANCTUARY AND THE LAW
A Decision-Making Activity

OVERVIEW: After reading about the sanctuary movement and one fictional case study, students are asked to make difficult decisions about whether Americans are bound first and foremost to the laws of the United States or to their own consciences.

AGE LEVEL: High school–adults

TIME: About 45 minutes

MATERIALS:

- Handout 24: The Sanctuary Movement in the United States
- Handout 25: A Case of Sanctuary

SUBJECT AREAS: Current events, U.S. history

OBJECTIVES:

- To understand U.S. immigration laws and the granting of asylum
- To develop an understanding of how the judicial branch interprets laws based on complex notions of public policy
- To develop an appreciation for the difficulty of making decisions in which the notion of the public good may be hard to discern

PART 1

Distribute **Handout 24: The Sanctuary Movement in the United States** and **Handout 25: A Case of Sanctuary** to students. Students might read the handouts as homework. Instruct students to focus on what should happen to the Gordons, who are on trial for violating U.S. immigration law, as they read **A Case of Sanctuary.**

NOTE: The case study included with this lesson is fictional, though the characters and situations are based on true stories.

PART 2

After students have read the case study, ask them to list all possible alternative courses of action they could follow as the judge in this case. For each alternative, have students identify the likely consequences of that course of action. Remind them to consider the immediate and long-term consequences to the Gordons, other persons in the sanctuary movement, the Riveras and others in their position, and the U.S. legal system.

Ask students to select a course of action from the alternatives and make a decision about what to do with the Gordons based on their interpretation of the law. Ask if their decision would change if they based it only on what was best for the individuals involved (both the Gordons and the Riveras) or only according to the U.S. legal system.

FURTHER ACTIVITIES

1. Students may want to stage the case of sanctuary as a mock trial. (See page 98 for examples of how to stage a mock trial.) The judge in the mock trial can issue instructions to the defense exactly as described in the handout or change them to allow the defendants greater latitude in introducing evidence on their behalf. Another possibility is to stage two separate trials, one greatly restricting the defense, the other allowing greater freedom in introducing evidence on behalf of sanctuary. The class can then examine the outcome of each trial, compare the decisions, and discuss how the kinds of evidence introduced may have influenced the judgment.

2. Have students write a brief essay explaining how they feel about having to decide such a case. Ask them to explain why the choices they had to make were either relatively simple and easy or complicated and difficult. Depending on the emphasis of the class, students can focus on the moral principles or the legal aspects of their choice.

THE SANCTUARY MOVEMENT IN THE UNITED STATES

In July of 1980 a *coyote,* a person who smuggles illegal aliens into the United States, left 26 Salvadorans without water in the desert near Tucson, Arizona. Half the Salvadorans died; the other half, near death, were picked up by the border patrol. The sanctuary movement got its start when religious congregations in Tucson took in the surviving Salvadorans, posting bond to get them released from detention as well as providing them with food, shelter, medical assistance, and legal advice as they began the process of asking for political asylum. During the 1980s the sanctuary movement grew to include hundreds of congregations that risked legal action against them as they worked on behalf of Central Americans seeking asylum.

HOW THE SANCTUARY MOVEMENT WORKS

The sanctuary movement functions as a "shadow" refugee program. Religious communities providing sanctuary screen refugees to protect those in the greatest danger of facing murder, torture, or other reprisal if sent back to their homes. Screening committees look for credible stories but do not require the kind of documentation required by the Immigration and Naturalization Service (INS) for those seeking asylum. The refugees travel to the southern United States border, stopping along the way at a series of "safe" houses that function like stops on an underground railroad. Typically, sanctuary workers meet the refugees in the desert to bring them across the border, avoiding official points of entry and INS officers. Once in the U.S., the congregations use their own financial resources to shelter, feed, and clothe the refugees. They also try to meet the emotional needs of refugees, many of whom suffer from on-going post-traumatic stress syndrome, the result of constantly being hunted and needing to flee. Some refugees go into "public sanctuary," speaking out about their persecution and need for asylum. Most refugees, however, do not. They find it too difficult to speak of the traumas, including murder, rape, and persecution, that forced them into flight. Furthermore, many worry about reprisals against family, friends, and neighbors at home if they speak out.

ARGUMENTS FOR AND AGAINST THE SANCTUARY MOVEMENT

Although members of the sanctuary movement are motivated by conscience to act on behalf of refugees, the movement faces two kinds of opposition. One form of opposition is from those who believe that no matter how well-intentioned, sanctuary is wrong because it is illegal. The first amendment to the United States Constitution guarantees freedom of speech to those speaking out on behalf of sanctuary, and it protects the practice of religions that participate in the sanctuary movement. No part of the Constitution, however, protects actions, even those motivated by humanitarian or conscientious considerations, that are against the law. The INS believes the sanctuary movement is violating the law by transporting illegal aliens and keeping them out of the reach of the government.

Other people who oppose sanctuary insist that economic opportunism is the real reason why Central Americans come to the United States. They believe there is no longer any danger to civilian human rights in these countries and that the sanctuary movement is more

From *The Uprooted: Refugees and the United States* ©1995 Nancy Flowers and David M. Donahue, published by Hunter House Inc., Publishers, 1-800-266-5592.

interested in aiding left-wing revolutions than refugees. These opponents often claim that sanctuary workers are not only a threat to refugee laws but to U.S. foreign policy as well.

Most supporters of sanctuary would respond by saying that humanitarian concerns for the refugees are their prime motivation for assisting the movement. In general they consider themselves law-abiding people and do not see themselves as willing breakers of the law. For some sanctuary workers the decision of whether to follow the government's laws or some "higher" laws of religion or conscience is not an easy one. To a large degree, however, sanctuary workers feel they have few options but to take their positions on behalf of refugees.

THE SANCTUARY MOVEMENT AND UNITED STATES LAW

Stacey Merkt is one such person who made the decision to join the sanctuary effort. She was also the first person to be arrested for her work in the movement. A volunteer worker at Casa Oscar Romero, which provided shelter for Central American refugees in San Benito, Texas, she was driving two Salvadorans to San Antonio to apply for political asylum in February, 1984, when she was arrested for transporting aliens. At the same time agents of the INS were working undercover within the sanctuary movement. Although the INS said it was not "going to go out and bust down the doors of churches," it did arrest 60 sanctuary workers in cities from Tucson to Rochester, New York, as a result of this work. Undercover agents audiotaped conversations in various sanctuaries, where they heard stories about atrocities committed by the Salvadoran army against civilians, including the massacre of 60 children in a school where soldiers were searching for guerrillas. Perhaps because this evidence might have supported the sanctuary workers' claims of "necessity" for their work, this evidence was never introduced by the government during trial.

The defense of sanctuary workers was severely limited. A federal court judge ruled that defendants were not allowed to testify on political or other conditions in Central America. They could not introduce evidence that the United States had broken international laws designed to protect refugees. They were also not allowed to argue that they were acting according to their consciences or to discuss their religious motivations. In a trial where the central issue was the dictates of individual conscience versus the compulsion of government, the defendants suffered an enormous handicap. All were found guilty. The sanctuary workers in Tucson received suspended sentences. Stacey Merkt, who had received a suspended sentence, was arrested a second time for her continued involvement with sanctuary and her second sentence was not suspended. In February, 1987, she was adopted as a prisoner of conscience by Amnesty International, which defended her for assisting refugees who "could have been in danger of human rights violations . . . including arbitrary seizure, torture, "disappearance," and extrajudicial execution if returned to their country of origin." She was later released after an international letter-writing campaign.

While the sanctuary movement has provided help to hundreds of asylum seekers, it has also served as a challenge to U.S. refugee policy. Sanctuary workers have worked to change the law at the same time they have broken it. They have forced the government and all Americans to examine the inequities in the asylum process and to look for ways to prevent refugee problems, not by building higher walls at the borders but by addressing the problems that force refugees to leave their homes in the first place.

A CASE OF SANCTUARY

NOTE: This case study is fictional, although the characters and situations are based on true stories.

Pedro Rivera, his wife Violeta, and their two daughters Anna and Maria are from a Central American country. Pedro is a peasant farmer, and neither he nor his wife has been active in politics or has advocated the use of violence against the government.

Anti-government rebels have been active in the country for many years and took control of the Riveras' village about two years ago. Although they maintained the village as a military camp, they tended not to harm the villagers because they wanted their support in the struggle against the government.

Government troops recaptured the village after about a year and, believing the villagers might be either rebel spies or at least sympathizers, began systematically persecuting the villagers. Over the past two years, the government of the Riveras' country has arrested and tortured about 50,000 people and killed about 15,000 of them.

Pedro Rivera was himself arrested and tortured by the troops, but later released. While he was in jail, government troops went to his house and, holding the family at gunpoint, searched for evidence of rebel contacts. Finding none, they beat up his family. Several of the Riveras' neighbors were arrested at the same time as he was. They too were tortured and, following brief trials, some were put to death.

When they learned of the death of their neighbors, the Rivera family left their village. They realized that this would be interpreted by the government troops as an admission of sympathy for the rebels. Yet they were sure that if they remained at home the family would be continually persecuted and possibly tortured or killed. Like many before them, they headed north and entered the United States illegally.

U.S. immigration law allows for two types of immigrants: quota immigrants (a set number of people from any particular country allowed to enter each year) and asylum immigrants (persons outside the quota who flee to the U.S. because of persecution and who, for humanitarian reasons, are allowed to stay). Quota immigration slots for Central American countries tend to be filled early by more affluent immigrants who can afford legal help in their relocation efforts. Moreover, because the United States supports the government in power in the Riveras' country, it does not want to recognize officially that the government there engages in or permits the persecution of its citizens. Therefore, only about 12% of Rivera's compatriots who seek asylum in the U.S., claiming a well-founded fear of persecution, are allowed to stay. The other 88% are routinely deported home.

Since the Rivera family knew they stood virtually no chance of obtaining political asylum, they did not apply for it, despite their well-founded fear of persecution. Instead, when they arrived in San Diego, they sought and found Tom and Mary Gordon, members of the sanctuary movement. During their journey to the United States the Riveras had heard about the sanctuary movement, and a church worker in Mexico had told them how to get in touch with someone who would help them once they reached California. Although the Gordons knew their actions were in direct violation of U.S. law, which makes it a felony to harbor illegal aliens, they gave the Rivera family a place to live.

From *The Uprooted: Refugees and the United States* ©1995 Nancy Flowers and David M. Donahue, published by Hunter House Inc., Publishers, 1-800-266-5592.

The Immigration and Naturalization Service (INS) eventually located the Rivera family, and they are now awaiting deportation. The INS also arrested the Gordons and charged them with violating US immigration law. At their trial, the Gordons admitted they hid the Rivera family in violation of the law. Their only defense was that U.S. policy—which systematically denies asylum to refugees and deports them to face almost certain arrest, probable torture, and possible death—is immoral.

In prosecuting the case against the Gordons, the U.S. attorney did not dispute their facts. For example, he agreed that if the Rivera family applied for asylum, their application probably would have been rejected. The lawyer nonetheless held that their argument was not a proper legal defense to the crime charged. Rather, because the Gordons knowingly and willfully violated U.S. immigration law and because they have shown no regret, the prosecution argued the Gordons should receive the maximum sentence provided in the statute—two years in prison.

From *The Uprooted: Refugees and the United States* ©1995 Nancy Flowers and David M. Donahue, published by Hunter House Inc., Publishers, 1-800-266-5592.

CROSSING THE SCHOOLHOUSE BORDER
Determining Responsibility for Helping Refugees Adjust to a New School

OVERVIEW: As students try to "pass the buck" on responsibility for aiding refugee children in their school, they wrestle with the question of social responsibility and gain insight on why sympathy for refugees can be inadequate.

AGE: High school–adult

TIME: About 45 minutes

MATERIALS:
- Handout 26: Voices of Refugee Schoolchildren
- Handout 27: My Story by "Rebeca Rivera"

SUBJECT AREAS: Current events, world studies

OBJECTIVES:
- To develop listening skills
- To make an argument and support it with evidence
- To begin developing a philosophy of social responsibility.

PART 1

Divide the class into five groups to represent the following categories:
- refugee students
- "native" American students (born in the U.S.)
- refugee parents
- teachers
- school administrators

Ask each group to come up with as many reasons as possible why they are not responsible for doing something about helping refugee children adjust to a new school in the United States. In addition, they must also try "to pass the buck" to the other groups, coming up with as many reasons as they can for why others should be responsible for helping refugees adjust.

The first group will have a chance to present its case and "pass" responsibility. Each group following can respond and make its own case as well as blame others. Finally, the first group can respond to any criticisms made of it by the other groups.

PART 2

After all the groups have presented, students should consider the following questions:

1. Which group made the best case? Which group made the worst case?

2. Who do you think was primarily responsible for helping the refugees adjust? Why?

3. In what ways do nations, institutions, or individuals respond similarly or differently to refugee problems in the world today?

4. In what ways do nations, institutions, or individuals respond similarly or differently to other social problems today?

VOICES OF REFUGEE SCHOOLCHILDREN

"My family problems are heavy to bear. My mother cries all night. I hold my little sister because she is scared and I try not to think about our father. He was shot before we left. I don't do my homework most nights because it is so sad at home and I try so hard to help. Now I am repeating the tenth grade. I sometimes think I should drop out of school. I cannot keep up."

—tenth-grade Salvadoran girl
  immigrated at age 12

"It is important to my family that I do well. We want our life in this new country to be a good one. I work very hard at school. My father makes me study even when I have no homework. He tells me this is how I can have a better life. America is a wonderful place to have free schools. Sometimes I cry because I am so tired of studying, but I know it is the way."

—tenth-grade Vietnamese boy
  immigrated at age 14

"My family has such set values and they hold to them strongly. They hold onto the old ways. It is very difficult to explain something to them about my life now. We end up always arguing—about school, religion, how I dress, what I can and can't do. They even get mad at me for arguing. They say I shouldn't talk back. I hate my family. We fight all the time."

—eleventh-grade Cambodian girl
  immigrated at age 10

"The Americans tell us to go back to our own country. I say we don't have a country to go back to. I wish I was born here and nobody would fight me and beat me up. They don't understand. I want to tell if they had tried to cross the river and were afraid of being caught and killed, and lost their sisters, they might feel like me, they might look like me, and they, too, might find themselves in a new country."

—tenth-grade Cambodian boy
  immigrated at age 12

"I'm not even Chinese and they call me *Chink*. It gets me so mad. Some of my friends just walk away, but I cannot. I am a troublemaker when that happens. I fight back hard. My father says not to fight. But I feel ashamed to just turn my back."

—tenth-grade Vietnamese boy
  immigrated at age 11

From *The Uprooted: Refugees and the United States* ©1995 Nancy Flowers and David M. Donahue, published by Hunter House Inc., Publishers, 1-800-266-5592.

"It was too hard for me. I didn't know anything. I didn't know the ABCs or the arithmetic and I felt so stupid. I should have been in 1st or 2nd grade, not in the 5th. I told my parents I want to change, but the teacher said no because it depends on your age. I cried because I didn't understand."

—ninth-grade Lao child
   immigrated at age 10

"For the refugees, many students have spent years in camps where their education was interrupted—there's no school over there. And some have never gone to school, so when they come here and are placed by age, they face not only the language problem, they face the gap of information and knowledge which is not easily remedied. For the younger children it can probably be remedied quickly, but for the older child it is very difficult.

"The refugee parents are frustrated. On the one hand they want to push their children academically, to become someone in the society, to work hard and study well. On the other hand, they cannot effectively intervene in the educational process. They cannot attend school functions, PTA meetings, even school conferences because of language and not understanding the process. The relative solution would be two-sided. Parents have to be educated on how to access the system, how to be influential, who to go to. And on the other hand, the school itself needs to outreach to bring in the parents of the new students in the system, because unless the parents work cooperatively with the schools, we will not get the education for the children that they need."

—Vu-Duc Vuong, Executive Director, Center for Southeast Asian Resettlement
   public testimony, San Francisco

"You don't know anything. You don't even know what to eat when you go to the lunchroom. The day I started school all the kids stared at me like I was from a different planet. I wanted to go home with my dad, but he said I had to stay. I was very shy and scared. I didn't know where to sit or eat or where the bathroom was or how to eat the food. I felt that all around me activities were going on as if I were at a dance but no one danced with me and I was not a part of anything. I felt so out of place that I felt sick. Now I know more, but I still sit and watch and try to understand. I want to know, what is this place and how must I act?"

—eighth-grade Vietnamese girl
   immigrated at age 9

"The school was so big! There were students everywhere all the time—not just in classes. I didn't know how you were supposed to know where to go when. There was no one who could speak Mien and explain to me. My uncle had told me if I needed any help to go to the Dean. My teacher asked me something and I didn't understand her. So I just said 'Dean, Dean,' because I needed help. That is how I got my American name. She was asking me, 'What is your name?' and I kept saying 'Dean.' Now everybody calls me Dean. Now it is funny, but it is also sad. My name comes from not knowing what was going on."

—twelfth-grade Lao Mien boy
   immigrated at age 14

"The issue came up so unexpectedly. It really caught me off guard. The children were painting pictures. Inadvertently some red paint got splashed on the picture a child from El Salvador had just drawn of a person. The child burst into tears, tore up the picture and was inconsolable for hours. Later she told me that red was blood, and she didn't want blood on her picture. It later came out that her father had been murdered when their village was destroyed by soldiers. The poor child. I really didn't know what to do!"

—elementary school teacher
   public testimony, San Francisco

"My parents will not let me stay after school to play soccer. They say I have to study. I study and I study and I study. That is what they believe I need to do. If I don't have homework, still I study. They make me do it over and over again. They really want me to do well, but they don't understand about the schools here."

—tenth-grade Cambodian boy
   immigrated at age 9

"Since I and other Cambodians did not know how to speak a word of English at first, most of the American people did not want to talk to us because they thought that we were nothing like them. When I walked to school (I knew how to speak a few words of English at that time) I would say 'Hi' or I would give a grin to every American student I encountered, but they paid no attention to me at all. They pretended that they didn't hear me. Another time in English class, I didn't understand what the teacher was trying to say so I asked classmates sitting next to me to explain it, but they pretended they were busy. They felt that their friends might laugh at them if they answered me. They acted like that because I was different, I came from another country, spoke broken English and looked different.

   "At school I was like a person from another planet. I was totally confused, my ears hurt. I got a headache almost every other day because I couldn't understand what other people were saying. It drove me crazy! After three months, we were put in school. I was then eleven years old, but I was placed in the same classroom with my two other brothers. That classroom combined all Southeast Asians from first to sixth grade. I was placed in sixth grade, but because I knew very little English, I still had to learn to write my name, color pictures, and other things. After I knew how to write my name and how to greet people, my teacher told me that there was no more for me to stay in that class any longer."

—Horng Kouch
   refugee from Cambodia

All quotes except the last one are from Laurie Olsen, Crossing the Schoolhouse Border, California Tomorrow Policy Research Report, 1988. *Reprinted with permission. The last quote is from Lucy Nguyen-Hong-Nhiem and Joel Martin Halpern, eds.* The Far East Comes Near: Autobiographical Accounts of Southeast Asian Students in America. *Reprinted by permission of Amherst: University of Massachusetts Press, 1989. Copyright © 1989 by The University of Massachusetts Press.*

From *The Uprooted: Refugees and the United States* ©1995 Nancy Flowers and David M. Donahue, published by Hunter House Inc., Publishers, 1-800-266-5592.

MY STORY
by "Rebeca Rivera"

My name is Rebeca Rivera. I am a Kennedy High School student, in the 11th grade, and I am Salvadoran-American . . . . I call myself a Salvadoran-American because no matter how "American" I become, I will never forget my Salvadoran culture, my country, and my traditions. I will also never forget some of the suffering that I left behind.

I came to this country when I was in third grade. I spoke no English, and I was scared. I was probably too young to even know what my real fears should be, but I was feeling lucky to be able to leave with my mother and most of my sisters—some of my friends' families were split apart—some have never seen family members again.

The way we came to the United States is a complicated story. My older sister came first, by boat at night, with her two children and arrived in California across the *frontera* . . . . My mother and the rest of the kids could not get the money until seven years later. When we were able to go, we all left El Salvador together, but when we got to the frontera my mother and my older sister walked across at night. My little sister and I could not walk that far, so we waited until morning. Someone put us in a closed trunk of a car and told us to be quiet. We were hungry and scared of suffocating.

Of course, life was difficult for my family when we arrived, but we were so thankful to be safe, that we didn't care at first. My mom worked almost 18 hours a day to get rent money, and I started school. The schools are large and impersonal. Even though I was immersed in English, my first teacher spoke Spanish. She was very nice, and it was a good feeling to communicate with someone. But it was also embarrassing to me to be spoken to in Spanish. Everyone would stare. I did learn English quickly, but the memories of "being different" and being singled out still come back. Now, I have learned the difference between positive help and negative help, but as a new kid in this country, everything seemed to be just different.

When we came to Montgomery County, I already spoke English and starting school here seemed like a dream. The classes were smaller, the teachers seemed to really care; the kids were nice, and there was even a small population of Salvadoran students that I had a lot in common with. The work was harder though. My mother was still working long hours. My older sister had moved out. Much of the household responsibilities fell upon me. Sometimes coming straight home every day, so that someone would be home when the little ones get out of school, is no fun. To have some fun, it was easier to cut school. No one is home during the day in most of my friends' apartments. Once in the habit of cutting, it's a hard habit to break. One child in my family even had his first encounter with the police at the age of eleven—while cutting school! Here my family had been through so much, and we, as kids, were messing up. It is like a bad cycle. You really do not know how to get out.

I had a rough year last year, but now I have straightened out and am doing well. I enjoy going to the Edison Center [a youth center] and I work every day after school until 7:30. I feel better bringing some money home. Maybe in the future my mother will not have to work so hard. I am receiving career counseling at school, and I do see that there are jobs that

From *The Uprooted: Refugees and the United States* ©1995 Nancy Flowers and David M. Donahue, published by Hunter House Inc., Publishers, 1-800-266-5592.

I will be able to qualify for after high school. I would like to go on with technical training or even community college, but I must face the fact that right now my family is just making it financially, and this might not be possible directly after high school. I know that I have been fortunate; I have supporters and understanding teachers in my school who have allowed me to make up missed work or pulled me back up when I began to feel down.

One day I would like to go back to my country. I would to go back as an educated woman, one with a career. I would like to go back to my country when there is peace and harmony and no danger.

Rebeca Rivera is the pseudonym of a Montgomery County, Maryland, high-school student who shared this description of her life at a workshop for teachers and administrators on the background of Central American students in December, 1990.

Reprinted courtesy of the Network of Educators for Central America.

From *The Uprooted: Refugees and the United States* ©1995 Nancy Flowers and David M. Donahue, published by Hunter House Inc., Publishers, 1-800-266-5592.

CALCULATING THE ESCAPE
A Math Activity

OVERVIEW: Using a typical voyage by refugees from Haiti to Miami, students are asked to make calculations that would be necessary to survive this journey.

AGE LEVEL: High school

TIME: Varies according to ability

MATERIALS:
- Handout 28: Human Rights Abuses in Haiti
- Handout 29: Calculating the Escape: Problems

SUBJECT AREAS: Pre-algebra, geometry, algebra II, calculus

OBJECTIVES:
- To build math and map-reading skills using real-life problems
- To foster understanding of the risks involved in fleeing to another country

PART 1

Introduce the Haitian refugee problem by eliciting information the class may already have on Haiti and the reasons so many Haitians have fled to the United States. Ask students to read **Handout 28: Human Rights Abuses in Haiti** and to locate Haiti on the accompanying map.

PART 2

Assign the problems in **Handout 29: Calculating the Escape** that are appropriate to the class level.

PART 3

When going over the completed problems, invite the class to discuss what the results of the calculations mean in human terms.

HUMAN RIGHTS ABUSES IN HAITI
Recent Background on Human Rights Violations

Human rights conditions in Haiti during the 1980s and 1990s have compelled many of its citizens to leave the country and seek protection elsewhere, especially in the United States. Patterns of severe human rights violations, including arbitrary arrest, torture, "disappearance," and political killings have occurred over decades in Haiti. In a 1989 report, Amnesty International concluded that "abuses by the security forces were so widespread and the lack of effective action so evident that it is hard to avoid the conclusion that the government condones their action, despite its well-publicized pledges to respect human rights."

In its 1993 annual report, Amnesty International stated that "hundreds of prisoners of conscience were detained, the majority for brief periods after which they were released without charge. Most detainees were tortured or ill-treated, and at least 10 people allegedly died as a result of torture. Prison conditions continued to be extremely harsh. At least 100 people were killed in circumstances suggesting they had been extrajudicially executed, and at least 10 'disappeared.'"

HAITIAN "BOAT PEOPLE" FLEE TO THE UNITED STATES

Since the mid-1970s thousands of Haitian refugees have fled by boat toward the southern coast of Florida. In 1981 the U.S. Immigration and Naturalization Service (INS) initiated a program to slow this migration of refugees from Haiti. After 1981 the Coast Guard began to intercept boats carrying Haitian migrants to the Florida coast. If the passengers were attempting to enter the U.S. without proper documentation and could not prove that they were legitimate refugees, i.e., faced "well-founded fear" of death or persecution, they were returned to Haiti. However, by March 1989 fewer than 10 of the more than 20,000 Haitians interviewed at sea since 1981 had been permitted to the United States to pursue their asylum claims. Few independent observers have traveled aboard the Coast Guard vessels which carry out the program to prevent Haitian "boat people" from landing in the United States. Haitians' ability to apply effectively for asylum, therefore, remains unclear.

According to the United States Committee for Refugees, "these Haitians are often crowded into boats well beyond the limits of health and safety, with inadequate provisions. They are at the mercy of often ruthless smugglers to whom they have paid enormous amounts to take them to the United States. The Coast Guard and the INS estimate that half perish at sea. Those who survive are often seasick, malnourished, and dehydrated when they are stopped. Their usual fear of authority is likely to become overwhelming. Without access to legal counsel, it is difficult for these poor, largely rural, and uneducated Haitians to properly convince an INS official that they have a real fear of return that meets the legal 'well-founded fear' standard."

THE BUSH POLICY TOWARD HAITIAN REFUGEES

After the September 30, 1990, coup against Haiti's first elected government under President Jean-Bertrand Aristide, tens of thousands of persons fled, seeking asylum in the United States.

From *The Uprooted: Refugees and the United States* ©1995 Nancy Flowers and David M. Donahue, published by Hunter House Inc., Publishers, 1-800-266-5592.

More than 10,400 were picked up at sea by the Coast Guard in May 1992, alone. Claiming that more recent refugees had not been persecuted and were without reasonable fear of persecution after their return, the U.S. government forcibly repatriated the Haitian refugees to their homeland. "Double-backers," who fled, were repatriated, and fled again, reported visits to their homes by police forces in Haiti, threats, arrests, beatings by soldiers, and even killings. The U.N. High Commissioner for Refugees warned that many returnees were "exposed to danger."

The U.S. Supreme Court refused to block the repatriations. In January 1992, the Supreme Court overturned a Miami federal judge's order blocking the forced returns, thus starting a wave of repatriation. In response to pleas that those being returned faced serious human rights abuses, the court refused in February 1992, to issue an order stopping repatriation.

As the flow of refugees continued despite repatriations, then-President George Bush ordered even further efforts to discourage refugees. In May 1992, the President issued an executive order authorizing the Coast Guard to halt all boats carrying Haitians from their homeland and escort them back to Haiti. Before the order refugees were being escorted to the U.S. naval base at Guantanamo Bay, Cuba, to investigate their claims for asylum. The Bush administration claimed that Guantanamo Bay was overflowing with more than 12,000 refugees and that no alternatives for housing additional Haitians were available. After over 1,000 refugees were repatriated from Guantanamo Bay in the days following the executive order, the base was no longer at capacity, but President Bush's policy of halting all boats still stood. Boatloads of refugees being escorted back to Haiti were not screened by the INS for valid political asylum-seekers. Instead, Haitians were told to apply for admission at the U.S. Embassy in Port-au-Prince, the Haitian capital. However, few Haitians who tried to take advantage of that opportunity succeeded. President Bush worried about the "appearance" of the executive order, but said, "Yes, the Statue of Liberty still stands, and we still open our arms under our law to people that are politically oppressed. [But] I will . . . not open the doors to economic refugees all over the world."

The U.N. High Commissioner for Refugees, Sadako Ogata of Japan, criticized the Bush policy, saying it was in violation of international agreements prohibiting the forced return of refugees rescued on the high seas. She said the order "denies those Haitians genuinely in need of international protection the opportunity to present their claims, thus exposing them to risk upon their return to Haiti."

THE CLINTON POLICY TOWARD HAITIAN REFUGEES

Bill Clinton, a presidential candidate at the time of Bush's executive order, said he was "appalled" by the policy "which must not stand. . . . It is a blow to the principle of first asylum and to America's moral authority." He said if he were president he would grant temporary asylum to the refugees until the U.S. restored Haiti's elected government.

After being elected, however, Clinton said he would continue the Bush policy of returning Haitians trying to emigrate to the United States. Clinton claimed his reversal was based on concern for Haitians. Approximately 1,000 boats able to accommodate as many as 150,000 people were set to sail from Haiti to southern Florida after Clinton's inauguration. In a radio appeal aimed at Haiti, Clinton warned Haitians to stay home, but said he would work "with energy and determination to promote agreement among all Haitian parties on a political solution" for the island. At the same time the Coast Guard also began a blockade of Haiti to stop the potential surge of people fleeing the island. Human rights groups, including Amnesty International, criticized the moves as a breach of campaign promises and a slight to Haitian refugees' human rights.

In May 1994, Clinton finally changed U.S. policy, as he had promised during the campaign, to allow shipboard interviews for asylum seekers from Haiti. The change, which was perceived by Haitians as increasing their chances of receiving asylum, sparked a surge in refugees from the island nation. Some Haitians headed out to sea in boats as small as 30 feet, hoping to reach Coast Guard ships, not the Florida mainland. The change in U.S. policy to allow shipboard applications for asylum came after pressure from U.S. supporters of Aristide, the ousted Haitian president. Aristide called the previous policy of returning boat people "racist."

As a result of the increased flow of refugees and the backlog of asylum claims, Clinton decided to reopen the refugee processing facility at Guantanamo Bay at the end of June 1994. During the last two weeks of June 1994, over 5,000 Haitians were picked up by the Coast Guard. Approximately a fifth of that number were screened for asylum. Only 38 were granted asylum, while 773 were returned to Haiti.

The Guantanamo Bay refugee center is a short-term solution. Ultimately, the cause of Haitians' exodus—the rule of terror by the nation's military regime—must be addressed. Currently the U.S. has instituted economic sanctions against Haiti, including an oil embargo, bans on commercial air flights, and freezes on U.S.-held Haitian assets.

Photo courtesy of Eric Avery

A correctional facility in Brooklyn, New York, where Haitian and other refugees are detained.

CALCULATING THE ESCAPE
Problems

A group of Haitians decide to flee their homeland and attempt to reach Miami, Florida, by boat. Because they will necessarily encounter many difficulties en route, some of which could be life-threatening, they must anticipate as many of these problems as possible. The following exercises are only suggestive of the serious challenges faced by Haitian and other "boat people."

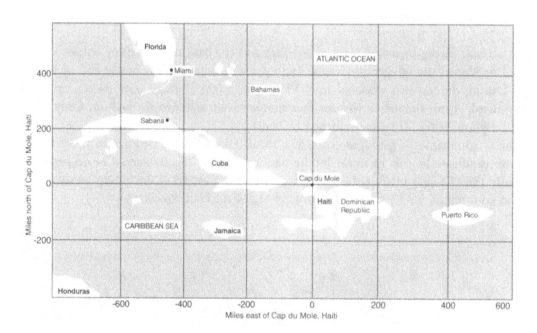

I. PRE-ALGEBRA: PROPORTION PROBLEMS

1. With a ruler, measure in centimeters the distance between two horizontal or vertical lines on the map. This distance is approximately 200 miles. Now measure the distance in centimeters from Cap du Mole to Miami. Write a proportion and solve it to find the distance between Cap du Mole and Miami in miles.

2. For most of the voyage the refugees can sail along the north coast of Cuba. Keeping land in sight makes navigation easy. Traveling from Cuba to Miami is more difficult because the refugees must cross the open sea. Measure the distance from Cap du Mole to Sabana in centimeters and set up a proportion to find this distance in miles.

From *The Uprooted: Refugees and the United States* ©1995 Nancy Flowers and David M. Donahue, published by Hunter House Inc., Publishers, 1-800-266-5592.

3. Measure the distance from Sabana to Miami in centimeters and use a proportion to find the distance in miles.

4. What is the total distance the refugees must travel if they follow the coast of Cuba and then turn north to Miami?

5. What percent of the total trip will be spent crossing the open sea?

II. PRE-ALGEBRA: MULTIPLICATION PROBLEMS

A typical boat used by the refugees can carry a maximum load of 2,000 pounds. What can the refugees bring with them?

1. People: Suppose a boat carries 10 refugees each weighing about 120 pounds. What is the combined weight of the people?

2. Fuel:

　a. The refugees can either travel 24 hours per day (i.e., day and night) for 3.5 days or 12 hours per day (daytime only) for 7 days. What is the total travel time in hours?

　b. If the boat uses one gallon of fuel during every hour of travel time, how many gallons will be used to get to Miami?

　c. If the fuel weighs eight pounds per gallon, what is the total weight of the fuel?

3. Food: An average healthy adult eats about 0.8 pounds of food per day.

　a. If the refugees ate similarly, how many pounds of food would a single refugee eat during 3.5 days? During 7 days?

　b. How many pounds of food would 10 refugees eat during 3.5 days? During 7 days?

From *The Uprooted: Refugees and the United States* ©1995 Nancy Flowers and David M. Donahue, published by Hunter House Inc., Publishers, 1-800-266-5592.

4. Water: An average healthy adult drinks about 4.5 pounds of water per day (about ½ gallon).

a. If the refugees drank a similar amount, how many pounds of water would a single refugee drink in 3.5 days? In 7 days?

b. How many pounds of water would 10 refugees drink in 3.5 days? In 7 days?

5. Find the total weight of people, fuel, food, and water:

a. If the trip lasts 3.5 days:

b. If the trip last 7 days:

Can the boat hold this much weight?

6. In order to keep the boat afloat, each refugee is allowed to bring only 1 pound of food and 9 pounds of water.

a. One pound of food is what percent of what an average adult would eat during 3.5 days?

b. Nine pounds of water is what percent of what an average adult would drink during 3.5 days?

III. ALGEBRA I: DISTANCE, RATE, TIME PROBLEMS

Before doing these problems, complete the proportion problems above or use the following information:

distance from Cap du Mole to Miami = 616 miles

distance from Cap du Mole to Sabana = 496 miles

distance from Sabana to Miami = 192 miles

1. If the boat travels at a rate of 8 miles per hour, how many hours will it take to travel straight from Cap du Mole to Miami?

From *The Uprooted: Refugees and the United States* ©1995 Nancy Flowers and David M. Donahue, published by Hunter House Inc., Publishers, 1-800-266-5592.

2. If instead the boat travels along the coast of Cuba and then turns due north to Miami,

a. How many hours does it take to travel from Cap du Mole to Sabana?

b. How many hours does it take to travel from Sabana to Miami?

c. What is the total time required for the voyage in hours? In days, rounding off to the nearest half-day?

3. In questions 1 and 2 you assumed the boat travels 24 hours per day. Traveling at night is dangerous because boats can easily run aground or become lost at sea. How many days would the voyage along the coast of Cuba and then north across the open sea to Miami take if the boat traveled only during the day (12 hours per day)?

IV. GEOMETRY/ALGEBRA II: COORDINATE GEOMETRY PROBLEMS

1. Find the coordinates of Cap du Mole, Miami, and Sabana.

2. Use the distance formula to find the distance between Cap du Mole and Miami.

3. To make navigation easier, the refugees will travel along the coast of Cuba and then turn due North toward Miami. Do you expect this trip to be longer, shorter, or the same length as the distance you found in question 2?

Optional Question: What theorem of geometry could you use to prove this trip is longer than the distance you found in question 2?

4. Use the distance formula to find:

a. The distance from Cap du Mole to Sabana:

b. The distance from Sabana to Miami:

5. What is the total distance if the refugees travel along the coast and then turn north?

From *The Uprooted: Refugees and the United States* ©1995 Nancy Flowers and David M. Donahue, published by Hunter House Inc., Publishers, 1-800-266-5592.

CALCULATING THE ESCAPE
Solutions to a Math Activity

I. PRE-ALGEBRA: PROPORTION PROBLEMS

1. $\dfrac{2.5 \text{ cm}}{200 \text{ miles}} = \dfrac{7.7 \text{ cm}}{n}$

   $2.5n = 1540$

   $n = 616$ miles

2. $\dfrac{2.5 \text{ cm}}{200 \text{ miles}} = \dfrac{6.2 \text{ cm}}{n}$

   $2.5n = 1240$

   $n = 496$ miles

3. $\dfrac{2.5 \text{ cm}}{200 \text{ miles}} = \dfrac{2.4 \text{ cm}}{n}$

   $2.5n = 480$

   $n = 192$ miles

4. $496 + 192 = 688$ miles

II. PRE-ALGEBRA: MULTIPLICATION PROBLEMS

1. $10 \times 120 = 1200$ lb.

2. $3.5 \times 24 = 84$ hours
   or $7 \times 12 = 84$ hours

3a. $3.5 \times 0.8 = 2.8$ lb.
    $7 \times 0.8 = 5.6$ lb.

3b. $10 \times 2.8 = 28$ lb.
    $10 \times 5.6 = 56$ lb.

4a. $3.5 \times 4.5 = 15.75$ lb.
    $7 \times 4.5 = 1.5$ lb.

4b. $10 \times 15.75 = 157.5$
    $10 \times 1.5 = 15$ lb.

5a. $1200 + 672 + 28 + 157.5 = 2057.5$ lb.

5b. $1200 + 672 + 56 + 15 = 2243$ lb.

6a. $1 = (n)(2.8)$

    $n = \dfrac{1}{2.8} = .36 = 36\%$

6b. $9 = (n)(15.75)$

III. ALGEBRA I: DISTANCE, RATE, TIME PROBLEMS

1. $616 = 8t$

   $t = \dfrac{616}{8} = 77$ hours

2a. $192 = 8t$

    $t = \dfrac{192}{8} = 24$ hours

2b. $496 = 8t$

    $t = \dfrac{496}{8} = 62$ hours

2c. $24 + 62 = 86$ hours

    $\dfrac{86}{12} = 3.5$ or about 3.5 days

3. $\dfrac{86}{12} = 7.17$ or about 7 days

IV. GEOMETRY/ALGEBRA II: COORDINATE GEOMETRY PROBLEMS

1. Cap du Mole: $(0, 0)$
   Sabana: $(-440, 220)$
   Miami: $(-460, 420)$

2. $D = \sqrt{(x_2 - x_1)^2 + (y_2 - y_1)^2}$

   $= \sqrt{388,000}$

   ≈ 623 miles

3. Longer. (The sum of the lengths of any two sides of a triangle is greater than the length of the third side.)

4a. $D = \sqrt{242,000}$
    $= 492$ miles

4b. $D = \sqrt{40,400}$
    $= 201$ miles

5. $492 + 201 = 693$ miles

From *The Uprooted: Refugees and the United States* ©1995 Nancy Flowers and David M. Donahue, published by Hunter House Inc., Publishers, 1-800-266-5592.

USING THE MOVIE *EL NORTE* IN THE CLASSROOM
Discussion Questions and Suggested Activities

OVERVIEW: The movie *El Norte* presents the story of a brother and sister fleeing the violence of Guatemala during the early 1980s for a safe haven in the United States.

NOTE: Because of strong language this film is rated R.

AGE LEVEL: High school–adult

TIME: 150 minutes

MATERIALS: *El Norte* videocassette, videocassette player

SUBJECT AREAS: Current events, geography, U.S. history

OBJECTIVES:
- To increase information about the journey of refugees from Central America to the United States
- To develop empathy for refugees and the problems they face

Photo courtesy of Eric Avery

The "Tortilla Curtain" separating Tijuana, Mexico, from San Diego, California, as seen from the U.S. side.

For classroom purposes the movie can be divided into three parts, which are best shown on separate days to facilitate discussion. The first part, which is set in Guatemala, gives background on why the main characters, Enrique and Rosa, flee their country. The second part describes their journey to the United States, and the third part illustrates their lives in Los Angeles as illegal aliens. You may wish to distribute the discussion questions or pose the questions after students view each part.

FURTHER ACTIVITIES

1. Have students write a letter in the voice of Rosa or Enrique to a relative in Guatemala telling about their impressions of the United States.

2. Assign students to write an essay describing what might happen to Enrique in the next 10 years.

3. Have students write a diary entry from the point of view of Enrique or Rosa.

4. Ask small groups of students to write a 30-second commercial or design a poster advertising *El Norte.*

5. As a class, conduct a political asylum hearing for Enrique. See **Activity 11: You Be the Judge,** page 98, for examples and guidance.

6. Have students use an atlas to draw Guatemala, Mexico, and the United States, and then trace the journey of Rosa and Enrique.

7. Invite students to investigate the human rights situation of Indians in Guatemala and to report their findings to the class.

8. Assign students to write an essay comparing *El Norte* to the film *Voyage of the Damned.*

QUESTIONS FOR DISCUSSION

PART 1: GUATEMALA

1. Describe the working conditions of the peasants.

2. Why do the peasants hold a secret meeting?

3. Why do the soldiers attack the peasant meeting?

4. What human rights violations occur after soldiers enter the village?

5. Why is the mother taken away?

6. Why is the son Enrique going to be killed?

7. What hopes do Enrique and Rosa have for the "promised land" in the north?

PART 2: THE JOURNEY TO THE UNITED STATES

1. What is a *coyote?*

2. Describe the living conditions Enrique and Rosa encounter in Tijuana.

3. Describe the various types of dangers Enrique and Rosa face in crossing the border.

4. Describe your feelings during the tunnel ordeal.

PART 3: LOS ANGELES

1. Describe the culture shock Rosa and Enrique face when they begin work in Los Angeles.

2. Describe how "illegals" are treated in the work sector.

3. Describe the constant pressures "illegals" face.

4. What personal qualities do Enrique and Rosa possess that give them some degree of success in Los Angeles?

5. When Rosa tells Enrique, "We're not free," what does she mean?

6. Why doesn't Rosa want to go to the hospital? Is she correct in her fear?

7. Why does Enrique tell Gacha that he can't stay to see his sister? What change seems to have come over Enrique while living in the United States?

8. Why does Enrique change his mind about seeing his sister, thereby losing his chance for a good job and legal status?

9. Does the end of the film offer any hope for Enrique's life? Why does the film end with a close-up of the father's decapitated head?

AFTER VIEWING THE ENTIRE FILM

1. Are Enrique and Rosa refugees, according to American law which defines a refugee as a person facing:

   persecution or a well-founded fear of persecution on account of race, religion, nationality, membership in a particular social group, or political opinion . . . .

2. What do you think would happen to Enrique or Rosa if they were sent back to Guatemala from the United States?

3. Do you think people like Enrique and Rosa should be allowed to stay in the United States, even if they are here illegally. Why or why not?

4. Is this film sympathetic to persons from Central America who cross into the United States? Explain. Describe which segments of U.S. society are portrayed in the film as sympathetic to such persons?

5. How has this film influenced your attitude toward refugees?

PART IV

REFUGEES AND YOUR COMMUNITY

✦

REFUGEES IN YOUR COMMUNITY

The majority of the world's 20 million refugees are not in the United States. Most refugees flee just across the border from their homeland, and wait for conditions to improve so that they can return home. However, going back is not always possible, and many thousands of refugees have found a permanent haven in the United States.

Many factors influence where a refugee family might choose to settle in the United States. In some cases, people flock to an area close to their former home. For example, large numbers of Cubans settle in Florida, especially in Miami, the largest port city close to Havana. In other cases, refugees go wherever they find family members, friends, or a community of people from the same city or country. San Jose, California, for example, has attracted the greatest number of Vietnamese in the world outside Vietnam itself. Having to cope with a climate and a culture that may be drastically different is worth the effort in order to find a community that speaks the same language and shares customs of the former life. Thus many refugees from tropical Laos make their homes in New England, and many Hmong people from rural Cambodian mountains thrive in urban Minneapolis.

Although we are often unaware of their presence, refugees are our neighbors! Refugee communities exist in every city and state in the United States, as well as in small towns and rural areas. Getting to know who they are, where they came from and why, appreciating their problems, and enjoying the contributions they have to make to our society is an important aspect of understanding our own communities.

> "We didn't want to come here; we just were trapped, you know. We couldn't go back. I had great hope that everything will stabilize and we'll go back . . . . [I]t's not normal for anybody that you leave your country and you go to another. It's a very disturbing situation—they can't be happy; it's impossible . . . . We lived all our life with hope that we would go there [i.e., back to Russia], but our children were born and the children were getting their lives, with school, with friends. So it was again hard for us to part with that because they would suffer. And they didn't know the language, and then it wasn't so good at that time to return back . . . . So that was going on and on and on. You're in a safe place; it's very natural with a human being not to go into a fire. That's the main reason why we remained here, and the reasons are emotional. You know, whatever we lived through, it was very, very bitter.
>
> —Anuta Sharrow, in her 80s
> Russian refugee in the U.S. since 1919

ORGANIZATIONS WORKING FOR REFUGEES

Leaving home—the single, momentous act that turns an ordinary citizen into a refugee—epitomizes how much courage, resourcefulness, endurance, and independence a person needs even to become a refugee. But refugees also can use a great deal of help and many people are working to improve their conditions. This assistance comes from four major sources: United Nations sponsored organizations, the United States government, nongovernmental organizations, and volunteers.

Refugees cannot, of course, claim protection under the laws of the country they have fled. What rights can they expect from their host country? In particular, what can they expect if the United States is their host country?

THE WORK OF THE UNITED NATIONS

The United Nations has established three organizations for the protection of refugees, all of which are supported by donations from governments that belong to the U.N. The largest of these organizations is the **U.N. High Commissioner for Refugees** (UNHCR). From its headquarters in Geneva and offices in more than 70 countries, the UNHCR works to carry out three major responsibilities:

1. To observe countries that have signed the 1951 **Convention Relating to the Status of Refugees** and to ensure they are carrying out their promise to treat refugees according to international law

> "I like the United States. I love it . . . . But I'm still missing my country. Every day I wonder where I belong. When do I stop being a refugee? How do I relate to the majority culture? How do I preserve my own culture without isolating myself? Where do my children belong? How will I ensure that my children will understand people of my own generation?"
>
> —Chilean refugee, 26 years old
> A resident of Great Britain for 16 years

> "It has not been easy for our old people to adjust from one culture to another. As we Mien say, 'Moving mountains is more easy than moving your mind . . . . If the children become too Americanized, then they won't care who they are so in the future we may be totally lost. We can become American, but our hair color won't change, our faces won't change. We don't belong to American. We don't belong to Mien. We are just nothing."
>
> —Ay Choy Saelee
> Mien refugee from Cambodia (quoted in *Moving Mountains*, a film by Elaine Velazquez)

2. To collaborate with other organizations to ensure aid reaches refugees

3. To work for long-term solutions for refugees, returning them to their home countries when conditions become safe or helping them to resettle in new countries

GOVERNMENTAL ASSISTANCE

In addition to U.N.-sponsored organizations, individual governments throughout the world also provide help for refugees. In the United States the **Immigration and Naturalization Service (INS)** is the agency charged with working for and with refugees. Many services and agencies work under its supervision to help refugees in a variety of ways.

NONGOVERNMENTAL ORGANIZATIONS

Nongovernmental organizations (NGOs), private institutions that do not receive government money, also work to assist refugees. Some, such as the International Red Cross or Red Crescent, are international humanitarian groups that address all kinds of disasters, not just those that involve refugees. Many, like the Church World Service, Catholic Charities, and the Lutheran Immigration and Refugee Service are sponsored by religious denominations.

Other U.N. Agencies Assisting Refugees

Two other U.N. organizations work in regions where there have been long-term concentrations of refugees. The **U.N. Relief and Works Agency for Palestine Refugees** (UNRWA) was established in 1949 to help Palestinian people who became refugees because of the war between Israel and its Arab neighbors. Working under extreme difficulties caused by continual violence in the area, this agency provides education, training, and health care for Palestinian refugees who live in the West Bank, Gaza Strip, Lebanon, Syria, and Jordan.

Since 1975 the people of Kampuchea (Cambodia) have endured terrible suffering from a civil war, oppressive regime, and invasion by Vietnamese forces. The **U.N. Border Relief Organization** (UNBRO) was set up to provide food and health care for the more than 300,000 Kampucheans who fled their country and are living in camps just inside the border of Thailand.

Also working for the welfare of refugees, especially those living in camps, is **UNESCO** (the United Nations Educational, Scientific and Cultural Organization), which provides schools for refugee children, and **UNICEF** (United National Children's Fund), which tries to ensure that children are properly fed, protected from disease, and have at least an elementary education.

147

Refugees and U.S. Government Support

Refugees are eligible for the following government support:

Reception and Placement Grants These grants are provided by the Bureau for Refugee Programs to voluntary resettlement agencies to support pre-arrival activities (identification and orientation of sponsors, travel arrangements to bring refugees to their final destinations); reception (assistance in obtaining initial housing, furnishings, food, and clothing); and orientation and referral services in the areas of health, employment, and training.

Cash Assistance Refugees who are eligible for Aid to Families with Dependent Children (AFDC), Supplemental Security Income (SSI), or state and local General Assistance programs may receive such assistance during the refugees' first 24 months in the United States. Refugees who meet income eligibility requirements but not family composition requirements for AFDC may receive Refugee Cash Assistance during their first 12 months in the U.S., with full federal reimbursement of all state costs.

Medical Assistance Refugees who are eligible for Medicaid may receive such assistance. Refugees who meet income eligibility requirements but not family composition requirements for Medicaid may receive Refugee Medical Assistance during their first 12 months in the U.S.

Social Services States receive funds, based on the number of refugees in the state who have been in the United States for 36 months or less, to support a range of services, including employment services, English as a Second Language training programs, health referral services, translating and interpreting services, and social adjustment services. Priority is given to those employment and language services that promote economic self-sufficiency.

Targeted Assistance "Impacted Areas" (localities with high concentrations of welfare-dependent refugees) receive funds to support supplemental services to promote self-sufficiency.

Transitional Service to Refugee Children Administered by the Department of Education, this program provides funds to the states for educational services for refugee children.

Health Program for Refugees Administered through the Centers for Disease Control, this program awards grants to states and localities to identify health problems that might impede effective resettlement of refugees and refer refugees for appropriate diagnosis and treatment.

English as a Second Language and Cultural Orientation Program Administered by the Bureau for Refugee Programs, this program provides training to U.S.-bound refugees in processing centers; for Southeast Asian refugees these programs are provided in Thailand and the Philippines.

Reprinted from The Refugee Information Resource Directory, *Denali Press, 1989.*

Others agencies concern themselves with particular needs or special groups of refugees. For example, groups like Save the Children address the needs of young children and their mothers. OXFAM and CARE are two examples of organizations that seek to provide food and medicine. Others like Doctors Without Frontiers provide health care in emergency situations. Amnesty International and other human rights organizations help ensure that refugees receive the treatment guaranteed them under international law. For example, some refugees suffer **refoulement,** forcible return to their home countries where they may run the risk of being arbitrarily imprisoned, tortured, or killed.

Some voluntary organizations offer assistance to refugees from a particular country. In the United States the sanctuary movement has offered support and protection to those people fleeing from Central America whom the United States government does not recognize as refugees. Often groups assisting refugees are largely composed of former refugees from that area. For example, Vietnamese who have been resettled in new countries often form groups to help other Vietnamese. Some raise money to improve coast guard protection against pirates in the waters off the coast of Vietnam. Other groups provide assistance to Vietnamese refugees in resettlement camps, where they may wait for years before being accepted by a new country. Still others help Vietnamese refugees who have finally arrived in a new country to learn the language, acquire new skills, and find housing and employment.

YOU CAN MAKE A DIFFERENCE

The welfare of refugees is not just the responsibility of the United Nations, governments, or big institutions. Local organizations and individual people play a vital role in seeing that the rights of refugees are respected, that they can live a decent life while they wait to return home, or that they can build a new life in the United States if return is impossible. Teenagers might babysit for refugee parents while they look for work, or retired people could teach English to newly arrived refugees. Sometimes assistance to refugees is as direct and simple as a kind neighbor who explains how to use a coin-operated washing machine or read the bus schedule, or a fellow student who helps with homework or simply offers friendship.

ASYLUM SUMMER

The following poem was written by Melissa Jameson a college student from Redlands, California. During the summer of 1990 she served as a volunteer with Amnesty International's Asylum Summer program in south Texas. She assisted asylum seekers and refugees in filling out forms and provided them with emotional support and empathy as well. The poem "Como se dice," which means "How do you say" in Spanish, presents some of the realities she encountered working with asylum seekers and refugees from Central America.

Como se dice

How do you say
I'm sorry
the kind you use to say
I'm sorry your sister was
disappeared
How do you word the question
that asks
What type of torture
and for how long
and where

Today I learned the word for
the rubber hood, filled with
powder that
burns your eyes and lungs until
you "confess" (say what they
want to hear or
say anything to stop the fire and
blood in your throat)
that government interrogators use

How do you ask, again,
Who killed your father
What did they use
When did you discover his
mutilated hands
Why did you leave your country
Who threatened you
How do you say
Where are your children?
How did they die?

Today I learned the word for
    threaten
    death
    torture
    body
    rape
    hide
    escape
    shoot
    beat
    hit

How do you say
Where did you go
after they raped you
after they killed your husband
after they kidnapped your son

Today I learned to say
I'm sorry
the kind you use to say
No,
We cannot take your case
I cannot help you.

REFUGEES IN YOUR COMMUNITY
A Cooperative Fact-Finding Activity

OVERVIEW: This activity relates information about refugees and human rights to students' home communities, and offers active, meaningful ways for students to respond to what they have learned.

AGE LEVEL: Grades 7–12

TIME: 1–3 hours

MATERIALS:

■ Handout 30: Refugees in Your Community

■ Handout 31: Verifying and Expanding Your Information

■ Handout 32: Compiling Your Investigation Results

■ World map, local telephone book and access to local telephone

SUBJECT AREAS: Language arts, government, journalism, religious studies

Refugees become integrated socially and economically in their new communities.

151

OBJECTIVES:

- To learn how to gather information about the local community
- To recognize the impact of international events on local life
- To become familiar with state and local agencies and legislators
- To find opportunities for an active response to social concerns
- To practice group cooperation
- To assess the validity of potentially conflicting information sources

NOTE: This exercise is designed to work both in communities with many groups of refugees and immigrants as well as in those with very few. The teacher is *not* expected to know the answers to the questions asked but rather to assist students in their investigations.

In preparing this activity, however, the teacher should become informed about what major refugee groups are present in the community.

Some information sources to suggest to students are the local Red Cross, mayor's office, Chamber of Commerce, clergy, county courthouse, and the State Department of Education. Some communities, especially those near national borders, may have an office of the Immigration and Naturalization Service, as well as an INS detention center. Some optional activities are suggested for communities with detention centers.

In this and all human rights education lessons, students should always be offered opportunities for appropriate action in response to the problems they learn about. **You Can Do More,** page 162 provides some suggestions.

PART 1

Distribute or display on an overhead projector **Handout 30: Refugees in Your Community.** Ask the group as a whole to generate answers to the questions from their own experience and information. Encourage students to cite and evaluate their sources of information. Locate on the world map the countries students suggest.

You may need to clarify for students the difference between *refugee* and *immigrant* and help the class think of information sources readily available to them such as the telephone book, as well as local social agencies.

PART 2

Break the group into teams of three or four. Explain that students are to work cooperatively on the rest of this assignment, dividing the information-gathering tasks among themselves. Then assign each team one or more groups of refugees to investigate and give them a separate copy of **Handout 31: Verifying and Expanding Your Information** to complete for each refugee group assigned. Because each student will need access to a local telephone, this activity is ideal for homework.

PART 3

After Part 2 is complete, have the class complete **Handout 32: Compiling Your Investigation Results** on the basis of the information they have gathered. Use the board, an overhead projector, or individual handouts. Be sure to include the name of each information source.

Encourage students to report their experiences in fact-finding and to discuss their personal responses to what they have learned. When information sources conflict, help students evaluate the validity of the sources and strategize how to resolve the conflict of information. Discuss what new insights students have gained about refugees, world conditions, and their own communities. Ask for suggestions about other topics for which students might use the same fact-finding skills.

PART 4

Build on this student-generated information by following up with one or more of the further activities described in **Activity 21: You Can Do More.**

FURTHER ACTIVITIES

1. Have students include the activities of the Immigration and Naturalization Service (INS) in their community investigations. Suggest they find out if there is a local INS office and what it does. Encourage them to find out if a detention center is in the area and, if so, to try to find out where it is, who runs it, how many people are there and for how long, and what agencies are helping people in the detention center.

2. Suggest students include activities of the sanctuary movement in their community investigations. (See **Handout 24: The Sanctuary Movement in the United States,** page 121.) Ask them to try to find out if local chuches are engaged in this movement, and, if so, to learn about what they do and why they do it.

REFUGEES IN YOUR COMMUNITY
Assessing What You Already Know

Because people often think of refugees as living in distant countries, they are surprised to learn that refugees also are living in their own communities. The following activity is designed to help you find out about refugees in your own town, city, or state.

1. Make a list of any groups of refugees you think may have settled in your community at any period in its history. Locate each country of origin on a world map.

Name of group	*Country/continent of origin*	*When arrived*
_____	_____	_____
_____	_____	_____
_____	_____	_____
_____	_____	_____
_____	_____	_____
_____	_____	_____
_____	_____	_____

2. What reasons do you think caused these refugees to leave their homes?

_____

_____

_____

_____

_____

3. What reasons do you think brought these refugees to your particular community?

_____

_____

_____

_____

_____

From *The Uprooted: Refugees and the United States* ©1995 Nancy Flowers and David M. Donahue, published by Hunter House Inc., Publishers, 1-800-266-5592.

4. Do you think it is easy for these refugees to settle in your community? What aspects of your community make settlement easy? What aspects of your community make settlement difficult?

_____

_____

_____

_____

5. Do you know any refugees personally? If so, how did you come to know them?

_____

_____

_____

_____

6. Make a list of any groups of recent immigrants you think may live in your community. Locate each country on a world map.

Name of group	_Country/continent of origin_	_When arrived_
_____	_____	_____
_____	_____	_____
_____	_____	_____
_____	_____	_____
_____	_____	_____

7. What reasons do you think caused these immigrants to leave their homes?

_____

_____

_____

_____

8. What reasons do you think brought these immigrants to your particular community?

_____

_____

_____

_____

From _The Uprooted: Refugees and the United States_ ©1995 Nancy Flowers and David M. Donahue, published by Hunter House Inc., Publishers, 1-800-266-5592.

9. What kind of help do you think immigrants may need when they come to your community? List your ideas below.

_____

_____

_____

_____

_____

10. What kind of help may refugees need when they come to your community that are different from those of immigrants?

_____

_____

_____

_____

11. What people or groups in your community offer help to refugees and immigrants?

Kind of help needed   _Group(s) offering this help_

_____   _____

_____   _____

_____   _____

_____   _____

_____   _____

_____   _____

12. Make a list of information sources you think might be able to answer your questions about refugees in your community.

_____

_____

_____

_____

_____

REFUGEES IN YOUR COMMUNITY
Verifying and Expanding Your Information

INSTRUCTIONS: Complete this form for each refugee group you investigate.

Name of refugee group: _____

Country/continent of origin: _____

Size of this refugee group in community: _____

Period of arrival in community: _____

1. Explain the reasons people from this group of refugees left their homes. Give the source of your information about each reason.

Reason for leaving home country   *Information source*

_____   _____

_____   _____

_____   _____

_____   _____

2. What route did most of these refugees take to get from their home countries to this community? By what means did they travel?

_____

_____

_____

_____

3. What reasons have you learned that may have brought this refugee group to your particular community? Give the source of your information about each reason.

Reason for coming to this community   *Information source*

_____   _____

_____   _____

_____   _____

_____   _____

4. Do any of your sources disagree on the reasons these refugees left their homes or came to your community? If so, how do you explain the differences in these points of view?

_____

_____

_____

_____

_____

_____

5. What kind of help do these refugees need when they come to your community? What people or groups in your community are offering help to these refugees? Give the source of your information about each need. Do any of your sources disagree?

Kind of help needed	_Group(s) offering this help_	_Information source_
_____	_____	_____
_____	_____	_____
_____	_____	_____
_____	_____	_____
_____	_____	_____
_____	_____	_____

6. Make a list of information sources (including telephone numbers) you used to answer your questions about refugees in your community. Place a star next to those sources that were especially helpful.

Information source	_Address_	_Telephone number_
_____	_____	_____
_____	_____	_____
_____	_____	_____
_____	_____	_____
_____	_____	_____
_____	_____	_____

REFUGEES IN YOUR COMMUNITY
Compiling Your Investigation Results

INSTRUCTIONS: Complete this chart using the information each team has gathered about refugees in your community.

1. What are the main refugee groups in your community? Place a star next to the largest groups.

Refugee group	Country/continent of origin	Period of arrival	Size of group
_____	_____	_____	_____
_____	_____	_____	_____
_____	_____	_____	_____
_____	_____	_____	_____
_____	_____	_____	_____

2. What is the total population of your community? _____

3. What is the approximate refugee population in your community? _____
(Add up the figures in the last column above.)

4. What percentage of the total population are the refugees in your community? _____
(Divide the refugee population by the total population.)

5. What reasons have you learned for why these refugees may have left their homes? List reasons for each group separately.

Group	Reason(s) for leaving home	Information source
_____	_____	_____
_____	_____	_____
_____	_____	_____
_____	_____	_____
_____	_____	_____
_____	_____	_____

From *The Uprooted: Refugees and the United States* ©1995 Nancy Flowers and David M. Donahue, published by Hunter House Inc., Publishers, 1-800-266-5592.

6. Based on your investigations, what are the main reasons people become refugees?

_____

_____

_____

_____

_____

_____

7. What reasons have brought these refugees to your particular community? List reasons for each group separately.

Group	Reason(s) for coming here	Information source
_____	_____	_____
_____	_____	_____
_____	_____	_____
_____	_____	_____
_____	_____	_____
_____	_____	_____
_____	_____	_____
_____	_____	_____
_____	_____	_____
_____	_____	_____
_____	_____	_____

8. Based on these investigations, what are the main factors that draw refugees to your community?

_____

_____

_____

_____

_____

_____

_____

From _The Uprooted: Refugees and the United States_ ©1995 Nancy Flowers and David M. Donahue, published by Hunter House Inc., Publishers, 1-800-266-5592.

9. What kind of help do most refugees need when they come to your community? List these below.

Kind of help needed   *Group(s) offering this help*   *Information source*

_____   _____   _____

_____   _____   _____

_____   _____   _____

_____   _____   _____

_____   _____   _____

_____   _____   _____

_____   _____   _____

_____   _____   _____

_____   _____   _____

10. Are there any needs listed above that members of your class might be able to help provide?

From *The Uprooted: Refugees and the United States* ©1995 Nancy Flowers and David M. Donahue, published by Hunter House Inc., Publishers, 1-800-266-5592.

YOU CAN DO MORE
Activities Involving Refugees in Your Community

INVITE A GUEST SPEAKER

Invite a recent or former refugee and/or someone who works with refugees to visit your class and talk about the refugee experience. If you live near an INS office, try to include representatives of both the government and a service agency.

If you are fortunate enough to arrange such a speaker, impress upon students the importance of patience and tact in listening to their guest and asking questions about what may be very painful experiences. Help students prepare in advance any sensitive questions they would like to ask. Recognize that refugee speakers may be fearful that their activities may result in their deportation and/or endanger the lives of family members in their native country.

Sample questions for refugees:

- What do you miss most about your former home?

- How did you decide to leave your former home?

- What was the most difficult part of your experience as a refugee?

- How were you received when you arrived in this country? In this community? Did you feel welcome?

- What was the greatest help to you in settling into your new community?

Often, refugees must learn a new language. Here, refugees are being tutored in English.

Sample questions for refugee workers:

- How did you get involved in working with refugees?

- What has been the most difficult aspect of this work for you?

- What kinds of help could you use in your work?

FIND WAYS TO HELP REFUGEES IN YOUR COMMUNITY

Reconsider the list of needs the class made in **Handout 32: Compiling Your Investigation Results,** Questions 9 and 10. How can class members help to meet any of these needs? The following are some ideas:

- Collect food, clothing, furniture, kitchen utensils, household goods.

- Sponsor a refugee family.

- Babysit while adult refugees attend English classes or look for work.

- Collect bicycles and other toys for refugee children.

- Tutor refugee children or adults in English.

- Tutor refugee children in school subjects.

- Help provide refugee families with transportation to medical, legal, or other appointments.

- Help refugees prepare for the job-search process.

FIND WAYS TO MAKE YOUR SCHOOL COMMUNITY MORE AWARE OF REFUGEES

Here are some ideas:

- Plan a school assembly that draws attention to refugee concerns. You might use a film, a guest speaker or panel of speakers, a selection of readings, or a student-written skit.

- Create a school bulletin board depicting the hardships refugees face, the cultural gifts they bring, and the help they need.

- Create a bulletin board to post clippings and articles about refugees.

- Use the information compiled on **Handout 32: Compiling Your Investigation Results** to let others know about refugees in your own community.

WRITE LETTERS IN SUPPORT OF REFUGEES IN YOUR COMMUNITY

Writing letters can let others know about problems in your community and influence those who make decisions. If your investigations into refugees in your community have revealed some issues you feel should be more widely known or problems that should be addressed, consider writing to express your concerns. See **Activity 22: The Power of the Pen,** page 165.

Photos courtesy International Institute of the East Bay

Community agencies provide recreational and educational opportunities for refugee children, helping them adjust to their new culture.

THE POWER OF THE PEN
A Letter-Writing Activity

OVERVIEW: Students plan, execute, and assess a letter-writing effort.

AGE LEVEL: High school

TIME: 1–2 hours

MATERIALS:
- Handout 33: Writing Letters that Have an Effect
- Handout 34: Facts for Letter Writing

SUBJECT AREAS: Government, language arts, religious studies, U.S. history

OBJECTIVES:
- To practice letter writing with meaningful subject matter
- To gain experience with an important tool for social activism
- To become familiar with the names of the local press and elected officials

PART 1: DEFINING THE ISSUE

Help students clarify their understanding and articulation of the refugee issue they wish to write about using **Handout 33: Writing Letters that Have an Effect.** Individuals or groups may chose different topics, some local and some national or international.

PART 2: STRATEGIZING

Help students plan the best strategy for writing about the issue or issues they have chosen. The list of refugee organizations in Appendix D may be useful. Use **Handout 34: Facts for Letter Writing** to indentify appropriate places to send these letters.

PART 3: GATHERING INFORMATION

If students have completed **Activity 20: Refugees in Your Community,** they will already have a fund of information about their local situation. Other activities in this resource curriculum may stimulate concern about national or international issues. This activity is an excellent opportunity to encourage use of library resources, both reference books and guides to periodical literature. Some students will need only local information; others will need national addresses. Encourage them to work cooperatively to find the information and addresses they need.

PART 4: WRITING THE LETTERS

Some students may need direction on the correct format for a formal business letter.

PART 5: EVALUATING THE RESULTS

Provide a place and time for students to share any responses they receive. A bulletin board to display responses helps to emphasize that letter writing gets results. As the class shares their responses, help students determine how to evaluate whether their letters have been effective. Discuss with the class other local and international issues for which letter writing might be a means of effecting change or voicing concern.

WRITING LETTERS THAT HAVE AN EFFECT

DEFINE YOUR ISSUE OR CONCERN CAREFULLY

A. State the issue you want to write about concisely in a sentence or two:

_____

_____

_____

B. Consider the following questions about the issue you want to write about:

- Is your source of information reliable?

- Do you have enough information about the issue?

- Do you have the facts straight?

- What do you want your letter(s) to accomplish?

STRATEGIZE ABOUT WHOM TO WRITE TO

- Is this a local, state, national, or international issue?

- Is this an issue that needs to be more widely known? Would a letter to the editor of a newspaper be effective? What community response is desired?

- Is this an issue that needs attention from government agencies? Which agencies are involved? What response is desired?

- Is this an issue about which legislation is needed? Who are the legislators involved? What response is desired?

GATHER THE NAMES AND ADDRESSES YOU NEED

Handout 31: Verifying and Expanding Your Information may help you to organize this information. The class might work cooperatively to gather all the addresses you will need.

WRITE TO EXPRESS YOUR CONCERN

- Define the issue specifically.

- If you ask for a response, be sure what you are asking for is clear.

- Identify yourself. If you are a student, mention your age or grade. If you write as a class, mention your school's name.

■ Keep the letter as brief as you can to get your concerns across.

■ Always be polite.

■ Stick to information you have verified from your sources. Don't make claims you can't support with facts.

■ If possible, keep a copy of the letter(s) you send.

EVALUATE THE RESULTS

■ Report any responses to your letters. Post any written responses or published letters to the editors.

■ After a few weeks, discuss what kinds of letters seem most effective.

From *The Uprooted: Refugees and the United States* ©1995 Nancy Flowers and David M. Donahue, published by Hunter House Inc., Publishers, 1-800-266-5592.

FACTS FOR LETTER WRITING

NEWSPAPERS

A. Newspapers with local, neighborhood, and community circulation:

Name: _____ Address: _____

Name: _____ Address: _____

Name: _____ Address: _____

B. Newspapers with statewide circulation:

Name: _____ Address: _____

Name: _____ Address: _____

Name: _____ Address: _____

C. Newspapers with national circulation:

Name: _____ Address: _____

Name: _____ Address: _____

Name: _____ Address: _____

II. ELECTED OFFICIALS

LOCAL OFFICIALS

1. Mayor: Party: Address:

_____ _____ _____

2. City Council members in your district:

_____ _____ _____

_____ _____ _____

_____ _____ _____

3. Other local officials who might be helpful:

_____ _____ _____

_____ _____ _____

_____ _____ _____

From *The Uprooted: Refugees and the United States* ©1995 Nancy Flowers and David M. Donahue, published by Hunter House Inc., Publishers, 1-800-266-5592.

STATE OFFICIALS

A. Governor: Party: Address:

_____ _____ _____

B. State Senator for your district:

_____ _____ _____

C. State Legislator for your district:

_____ _____ _____

D. Other state officials who might be helpful:

_____ _____ _____

_____ _____ _____

_____ _____ _____

_____ _____ _____

FEDERAL OFFICIALS

A. U.S. Senators: Party: Address:

_____ _____ _____

_____ _____ _____

B. U.S. Congressional Representative for your district:

_____ _____ _____

C. Other federal officials who might be helpful:

_____ _____ _____

_____ _____ _____

_____ _____ _____

PUBLIC AGENCIES AND PRIVATE ORGANIZATIONS THAT MIGHT BE ABLE TO HELP:

_____

_____

_____

_____

From *The Uprooted: Refugees and the United States* ©1995 Nancy Flowers and David M. Donahue, published by Hunter House Inc., Publishers, 1-800-266-5592.

PART V

APPENDICES

✦

171

IMMIGRATION AND REFUGEE TERMS

alien (noun) [Latin *alius* "other," "different"] A person who is not a citizen of the country in which he or she lives.

    A **legal alien** is someone who lives in a foreign country with the legal approval of that country.

    An **illegal alien** is someone who lives in a foreign country without the legal approval of that country.

asylum (noun) [Greek *asulon*, "sanctuary": *a-*, "without" + *sulon*, "right of seizure"] Any place offering protection or safety.

    Political asylum is legal permission to live in a country given by its government to people fleeing danger or persecution in their original homelands.

    A **country of asylum** grants a person asylum.

    A **country of first asylum** gives a person temporary asylum until he or she leaves it for another country.

    A person who seeks safety in a foreign country from danger at home is an **asylum seeker**.

country of origin (noun) A refugee's native land.

country of first asylum (noun) A country that gives a refugee a temporary asylum until he or she leaves for another country.

coyote (noun) A slang expression for a person who guides illegal aliens across a border, especially in Central America. Like the coyote in Native American legends, modern coyotes are often sly and sometimes treacherous.

deport (verb) To force someone to leave a country.

    Deportation often occurs when a country regards a person as an "undesireable alien," usually because of criminal activity.

    A **deportee** is usually someone who is not a native of the country that ejects him or her.

detainee (noun) An alien in the custody of government authorities who is waiting for officials to decide if he or she may stay in the country or will be forced to leave. Also called **internee**.

    Detention Centers, where detainees may remain for periods of years, are often run like prisons. Detainees are held under guard and usually not allowed to leave the centers until their cases are settled.

displaced person (noun) A person who has been forced by dangerous circumstances to leave home for a place of safety within the home country.

    The dangerous circumstances could be natural disasters such as droughts or storms or they could be social unrest such as wars or revolutions.

    If a person flees to a place within the home country, he or she is called *displaced*. If that person flees to another country, he or she is called a **refugee**.

emigrate (verb) [Latin *emigrare*, "to move away from": *ex-*, "out" + *migrare*, "to move"] To go from one region or country and settle in another.

Emigrants are people who choose to leave their home countries to settle elsewhere.

The French word *emigré* (pronounced EM-UH-GRAY) is especially used to describe someone who has emigrated because of a revolution. This word came into common English usage during the eighteenth century French Revolution, when many French aristocrats fled to England.

exile (verb) [Latin *exilium*, "to exile"] To send someone out of a place; to banish.

Unlike a deportee, who is forced to leave a country where he or she is not a citizen, an **exile** is a person who is forced to leave his or her home country.

When circumstances cause a person to leave, he or she is in **voluntary exile**.

When a legal decree or banishment force a person to leave, he or she is in **involuntary exile**.

green card (noun) A slang term describing the permit that indicates a person who is not a citizen has been granted legal permanent resident status in the United States. Such a "resident alien" can live and work in the U.S. without fear of deportation unless he or she commits a serious criminal offense or lives outside the country for more than two years.

immigrate (verb) [Latin *immigrare*, "to go into": *in-*, "in" + *migrare*, "to move"] To come into a region or country where one is not a native.

Immigrants are people who choose to come to a country where they mean to settle permanently and obtain citizenship.

A **legal immigrant** is a person who comes to settle in a country with the legal permission of its government.

An **illegal immigrant** is a person who comes to settle in a country without the legal p 2ermission of its government. Unlike the illegal alien, an illegal im 3migrant wishes to settle permanently in
the new country.

I.N.S. (noun) Acronym for the United States Immigration and Naturalization Service.

haven (noun) [Old English *haefen*, "a harbor"] Any safe place; a shelter from danger.

migrate (verb) [Latin *migrare*, "to move"] To move from one place and settle in another.

Migratory people are those who must regularly move from place to place. Migration may occur when hunters must follow seasonal moves of game or herders need new grasses for their livestock; migration may also result from natural disasters such as volcanic eruptions or droughts, or from social disorders such as wars and revolutions.

A **migrant** is any person or animal that moves from place to place.

Migrant workers or **economic migrants** must travel from place to place, sometimes from country to country, to find employment. This migration is often determined by what crops need harvesting and in which season.

naturalization (noun) The process whereby an immigrant becomes a citizen. Naturalized citizens in the United States have all the rights of native-born citizens except election to certain public offices such as the Presidency.

NGO (noun) Acronym for NonGovernmental Organization, private organizations that receive no governmental financial support. The Red Cross, CARE, and OXFAM are examples of international NGOs.

refoulement (noun) When a person is forcibly returned to the home country where his or her life or freedom would be threatened; also called **forced repatriation.**

refuge (noun) [Latin *refugere*: *re-*, "back" or "away" + *fugere*, "to flee"] Protection or shelter; relief; anything or place to which one goes for help, comfort, or escape.

refugee (noun) A person who leaves his or her country of origin because of a "well-founded fear of persecution for reasons of race, religion, nationality, membership in a particular social group or political opinion." (Definition used by U.S. Refugee Act of 1980 and the United Nations.)
When a government acknowledges that someone has left their home country because of such a "well-founded fear of persecution," it grants that person **political asylum** or **refugee status.**
A significant number of refugees sharing a similar background is referred to as a **refugee community.**
A distinction is sometimes made between a **political refugee,** who seeks asylum because of the "well-founded fear of persecution" described above and an **economic refugee,** who flees a situation in which survival is threatened not by persecution but by conditions like poverty or famine.

repatriate (verb) [Latin *repatriare*: *re-*, "back" + *patria* "native country"] To return someone to his or her home country.
Voluntary repatriation is when a person chooses to return to the home country. In most cases voluntary repatriation occurs when the danger that threatened the person is over.
Involuntary repatriation or **refoulement** is when a person is caused unwillingly to return to the home country. In many cases involuntary repatriation results when the country where a person seeks asylum does not recognize that person as a refugee; i.e., a person with a "well-founded fear of persecution."

resettlement (noun) Moving a refugee from the country of first asylum to another country where he or she can settle permanently. Resettlement occurs when the refugee has no hopes of returning safely to the home country.
People waiting to be moved from the country of first asylum are often kept in **resettlement camps** until a place of resettlement can be found in another country.

sanctuary (noun) [Latin *sanctus,* "holy"] Any safe place.
The Sanctuary Movement is a cooperative action among many churches in the United States to help illegal refugees from Central America.

UNHCR (noun) Acronym for the United Nations High Commissioner for Refugees.

REFUGEES AND THE UNITED STATES
A TEACHING BIBLIOGRAPHY

FICTION

Angell, Judy, *One-Way to Ansonia*
Bradbury, 1985, 192 pp.
The life of a Russian immigrant girl in the U.S.A.,
1894–1899.

Bunting, Eve, *How Many Days to America: A
Thanksgiving Story*
Illustrated by Beth Peck
Clarion Books, 1988, 32 pp.
A beautifully illustrated book for young children about
the flight of a young boy and his family from oppression
in an unidentified Caribbean country. After many dangers
adrift in an open boat, they arrive in America, where
they have a special reason to celebrate Thanksgiving.

Butler, Robert Olen, *A Good Scent from a Strange
Mountain*
Penguin, 1993
These masterful short stories are written in first-
person Vietnamese voices, and juxtapose the history
and culture of Vietnam and the American South.

Cather, Willa, *My Antonia*
A classic of American literature, this novel tells the
story of a lifetime friendship between Antonia, a
Bohemian immigrant to the Nebraska frontier, and
the native-born narrator who cherishes her courage
and vitality.

Chigas, George, ed. and trans., *Cambodia's Lament: A
Selection of Cambodian Poetry*
Mill Town Graphics, Millers Falls, MA, 1991, 97 pp.

Christen-Morris, G., *Who Am I? Refugee Voices*
Vantage, 1987, 138 pp.
Lyrical evocations in prose and verse that penetrate the
"compassion fatigue" about the plight of refugees today.

Crew, Linda, *Children of the River*
Delacorte, 1989, 213 pp.
Having fled Cambodia, 17-year-old Sundara is torn
between remaining faithful to her family and
community and enjoying herself as a "regular"
American high school student in Oregon.

Duong Huy Duong, *Paradise of the Blind*
Morrow, 1993, 270 pp.
The plight of three Vietnamese women.

Fahrmann, Willi, *The Long Journey of Lukas B.*
Bradbury, 1985, 280 pp.
A boy's immigration from Prussia to the United States
in the 1870s.

Geras, Adele, *Voyage*
Athenaeum, 1985, 193 pp.
A group of Jewish young people leave eastern Europe
to settle in the United States in the early twentieth
century.

Gibson, Jamie, *Hello, My Name is Scrambled Eggs*
Lothrop, 1985, 159 pp.
Twelve-year-old Harvey enjoys "Americanizing" Tuan,
a young Vietnamese boy.

Jen, Gish, *Typical American*
Houghton Mifflin, 1990, 296 pp.
The communist takeover of China prevents Ralph
Chang, his sister Theresa, and her friend Helen from
ever returning home. The three young people ally
themselves, living together as a traditional extended
family in an alien culture.

Keneally, Thomas, *To Asmara: A Novel of Africa*
Warner Books, 1989, 290 pp.
A group of Europeans journey through Eritrea during
its civil war, a situation typical of the internecine
conflicts now current in Africa.

Laird, Elizabeth, *Kiss the Dust*
Dutton Children's Books, 1992, 278 pp.
Each phase of the refugee experience from flight to
resettlement is recounted in this story of a young
Kurdish girl and her family who are forced from Iraq.

Langford, Sondra Gordon, *Red Bird of Ireland*
Atheneum, 1983, 175 pp.
Thirteen-year-old Aderlyn is forced to flee famine,
disease, and political persecution in 1846 Ireland.

Law-Yone, Wendy, *The Coffin Tree*
Knopf, 1983, 195 pp.
A young Burmese woman's experience in New York City after she flees a political coup in Burma.

Lee, Gus, *China Boy*
Dutton, 1990, 322 pp.
The only Asian in an African-American neighborhood, Kai Ting must literally fight his way out of this ghetto.

Mark, Michael, *Toba*
Bradbury, 1984, 105 pp.
Individual stories about a young Jewish girl in Poland about 1910 as she prepares for her voyage to the United States.

McCunn, Ruthanne Lum, *Thousand Pieces of Gold*
Beacon, 1988, 308 pp.
Lalu, a Chinese-American pioneer, struggles through childhood poverty only to come to San Francisco and be sold as a slave. Lalu's triumph in a new world reflects the experience of many nineteenth century Asian immigrants.

Mukerjee, Bharati, *Jasmine*
Fawcett Crest, 1989, 214 pp.
Jasmine's journey from traditional India through the dark migratory world of refugees and illegal aliens to life as an Iowa farmer's wife in a household that also includes a Vietnamese refugee is a paradigm for the "new Americans" of the great immigration wave of the late twentieth century.

Mukerjee, Bharati, *The Middleman and Other Stories*
Fawcett Crest, 1988, 194 pp.
Mukerjee's short stories of displacement and dispossession portray the lives of new Americans from the Philippines, Iraq, India and other lands.

Tan, Amy, *The Joy Luck Club*
Putnam, 1989, 288 pp.
These intertwining stories narrated by four Chinese immigrant mothers and their four American-born daughters reflect typical conflicts of tradition and modernity, but the frictions and devotions between mothers and daughters are universal.

Townsend, Peter, *The Girl in the White Ship*
Holt, 1983, 171 pp.
Hue Hue, 13 years old, fleeing Vietnam.

Wartski, Maureen Crane, *A Boat to Nowhere*
Signet, 1980, 152 pp.
A Vietnamese family becomes "boat people" in a desperate flight to find refuge and a new life.

Wartski, Maureen Crane, *A Long Way Home*
Westminster Press, 1982
A sequel to *A Boat to Nowhere*.

PERSONAL NARRATIVES

Bode, Janet, *New Kids on the Block*
Franklin Watts, 1989
Oral histories of immigrant teens, some of whom are refugees.

Criddle, Joan and Teeda Butt Mam, *To Destroy You Is No Loss: The Odyssey of A Cambodian Family*
Anchor, 1987, 289 pp.
The story of one young woman and her family struggling for survival during the Pol Pot regime and their eventual flight to refugee camps in Thailand where the family awaits resettlement in the United States.

Fenton, James, ed., *Cambodian Witness: the Autobiography of Someth May*
Random House, 1986, 287 pp.

Filipovic, Zlata, *Zlata's Diary: A Child's Life in Sarajevo*
Viking, 1994, 200 pp.
The diary of a young girl living in war-torn Bosnia.

Freeman, James A.
Hearts of Sorrow: Vietnamese-American Lives
Stanford University, 1989

Haing Ngor, *A Cambodian Odyssey*
Warner Books, 1987
The story of a doctor who survived the brutalities of the Pol Pot regime.

Hayslip, Le Ly and Jay Wurts, *When Heaven and Earth Changed Places: A Vietnamese Woman's Journey from War to Peace*
Doubleday, 1989, 368 pp.
The memoir of a teenage Vietnamese girl who experiences the horrors of war, the disruption of life in a new country, and her own path to reconciliation with the past.

Jade Ngoc Quang Huynh, *South Wind Changing*
Graywolf Press, 1994, 305 pp.
The story of a young man's risky escape from
Vietnam to Thailand and the United States.

Katsuyo, Howard K., ed., *Passages: An Anthology of
the Southeast Asian Refugee Experience*
California State University: Fresno, 1990
A collection of essays and stories written by students
from Southeast Asia.

Keenan, Deborah and Roseann Lloyd, eds., *Looking
for Home: Women Writing about Exile*
Milkweed Editions, 1990, 288 pp.
A collection that offers many definitions of what exile
means, including being forced by circumstances to
make a new home in a strange land.

Kherdian, David, *The Road from Home: The Story of
an Armenian Girl*
Morrow, 1979, 238 pp.
Vernon's life is brutally disrupted as her family is
deported from Turkey and forced to live in the
deserts of Syria. Only Vernon (the author's mother)
survives the long trek, and after a sojourn in an
orphanage and an escape from the massacre of
Armenians and Greeks in Smyrna, she is sent at age
16 to the United States as a "mail order" bride.

Kramer, Sydelle and Jenny Masur, eds., *Jewish
Grandmothers*
Beacon, 1976, 174 pp.
A collection of first-person accounts of ten immigrant
Jewish women who came to the United States during
the first decades of the twentieth century.

Matthews, Ellen, *Culture Clash*
Intercultural Press, 1982, 125 pp.
A personal chronicle of the frustrations, conflicts, and
joys of an American family that sponsors a
Vietnamese refugee family.

Menchu, Rigoberta, Elisabeth Burgos-Debray, ed., *I,
Rigoberta Menchu: An Indian Woman in Guatemala*
Trans. Ann Wright.
London: Verso, 1984, 251 pp.
The personal narrative of this Nobel Peace Prize
winner's struggle for the rights of Guatemalan native
peoples and her ultimate exile.

Morrison, Joan and Charlotte Fox Zabusky, eds.,
*American Mosaic: The Immigrant Experience in the
Words of Those Who Lived It*
Dutton, 1980, 457 pp.

An extensive collection of narratives from immigrants
who span the century and the globe. A rich resource!

Nguyen-Hong-Nhiem, Lucy and Joel Martin
Halpern, eds., *The Far East Comes Near:
Autobiographical Accounts of Southeast Asian Students
in America*
University of Massachusetts, 1989, 213 pp.
A collection of narratives by American college students
who have lived through the refugee experience.

Philipson, L., *Freedom Flights: Cuban Refugees Talk
about Life under Castro and How They Fled His
Regime.*
Random House, 1980, 201 pp.
Twenty Cubans who chose exile from Castro's Cuba
tell their stories.

Portland Public Schools Foxfire Project, *Alive in
Portland*
Portland Public Schools Foxfire Project, Portland,
OR, 1981.
A collections of writings by Southeast Asian
immigrant high school students, including poetry,
folk tales, accounts of their traditional cultures, and
personal narratives.

Portuondo, M.F., *Ups and Downs of an
Unaccompanied Minor Refugee*
Ediciones Universal, 1984, 31 pp.
The narrative of a teenage Cuban girl as she flees her
country alone.

Santoli, A., ed., *New Americans: An Oral History:
Immigrants and Refugees in the U.S. Today*
Penguin, 1988, 392 pp.
The editor has complied 18 first-person narratives of
"new Americans" describing their exiles, struggles, and
difficulties in adapting to a new way of life.

Szymusiak, Molyda, *The Stones Cry Out: A
Cambodian Childhood, 1975-1980*
Hill and Wang, 1986, 245 pp.
A young girl and her family are driven from their
home by Pol Pot troops to live in work camps, where
most of the family dies from the brutal conditions.
She manages to escape to the refugee camps in
Thailand and ultimately is adopted by French parents.

Var Hong Ashe, *From Phnom Penh to Paradise: Escape
from Cambodia*
Hodder and Stoughton, 1988, 222 pp.

Watkins, Yoko Kawashima, *So Far from the Bamboo Grove*
Puffin Books, 1986, 183 pp.
A young Japanese girl living with her family in North Korea at the end of World War II struggles with her mother and sister to reach their devastated home in Japan.

BACKGROUND, HISTORY, AND DISCUSSION

Andre, Jacques, *The Stranger Within Your Gates*
World Council of Churches, 1987

Ashabranner, Brent, *Children of the Maya: A Guatemalan Odyssey*
Dodd, Mead, 1986, 97 pp.
Focuses on a large group of Mayan refugee children now living in Indiantown, Florida.

Ashabranner, Brent, *The New Americans: Changing Patterns in U.S. Immigration*, Photographs by Paul Conklin
Dodd, Mead and Company, 1983, 212 pp.
In describing the latest wave of legal and illegal U.S. immigrants and refugees, this book examines immigration issues in the context of immigrants themselves.

Bau, Ignatius, *This Ground is Holy: Church Sanctuary and Central American Refugees*
Paulist Press, 1985, 288 pp.
A historical and philosophical description of the sanctuary movement in the United States.

Bentley, Judith, *Refugees: Search for a Haven*
Messner, 1986, 160 pp.

Cartmail, Keith, *Exodus Indochina*
Heineman, 1983, 309 pp.
Coming to America: American Immigrants Series
1. Blumenthal, S., Coming to America: Immigrants from Eastern Europe, Delacorte, 1981
2. Blumenthal, S. and J. Ozer, *Coming to America: Immigrants from the British Isles,* Delacorte, 1980, 184 pp.
3. Garver, S. and P. McGuire, *Coming to North America: Immigrants from Mexico, Cuba, and Puerto Rico,* Delacorte, 1981, 161 pp.
4. Perrin, Linda, *Coming to America: Immigrants from the Far East,* Delacorte, 1980, 182 pp.
5. Rips, Gladys Nadler, *Coming to America: Immigrants from Southern Europe,* Delacorte, 1981, 143 pp.
6. Robbins, Albert, *Coming to America: Immigrants from Northern Europe,* Delacorte, 1981, 214 pp.

Cogswell, J.A., *No Place Left Called Home*
Friendship Press, 1983, 132 pp.
This books presents the global refugee situation and considers the ethical issues involved, including the question of just immigration policies for the United States and Canada, from a Christian perspective.

Conover, Tom, *Coyotes: A Journey through the Secret World of America's Illegal Aliens*
Vintage Books, 1987.

Davidson, Mariam, *Convictions of the Heart: Jim Corbett and the Sanctuary Movement*
University of Arizona, 1988, 187 pp.
A history of the sanctuary movement and one of its founders, Jim Corbett.

Dawson, Mark, *Flight: Refugees and the Quest for Freedom*
International Rescue Committee, 1993

Fields, Rick, *Taking Refuge in Los Angeles: Life in a Vietnamese Buddhist Temple*
Photographs by Don Farber
Aperture Foundation, 1987
A book of beautiful photographs and text that explores the lives of Vietnamese Buddhist refugees as they maintain their traditions as well as build a new life in the United States centering around their temple.

Freedman, Russell, *Immigrant Kids*
Dutton, 1980, 67 pp.
Forceful photographs of immigrant children to the United States at the turn of this century make their lives and hardships real.

Haines, David W, ed., *Refugees in the United States: A Reference Handbook*
Greenwood, 1985, 243 pp.
An invaluable reference book on immigration and refugee policy and statistics.

Helsinki Watch Staff and Lawyers Committee for Human Rights, *Mother of Exiles: Refugees Imprisoned in America*

Fund Free Expression, 1986, 59 pp.
This report catalogs the detention policies and centers of the INS, focusing on its abuses.

Higgins, J. and J. Ross, *Southeast Asians: A New Beginning in Lowell*
Mill Town Graphics, 1986, 131 pp.
A compilation of photographs of some of the 10,000 refugees from southeast Asia who have settled in Lowell, Massachusetts in the last decade. Includes a brief history of the Indochinese exodus and quotations from individual experiences.

Kismaraic, Carole, *Forced Out: The Agony of the Refugee in Our Time*
Human Rights Watch and J.M. Kaplan Fund in Association with William Morrow & Co., W.W. Norton & Co., Penguin Books Ltd., Random House, l989, 191 pp.
An extraordinary and moving collection of photographs, essays, and factual information that conveys the global refugee crisis.

MacEoin, Gard, ed., *Sanctuary: A Resource Guide for Understanding and Participating in the Central American Refugee Struggle*
Harper and Row, 1985, 217 pp.

Marrus, Michael R., *The Unwanted: European Refugees in the 20th Century*
Oxford, 1985, 414 pp.
A comprehensive history of the twentieth century refugee crisis in Europe and how the Great Powers have responded to it.

Martin, Susan Forbes, *Refugee Women*
Zed Books, 1992.
This useful book provides an overview of the situation and needs of refugee women and children and stresses the importance of women's participation in the design and implementation of all assistance programs.

Olsen, Laurie, *Crossing the Schoolhouse Border: Immigrant Students and the California Public Schools*
A California Tomorrow Policy Research Report, 1988, 128 pp.
Available through California Tomorrow, Fort Mason, Building B, San Francisco, CA 94123.
This report studies the problems, successes, and future of immigrant children in California's public schools.

Silk, James, *Despite a Generous Spirit: Denying Asylum in the United States*
US Committee for Refugees, 1986, 48 pp.
Available from USCR, 1025 Vermont Avenue, NW, Suite 920, Washington, DC 20005.
This accessible booklet summarizes U.S. policy toward refugees in the past decade.

Zucker, Norman and Naomi, *The Guarded Gate: The Reality of American Refugee Policy*
Harcourt, Brace, Javanovich, 1987
An excellent overview of U.S. refugee history, this text investigates the political, social, and personal issues that have shaped and reshaped refugee policy since legislation first distinguished refugees from immigrants in the early twentieth century.

CURRICULUM RESOURCES

Amnesty International USA, *Human Rights Education: The Fourth R*
Two issues of this periodical (Vol. 2, no 2, spring 1990, and Vol. 3, no 1, Spring 1991) focus on teaching about refugees. For information write to Educators' Network, AIUSA, 53 W. Jackson, Chicago, IL 60604.

A Curriculum for Teaching about Today's Refugees and Immigrants
Zellerbach Family Fund:
Available from San Francisco Study Center, 1095 Market Street, #602, San Francisco, CA 94103

Flight to Hope: A Catholic Refugee Awareness Education Project

Catholic Consortium on Refugee Awareness Education, 1990
Available from US Catholic Conference, 3211 4th St. NE, Washington, DC 20017-1194.

Jorgensen, Karen and Cynthia Stokes Brown, *New Faces in Our Schools: Student-Generated Solutions to Ethnic Conflict*
Zellerbach Family Fund, 1992
Available from San Francisco Study Center, 1095 Market Street, #602, San Francisco, CA 94103.
This curriculum for grades 9–12 addresses the conflicts that arise in schools among students of many backgrounds, especially new immigrants and refugees, by offering activities that dispel stereotypes and encourage dialogue and conflict resolution.

Nelson Thibaut, Amy, *The Chinese Immigrant Experience: A Simulation*
Center for Teaching International Relations, 2201 South Gaylord St., Denver, CO 80208, 1992
In this simulation students experience some of the legal and social problems that many immigrants encounter as they enter the country.

Stromberg, Jacqueline, *Encouraging Refugee Awareness in the Classroom: A Guide for Teachers*
US Committee for Refugees, 1993
Available from USCR, 1717 Mass. Ave.., NW, Washington, DC 20036

"Immigration." *Bill of Rights in Action*
Vol. 15, no. 1, Constitutional Rights Foundation, 1981, 24 pp.
For information write to Constitutional Rights Foundation, 601 Kingsley Drive, Los Angeles, CA 90005

United National High Commissioner for Refugees
A number of useful curriculum materials are available from this UN agency, including posters, slides, videos, and two teaching guides: *The Plight of the Refugees*, 1992 and *Combating Hate and Destruction*, 1994.

For information write UNHCR, Public Information, 1718 Connecticut Avenue NW, Suite 200, Washington, DC 20009.

Why Do People Move? Migration from Latin America
Stanford Program on International and Cross-Cultural Education (SPICE), Institute for International Studies, Littlefield Center, Room 14C, Stanford University, Stanford, CA 94305-5013
This unit of interactive activities for middle-school students examines the concept of migration through Latin American case studies. Poetry, music, drawings, and personal testimony convey the flight of political refugees and the quest for economic opportunities.

Women's Commission for Refugee Women and Children, *The Refugee Experience*
Women's Commission for Refugee Women and Children, 122 E. 42nd. St., New York NY 10168-1289, 1994
A Schools Project packet that includes a teaching guide by Ann Armstrong Craig, a video, and readings for students.

MAGAZINES AND INFORMATION BULLETINS

Refugee
A monthly publication of the United Nations High Commission for Refugees, this beautifully illustrated magazine features articles on refugee concerns around the world. Attractive format and clear prose make this magazine easily accessible to high-school students. Distributed free, though voluntary subscription donations are encouraged, *Refugee* belongs in every high-school library. For subscriptions write to: UNHCR, 1718 Connecticut Avenue NW, Suite 200, Washington, DC 20009.

Refugee Reports
Published monthly by the American Council for Nationalities Services/US Committee for Refugees, this magazine provides detailed, current information on government policy that affects refugees. Subscriptions are $20 a year: *Refugee Reports* subscriptions: Sunbelt Fulfillment Services, P.O. Box 41094, Nashville, TN 37204.

Refugee Voices
Published quarterly, *Refugee Voices* seeks to raise awareness about the plight of refugees recently arrived in the United States and those still in camps. For information write *Refugee Voices*, 713 Monroe Street NE, Washington, DC 20017.

World Refugee Survey
Published annually by the US Committee for Refugees, this publication provides up-to-date statistics and country reports as well as an overview of the year in review. A primary document for learning about refugees! Annual reports are $10 from the USCR, 1025 Vermont Avenue, NW, Suite 920, Washington, DC 20005.

United Nations High Commissioner for Refugees
Current information on specific refugee situations is available free of charge from the UNHCR, Public Information, 1718 Connecticut Avenue NW, Suite 200, Washington, DC 20009.

REFUGEE FILMOGRAPHY
Prepared by Edward Markarian

This refugee filmography is designed to provide summaries of 16mm films and videocassettes, both documentary and fictional, ranging in viewing time from a few minutes to feature length. Each entry contains the film title, length, year of distribution, and country of origin. A short description of the film is followed by a listing of its distributor and the recommended viewing age level (E = Elementary, JR = Junior High/Middle School, H = High School, A = Adult). A distribution index is included and several video distributors are provided for hard-to-locate foreign films.

GENERAL

"Ave Maria." 24 minutes. 1986. USA/Switzerland. Documentary depicting the suffering of refugee women and children in time of war. Available in all formats from the UNHCR. Level JR to A.

"HRC Spot 87." 10 minutes. 1987. Switzerland. A video without text on refugees, the causes of refugee movements, and the UN High Commissioner on Refugees' work. Available on video from the UNHCR. Level JR to A.

"Refugee: In Search of Haven." 12 minutes. 1979. USA. Overview of the refugee situation worldwide, with an emphasis on the special problems of hunger, shelter, lack of legal rights, and high personal risks. Available on filmstrip through the Church World Service. Level JR to A.

"Refugee Children." 40 minutes. 1987. Great Britain. Refugee children from Chad, Guatemala, and Vietnam are the focus of this film Available on videotape from the UNHCR. Level JR to A.

"Refugees: A Historical View." 22 minutes. 1981. Switzerland. The story of refugees, from early

civilization up to the creation of the UNHCR is told through paintings, sculptures, and drawings, both ancient and modern, and through archive film footage of the major upheavals of this century. Available in all formats from the UNHCR. Level JR to A.

"Refugee Women." 40 minutes. 1986. USA. Documentary depicting the lives of refugee women and their difficult circumstances worldwide. Available in 16mm from the Church World Service. Level JR to A.

"Si Ce N'est Ici." 8 minutes. 1978. Switzerland. Animated cartoon of a man forced to leave his country, who becomes a refugee. Available in all formats from the UNHCR. Level E to A.

"UNHCR: Caring for Refugees Since 1951." 27 minutes. 1987. Switzerland. Historical overview of the activities of the United Nations High Commissioner for Refugees. Available in all formats from the UNHCR. Level JR to A.

THE UNITED STATES

"Alambrista!" 110 minutes. 1978. USA. Drama of Mexican farmworkers who enter the country illegally. Available on videotape at specialty video stores. Level H to A.

"Alamo Bay." 105 minutes. 1985. USA. Drama of a Texas community unable to cope with Vietnamese refugees as they impact the fishing industry. Available

on videotape from most video stores. Level H to A.

"America, America." 174 minutes 1963. USA. Drama focuses on one young Greek boy who struggles in his attempt to reach America in the 1890s. Available on videotape from specialty video stores. Level H to A.

"An American Tail." 80 minutes. 1986. USA. Animated story of Feivel the Mouse, who is separated from his family after they escape persecution in Russia to find freedom in America. Available on videotape at most video stores. Level E to JR.

"Bittersweet Survival." 30 minutes. 1982. USA. The plight of Southeast Asian refugees in the U.S. is examined. Available in 16mm through Third World News. Level H to A.

"Becoming American." 40 minutes. 1983. USA. Documentary depicting the odyssey of a refugee family from Southeast Asia. Available on 16mm from the Church World Service. Level JR to A.

"The Border." 107 minutes. 1982. USA. Drama of honesty and corruption among U.S. border guards. Graphically depicts the exploitation of Mexican illegal immigrants. Available on videotape at most video stores. Level H to A.

"Ellis Island." 18 minutes. 1920. USA. Silent footage of the immigrants entering the gateway of the United States in the early twentieth century. Available on 16mm from The Film Center in Washington, D.C. Level E to A.

"El Mojado (The Wetback)." 20 minutes. 1974. USA. Activities of the U.S. Border Patrol and the plight of Mexican laborers are juxtaposed. Available on 16mm from the New York Museum of Modern Art. Level H to A.

"El Norte." 130 minutes. 1983. USA. Drama of Guatemalan refugees as they struggle to emigrate to the U.S. Their problems continue as they encounter American society. Available at most video stores. Level H to A.

"The Emigrants." 148 minutes. 1971. Sweden. Drama traces the hardships of a Swedish family who came to America in the nineteenth century. Available on videotape from video stores specializing in foreign films. Level JR to A.

"The Girl Who Spelled Freedom." 104 minutes. 1986. USA. A true-life story of a young Cambodian refugee who became a spelling bee champion in America a few months after fleeing her homeland. Available on videotape at most video stores. Level E to A.

"Hester Street." 90 minutes. 1975. USA. Drama of the immigration of a Jewish family to New York and the problems of assimilation. Available on videotape at most video stores. Level H to A.

"Illegal Aliens." 15 minutes. 1975. USA. Documentary of undocumented Mexicans in the U.S. and the problems they face. Available in 16mm from Third World News. Level H to A.

"The Immigrant." 20 minutes. 1917. USA. Charlie Chaplin's silent comedy melodrama, which portrays the difficulties refugees face on the voyage to the U.S. and their encounters with the new land. Available on videotape at most video stores. Level E to A.

"In Transit: Chinese in California." 26 minutes. 1977. USA. Historical view of Chinese immigration and the problems they faced. Available on 16mm from Lillian Woo. Level H to A.

"Journey to America." 60 minutes. 1984. USA. Presents the personal histories of immigrants and refugees coming to America between 1890 and 1920. Available on videotape from PBS Video. Level JR to A.

"Maricela." 60 minutes. 1985. USA. Story of a Salvadoran mother and daughter as they struggle to make a life in the U.S. Available on videotape from PBS Video. Level JR to A.

"Mississippi Triangle." 110 minutes. 1983. USA. Documentary of the relationship between Chinese refugees on the Mississippi and their interactions with the black and white community. Available on 16mm from Third World News. Level H to A.

"Molly's Pilgrim." 24 minutes. 1985. USA. Academy Award winning short portraying the plight of refugee children in this country, especially as they face insensitivity of American children in public schools. Appropriate for elementary level children. Available on 16mm through Budget Films. Level E to JR

"New Harvest, Old Shame." 60 minutes. 1990. USA. Sequel to Edward R. Murrow's "Harvest of Shame" documentary about the terrible conditions under which migrant workers and undocumented aliens live. Available from PBS Video. Level H to A.

"The New Land." 161 minutes. 1973. Sweden. Sequel to "The Emigrants" documents the hardships of a Swedish family as it attempts to build a new life in 19th century America. Available on videotape at stores specializing in foreign films. Level H to A.

"Peace Has Not Yet Been Made: A Case History of a Hmong Family's Encounter with a Hospital." 30

minutes. 1982. USA. Portrays the difficulties of a Hmong family and an American hospital staff in an emergency situation. Available on 3/4" videotape from Church World Service. Level H to A.

"Safe Haven." 60 minutes. 1988. USA. Documentary tells the story, through interviews with refugees, of the Roosevelt Administration's treatment of European exiles during World War II. Available on videotape from PBS Video. Level H to A.

"From Spikes to Spindles." 50 minutes. 1975. USA. Documentary history of the Chinese immigrants' experience of struggle and discrimination in the 19th

and 20 centuries. Available in 16mm from Third World News. Level H to A.

"The Statue of Liberty." 60 minutes. 1986. USA. Documentary of the interviews by famous immigrants. Available on videotape at stores specializing in documentaries. Level JR to A.

"Strozek." 115 minutes. 1982. West Germany. Drama following three West German eccentrics as they attempt to adapt to American culture. A commentary on the difficulties of assimilation for foreigners. Available on videotape at stores specializing in foreign films. Level H to A.

SANCTUARY

"Asylum." 60 minutes. 1985. USA. Depicts the plight of Central American refugees as they attempt to seek asylum in the north. Available on videotape from Amnesty International regional offices.

"The Defection of Simas Kudirka." 104 minutes. 1978. USA. True drama of a Russian seaman who defects to a U.S. Coast Guard cutter and who, through bureaucratic blunders is turned back to the Russians. Available on videotape at most video stores. Level JR to A.

"New Underground Railroad." 30 minutes. 1983. USA. The examination of the sanctuary movement in the United States and its efforts to help Salvadoran

refugees. Available on video through Indiana University. Level H to A.

"Sanctuary." 60 minutes. 1986. USA. A PBS documentary focusing on the sanctuary movement in the United States. Available on videotape from PBS Video. Level H to A.

"Sanctuary: An African Epic." 26 minutes. 1982. USA. Focuses on the problems of the daily life of a refugee. The film emphasizes the community spirit of the refugees in the face of tragedy. Available in 16mm through the Church World Service. Level H to A.

ASIA

"Adrift in the World: Indochina Refugees." 28 minutes. 1975. USA. Portrays the situation of the "boat" people of Vietnam, Laos, and Cambodia. Available in 16mm through CC Films. Level H to A.

"Another Chance." 29 minutes. 1986. Switzerland. Report on the efforts to help refugee boat people on the Malaysian island of Palau Bidong. Available in all formats from the UNHCR. Level H to A.

"Are You Listening? Indochina Refugees." 60 minutes. 1982. USA. Interviews with refugees from Vietnam, Cambodia, and Laos who describe their experiences in camps and later their resettlement in the United States. Available on 3/4" videotape from Stuart Films. Level H to A.

"Bamboo City." 28 minutes. 1980. Switzerland. Documents the establishment of a refugee camp near the Kampuchean border and the critical shortages of food and water it faced. Available in all formats from the UNHCR. Level H to A.

"The Boat People." 106 minutes. 1983. Hong Kong. Drama of Vietnamese "boat" people through the eyes of a Japanese journalist. Available on videocassette at video stores specializing in foreign films. Level H to A.

"The End of the Road." 20 minutes. 1979. Switzerland. Shows the Hmong hill tribes coping in refugee camps in Thailand in the late 1970s. Available in all formats from the UNHCR. Level H to A.

"Fire on the Water." 60 minutes. 1982. USA. Refugee Vietnamese fishermen come into conflict with Texans. Available in 16mm from Films Incorporated. Level H to A.

"Only When It Rains." 11 minutes. 1980. Switzerland. Documents the plight of Indochinese refugees in Thailand's Sadeo and Khao-I-Dang refugee camps. Available in all formats from the UNHCR. Level H to A.

"Pass." 30 minutes. 1983. USA. Documents the Pass Program for Southeast Asian teenage refugees as they are placed in a simulated American high school environment. Available on 16mm from the Center for Applied Linguistics in Washington, D.C. Level H to A.

"The Restless Wave: Boat People in South-East Asia." 16 minutes. 1979. Switzerland. Documents the horrible ordeal of the Vietnamese boat people. Available in all formats from the UNHCR. Level H to A.

"So Far From India." 49 minutes. 1983. USA. Documentary of a family facing alienation in the United States as well as the pain of separation. Available in 16mm from Filmmakers Library. Level H to A.

"Voyage of Dreams." 30 minutes. 1983. USA. Examines the plight of Haitian refugee "boat" people. Available in 16mm and videotape from Cinema Guild. Level H to A.

LATIN AMERICA

"After the Earthquake." 20 minutes. 1983. USA. Documentary follows a Nicaraguan refugee emigrating to the United States. during the Somoza dictatorship. Available in 16mm through Third World News. Level H to A.

"Against the Wind and Tide." 55 minutes. 1982. USA. Documentary following the Mariel boat lift of Cuban refugees and their efforts to be granted asylum. Available in 16mm from Filmmakers Library. Level H to A.

"Artists in Exile." 30 minutes. 1982. USA. Interviews with Cuban exiles and the art they create. Available on 3/4" videotape from Black Filmmakers. Level H to A.

"Casualties of Conflict: Parts One and Two." 53 minutes. 1985. Great Britain. A documentary look at Guatemalan refugees in Mexico, and Salvadoran and Nicaraguan Miskito Indians in Honduras. Available in all formats from the UNHCR. Level H to A.

"Central America." 15 minutes. 1987. Great Britain. Film focusing on a refugee from El Salvador, Rufina, describing the tragic events leading up to her flight (the massacre of her entire village). Available on videotape from the UNHCR. Level H to A.

"Eduardo Uruguayo." 45 minutes. 1984. Uruguay. An Uruguayan family faces exile from the political repression of the military dictatorship. Available in 16mm from Icarus Films. Level H to A.

"El Salvador: Nowhere to Run." 27 minutes. 1987. USA. Documentary looks at the plight of El Salvadoran refugees in Honduras. Available on videotape from Oxfam America. Level H to A.

"Gaijin." 105 minutes. 1979. Brazil. The problems of Japanese immigrants in Brazil at the turn of the century are examined in their feature drama. Available in 16mm from New Yorker Films and in videocassette at stores specializing in foreign videos. Level H to A.

"Improper Conduct." 115 minutes. 1984. France. Documentary interviews with Cuban exiles who recount the repression they faced. Available in 16mm from New Yorker Films. Level H to A.

"Nowhere to Run." 25 minutes. 1982. USA. Examines the plight of Salvadoran refugees at La Virtud refugee camp in Honduras. Available on videotape through Downtown Community TV. Level H to A.

DISTRIBUTOR INDEX

Amnesty International
National Headquarters
322 8th Avenue
New York NY 10001
212-807-8400

> Mid-Atlantic Office
> 1118 22nd Street
> Washington DC 20037
> 202-775-5161

> Midwest Office
> 53 West Jackson, #1162
> Chicago IL 60604
> 312-427-2060

> Northeast Office
> 58 Day Street
> Somerville MA 02144
> 617-623-0202

> Southern Office
> 730 Peachtree Street, Suite 982
> Atlanta GA 30308
> 404-876-5661

> Western Office—Los Angeles
> 9000 West Washington Boulevard
> Second floor
> Culver City CA 90232
> 310-815-0450

> Western Office—San Francisco
> 500 Sansome Street, #615
> San Francisco CA 94111
> 415-291-9233

Church World Service
28606 Phillips Street
Elkhart IN 46515
219-264-3102

Downtown Community Television
87 Lafayette Street
New York NY 10013
212-966-4510

Filmmakers Library
133 East 58th Street
New York NY 10022
212-355-6545

"The" Film Center
938 K Street, NW
Washington DC 20001
202-393-1205

Indiana University
Audio-Visual Center
Bloomington IN 47405
812-335-2103

The Museum of Modern Art
Department of Film
11 West 53rd Street
New York NY 10019
Information: 212-956-4205
Orders: 212-956-4204

New Yorker Films
16 West 61st Street
New York NY 10023
212-247-6110

Oxfam America
800-225-5800

PBS Video
1320 Braddock Place
Alexandria VA 22314-1698
800-424-7963

United Nations High Commissioner for Refugees
Geneva Switzerland
41-22-739-8512
USA
1718 Connecticut Avenue, NW
Washington DC 20009
202-387-8546

Lillian Woo
608 South Citrus
Los Angeles CA 90036

The following rent-by-mail video collections provide a wide assortment of foreign films and documentaries.

Facets Video
1517 West Fullerton
Chicago IL 60614
800-331-6197

Connoisseur Video Collection
800-FILMART

New Yorker Video
800-447-0196

DIRECTORY OF REFUGEE RESOURCES
Reprinted from the World Refugee Survey, 1994,
U.S. Committee for Refugees.

INTERNATIONAL ORGANIZATIONS

Centre for Documentation on Refugees (CDR),
Postal Address: Case postale 2500, 1211 Geneva 2,
Switzerland. Street Address: 62 rue de Vermont, 1202
Geneva (41-22) 739-8111. FAX: (41-22) 739-8682.
E-mail address: UNHCR.CDR@OLN.COMLINK.APC.ORG.

An open, integrated, computer-based
documentation center that gathers, stores, analyzes,
and disseminates information on all aspects of
refugees for UNHCR and outside users. Its former
quarterly publication *Refugee Abstracts* was replaced in
the Spring of 1994 by *Refugee Survey Quarterly*,
which includes abstracts, reviews, bibliographic
references, and other refugee-related information.
CDR also coordinates IRENE, the electronic network
of the International Refugee Documentation Network
(IRDN).

European Council on Refugees and Exiles (ECRE),
Bondway House, 3-9 Bondway, London SW8, UK.
Telephone (44-71) 582-9928. General Secretary:
Philip Rudge.

International forum for 60 West European
nongovernmental organizations that assist refugees or
are concerned with refugee and asylum policy.
Monitors national and international developments,
promotes legal and information networks, and
advocates progressive standards for the treatment of
refugees and asylum seekers. The European Legal
Network on Asylum (ELENA), a forum for legal
counselors, is a project activity of ECRE.

**International Catholic Migration Commission
(ICMC)**, 37-39 rue de Vermont, Case postale 96,
CH-1211 Geneva 20, Switzerland. (41-22) 733-4150.
FAX: (41-22) 734-7929. Secretary General: Dr.
André Van Chau. President: Mr. Michael Whitely. In
the U.S.: 1319 F St., NW, Suite 820, Washington,
DC 20004. (202) 393-2904.

Mandate covers refugees, migrants, and internally
displaced persons, regardless of creed. Task is to

coordinate Catholic assistance to these groups and
play an advocacy role on their behalf. Headquartered
in Geneva, the Commission operates through
subordinate offices in ten countries, through Regional
Liaison Offices in seven countries, and through a
network of local Catholic agencies at grassroots level
in some 80 countries.

International Committee of the Red Cross (ICRC),
19 avenue de la Paix, CH-1202 Geneva Switzerland.
(41-22) 734-6001. FAX: (41-22) 733-2057. Telex:
414-226. Delegations in 47 countries. In the U.S,
780 Third Avenue, 28th Floor, New York, NY
10017. (212) 371-0770. FAX: (212) 838-5397.
President: Cornelio Sommaruga.

Founder of the Red Cross and Red Crescent
Movement. A Swiss, independent, neutral
organization with the internationally recognized role
of humanitarian intermediary between belligerents
during armed conflicts. Promotes international
humanitarian law. Protects and assists the victims of
international and civil wars and of internal
disturbances and tensions by providing medical aid;
relief supplies; a tracing and information agency for
prisoners of war and missing persons; a service for
transmission of family messages; and visits to civilian
internees, prisoners of war, and political detainees.
Has observer status to the U.N. General Assembly.

International Council of Voluntary Agencies (ICVA),
13 Rue Gutier, 1201 Geneva, Switzerland, Postal
Address: C.P. 216, 1211 Geneva 21, Switzerland.
(41-22) 732-6600. Cable: VOLAG (Geneva). Telex:
412 586 ICVA-CH. FAX: (41-22) 738-9904.
Executive Director: Delmar Blasco.

Founded in 1962 to provide a forum for
voluntary agencies active in the fields of humanitarian
assistance and development cooperation. At present,
has 87 members comprising international and
national voluntary agencies.

Federation of Red Cross and Red Crescent Societies, 17 chemin des Crêts, P.O. Box 372, CH-1211 Geneva 19, Switzerland. (41-22) 731-5580. FAX: (41-22) 733-0395. Telex: 22555. LRCS-CH Secretary-General: George Weber.

The League is the international federation of 149 National Red Cross and Red Crescent Societies, which coordinates the relief operations for natural disaster victims, cares for refugees and internally displaced persons outside areas of conflict, and aims to promote peace in the world. In refugee and displaced persons situations, the Secretariat mobilizes the Federation's own financial and in-kind contributions and health, logistics, and managerial staff to supplement Red Cross and Red Crescent Societies' and UNHCR's resources.

International Organization for Migration (IOM), 17 route des Morillons, P.O. Box 71, CH-1211 Geneva 19, Switzerland. (41-22) 717-9111. FAX: (41-22) 798-6150. Director General: James N. Purcell, Jr. New York: Richard Scott, Room 717, 1123 Broadway, New York, NY 10010. Washington: Hans-Petter Boe, 1750 K Street, NW, Suite 1110, Washington, DC 20006 (202) 862-1826. Chicago: Pannee Peiffer, O'Hare Corporate Tower 1, 10400 West Higging Road, Suite 329, Rosemont, IL 60018 (708) 296-3583. Miami: Ada Peralta, 4471 N.W. 36th Street, Suite 236, Miami Springs, FL 33166 (305) 885-5426. San Francisco: James Gildea, 114 Sansome Street, Suite 1225, The Adam Grant Building, San Francisco, CA 94104 (415) 391-9796.

Established in 1951 to arrange resettlement processing and transportation for refugees and migrants. Conducts related programs for medical screenings, language training, and cultural orientation. Plans and implements programs for the transfer of specialized human resources through migration to developing countries. Undertakes research projects and organizes international seminars on major migration themes. Represented in 73 countries worldwide.

Office of the United Nations High Commissioner for Refugees (UNHCR), Case Postale 2500, CH-1211 Geneva 2 Dépôt, Switzerland. (41-22) 739-8111. High Commissioner: Sadako Ogata. UNHCR Liaison Office to the United Nations Headquarters, UN Plaza, New York, NY 10017. (212) 963-6200. UNHCR Branch Office for the United States, 1718 Connecticut Avenue, NW, Washington, DC 20009. (202) 387-8546.

Representative: Rene van Rooyen.

Established in 1951 to provide international protection to refugees who fall within the scope of its statute and to seek durable solutions for the problems of refugees. Also coordinates assistance programs for displaced persons in accordance with various subsequent General Assembly resolutions. Representation in more than 100 countries.

United Nations Children's Fund (UNICEF), 3 UN Plaza, New York, NY 10017. (212) 326-7000. FAX: (212) 888-7465. Executive Director: James Grant.

Established in 1946 to assist children of war-devastated Europe, UNICEF has, since the early 1950s, expanded its role to meet the needs of children in the developing world, with community-based, sustainable programs. Supports programs in nutrition, primary health care, water and sanitation, education, the environment, and women in development, among others. Provides emergency humanitarian assistance to victims of natural and human disasters. UNICEF has offices in 128 developing countries and territories and is supported by more than 30 National Committees in the industrialized world.

United Nations Department of Humanitarian Affairs (DHA), UN Headquarters, New York, NY 10017. (212) 963-1392 (Information). FAX: (212) 963-9489 or (212) 963-1312. Palais de Nations, CH-1211 Geneva 10, Switzerland. (41-22) 917-2142 (Information). Emergencies only (41-22) 917-2010. FAX: (41-22) 917-0023.

Created in April 1992 to provide a rapid and coordinated response by the U.N. system to natural disasters and major complex emergencies. Serves as a focal point for facilitating action on emergencies by coordinating U.N. action, fielding assessment missions, issuing appeals for funding humanitarian relief programs, publishing situation reports, monitoring status of donor contributions, etc. Administers a Central Emergency Revolving Fund that facilitates rapid humanitarian action in emergency situations. Incorporates the previous Office of the UN Disaster Relief Coordinator and the secretariat of the International Decade for Natural Disaster Reduction.

United Nations Relief and Works Agency for Palestine Refugees in the Near East (UNRWA), Vienna International Centre, P.O. Box 700, A-1400 Vienna, Austria. (43-1) 21131, Ext. 4530. Commissioner-General: Ilter Türkmen. New York Liaison Office: William Lee, UN Building, Room DC2-0550, New York, NY 10017. (212) 963-2255.

Since 1950, has provided assistance to registered Palestinian refugees, now numbering more than 2.8 million, in Lebanon, Jordan, Syria, and the occupied territories of the West Bank and Gaza Strip. Provides education, health, relief, and social services, as well as developmental assistance in the areas of vocational training, environmental health, and income-generation. Also extends emergency services to Palestinians who have been displaced or otherwise affected by war and violence.

World Council of Churches, Refugee and Migration Service, P.O. Box 2100, 1211 Geneva 2, Switzerland. (41-22) 791-6111. FAX: (41-22) 791-0361. Telex: 415730OIKCH. Coordinator: Melaku Kifle.

Works with local churches in about 70 countries in support of their refugee services, including both emergency and long-term assistance. Also, in cooperation with local churches, advocates on behalf of refugees, provides public information and training, and facilitates meetings between churches on refugee issues.

World Food Program (WFP), Via Cristoforo Colombo 426, 00145 Rome, Italy. (39-6) 522-821. Telex: (39-6) 626675WFPI. FAX: (39-6) 512-3700. Executive Director: Catherine Bertini. Liaison Office at UN Headquarters, NY. (212) 963-8440. FAX: (212) 963-8019.

The food aid organization of the United Nations Founded in 1963 to help combat world hunger, provides food aid to developing countries to promote economic and social development, and to help meet emergency needs in the wake of natural or human disasters. Coordinates food aid deliveries and assists bilateral donors with procurement and transportation of food. Helps developing countries with logistics problems in food emergencies.

U.S. GOVERNMENT OFFICES

Department of Health and Human Services, Centers for Disease Control and Prevention (CDC), 1600 Clifton Rd., NE, Atlanta, GA 30333. (404) 639-2101. FAX: (404) 639-0277. Associate Director for International Health: Joe H. Davis, M.D.

Provides technical assistance in refugee health to U.S. government agencies, multilateral organizations, nongovernmental organizations, and other agencies involved in refugee care. Assistance includes rapid needs assessments in health and nutrition, epidemiological evaluation, disease outbreak investigation and control, and establishing disease surveillance systems in refugee populations. Conducts training in refugee health.

Department of Health and Human Services, Office of Refugee Resettlement (ORR), Administration for Children and Families, 370 L'Enfant Promenade, SW, 6th Floor, Washington, DC 20447. (202) 401-9246. Director: Lavinia Limon.

Assists refugees in achieving economic self-sufficiency following their arrival to the United States. Assistance primarily provided through state-administered resettlement programs. Reimburses states for costs incurred in providing cash and medical assistance to newly arrived refugees in need. Provides social service and targeted assistance grants to states and nonprofit organizations primarily for making available English language and employment training services to refugees.

Department of Justice, Immigration and Naturalization Service, 425 I Street, NW, Washington, DC 20536. (202) 514-2000. Commissioner: Doris Meissner.

Administers immigration and naturalization laws relating to the admission, exclusion, deportation, and naturalization of aliens, including refugees and asylees.

Department of State, Bureau for Refugee Programs (BRP), Room 5824, 2201 C Street, NW, Washington, DC 20520. (202) 647-5822. Acting Director: Phyllis Oakley.

Formulates, implements, and directs U.S. refugee and migration policies and programs. The basic mission comprises international refugee protection and assistance as well as management of the U.S. admissions program and interagency coordination.

House Judiciary Committee, 2138 Rayburn House Office Building, Washington, DC 20515. Chairman: Henry J. Hyde; Subcommittee on International Law, Immigration, and Claims, Chairman: Lamar Smith.

Legislative and oversight responsibility for immigration and naturalization, citizenship, refugees, international law, and other relevant matters.

Senate Judiciary Committee, 224 Dirksen Senate Office Building, Washington, DC 20510. Chairman: Orrin Hatch; Subcommittee on Immigration, 520 Dirksen Senate Office Building, Washington, DC 20510. Chairman: Alan Simpson.

Studies and makes recommendations on the problems of refugees; has jurisdiction over immigration and naturalization legislation.

PRIVATE ORGANIZATIONS

The following are selected United States voluntary agencies and human rights and educational organizations that participate in programs to resettle refugees and/or provide assistance to or information about refugees. Readers may contact U.S. resettlement agencies (indicated by *) for information on sponsorship.

Africare, Inc., 440 R Street, NW, Washington, DC 20001. (202) 462-3614. Executive Director: C. Payne Lucas.

Dedicated to improving the quality of life in rural Africa through the development of water resources, increased food production, health services, and refugee assistance. Currently operates more than 220 programs, including refugee programs in East, Southern, and Francophone Africa, and many development education programs in the United States.

American Friends Service Committee, 1501 Cherry Street, Philadelphia, PA 19102. (215) 241-7000. FAX: (215) 241-7026. Executive Director: Kara Newell.

Quaker organization founded in 1917, supports reconciliation and development worldwide, especially in situations of conflict; provides relief and rehabilitation assistance to refugees in the context of community development; advocates for resolution of conflicts and for refugee rights in the United States.

American Jewish Joint Distribution Committee, Inc. (JDC), 711 Third Avenue, New York, NY 10017. (212) 687-6200. Executive Vice President: Michael Schneider.

Established in 1914 and funded predominantly by the campaigns of the United Jewish Appeal, JDC serves as the overseas arm of the organized American Jewish community, providing for rescue, relief, and rehabilitation of Jewish communities around the world. Current programs in 58 countries include Soviet Jewish emigres, Israel's social needs, glasnost-facilitated expansions in Eastern Europe and the former U.S.S.R., and nonsectarian development and disaster relief worldwide.

American Jewish Philanthropic Fund, c/o Tanenbaum, 27 East 61st Street, New York, NY 10021. (212) 755-5640. President: Charles J. Tanenbaum.

Provides relief, resettlement, and retraining services to Jewish refugees in Europe and the U.S. through programs administered by the International Rescue Committee.

American Red Cross, 17th & D Streets, NW, Washington, DC 20006. (202) 639-3306. Chairman: George F. Moody. International Social Services Division Director: Mary-Lou McCutcheon (202) 639-3308.

Works in cooperation with 150 agencies, including Red Cross/Red Crescent, Magen David Adom of Israel, and the International Federation of Red Cross and Red Crescent Societies. Assists refugees in locating missing family members through its tracing and social services. Other Red Cross programs include international disaster preparedness and relief and development of other national societies.

American Refugee Committee (ARC), Headquarters: 234 Nicollet Avenue, Suite 350, Minneapolis, MN 55404. (612) 872-7060. Illinois office: 317 Howard Street, Evanston, IL 60202. President and CEO: Anthony J. Kozlowski.

Provides health care and medical training to refugees, displaced people, and others affected by war and natural disasters. Founded in 1979, ARC currently serves more than a half million affected people and has trained more than 3,000 local people as health care workers. Programs currently operate in Somalia, Malawi, Mozambique, Croatia, Thailand, and Cambodia.

Amnesty International, International Secretariat, 1 Easton Street, London WCIX 8DJ, United Kingdom. Secretary General: Pierre Sané. U.S. Section: 322 8th Avenue, New York, NY 10001. Executive Director: William F. Schulz. Address requests for assistance to: National Refugee Office, 500 Sansome Street, Suite 615, San Francisco, CA 94111 (415) 291-0601. FAX: (415) 291-8722.

A worldwide independent movement, its main focus is to free all prisoners of conscience; ensure fair and prompt trials for political prisoners; abolish the death penalty, torture, and other cruel treatment of prisoners; end extrajudicial executions and "disappearances." Also opposes abuses by opposition groups. Provides information for asylum applications and opposes forcible return of people who risk imprisonment as prisoners of conscience, torture, "disappearance," or execution. Publishes annual report, monthly newsletter, and country reports on human rights conditions worldwide.

Boat People S.O.S., Inc., P.O. Box 2652, Merrifield, VA 22116. Telephone and FAX: (703) 204-2662. Executive Director: Dr. Thang Dinh Nguyen. Chairperson: Mr. Nguyen Ngoc Bich.

A private, nonprofit organization providing free legal counseling and assistance to Vietnamese asylum seekers in Southeast Asian refugee camps. Cooperates with other Vietnamese organizations to seek better treatment of Vietnamese asylum seekers. Publishes monthly *The Boat People S.O.S. News Bulletin.*

CARE, 151 Ellis Street, NE, Atlanta, GA 30303. (404) 681-2552. President: Dr. Philip Johnston.

An international aid and self-help development organization. Responds to the needs of refugees and displaced persons in emergency situations through effective delivery systems to facilitate the distribution of food and other aid. Also implements long-term development programs in health and nutrition education and natural resource management to improve living conditions and facilitate self-sufficiency

among refugees, displaced persons, and repatriates. Has programs for refugees and/or internally displaced people in 18 countries worldwide.

Catholic Relief Services (CRS), U.S. Catholic Conference (USCC), 209 West Fayette Street, Baltimore MD 21201. Executive Director: Kenneth F. Hackett.

Overseas relief and development agency of the U.S. Catholic community. Active in more than 70 countries with nutrition, water, agriculture, and small enterprise development projects. CRS also assists refugees, displaced persons, and returnees in 18 countries worldwide.

Center for Applied Linguistics, 1118 22nd Street, NW, Washington, DC 20037. (202) 429-9292. President: G. Richard Tucker.

Operates the Refugee Service Center in Washington DC under a cooperative agreement with the U.S. State Department. Acts as a liaison between the State Department-funded Overseas Refugee Training Program sites in Southeast Asia and educators, social service providers, and others assisting refugees in the U.S. Produces resettlement guides for newly arrived refugees, conducts surveys to gather information on refugees' resettlement experiences, gives presentations and workshops in U.S. resettlement sites and at professional conferences, and publishes information material for staff in the Overseas Refugee Training Program.

Center for Immigration Policy and Refugee Assistance (CIPRA), P.O. Box 2298, Georgetown University, Washington, DC 20057. (202) 298-0200. Director: Fr. Julio Guilietti, S.J.

Provides research, training, and consultation to contribute to the development of humane, reasonable, and enforceable immigration and refugee policies. Sponsors lectures, seminars, and public meetings on refugee policy and administers educational programs offering internships in refugee assistance. Tutorial programs offer community service to refugees, immigrants, and at-risk youth. Conducts research on migration in the Americas and on U.S. immigration legislation and its effects.

Center for Migration Studies (CMS), 209 Flagg Place, Staten Island, NY 10304-1199. (718) 351-8800. FAX: (718) 667-4598. Executive Director: Lydio F. Tomasi.

Founded in 1964, CMS encourages the interdisciplinary study of human migration and refugee movements through scientific research projects; publication of the quarterly *International Migration Review* and the bimonthly *Migration World Magazine*, as well as books, papers, and the *CMS Newsletter;* the CMS Annual National Legal Conference on Immigration and Refugee Policy in Washington, DC; other occasional national and international conferences on migration and refugees; and a specialized library and archives on migration and refugees.

*Church World Service/Immigration and Refugee Program, 475 Riverside Drive, New York, NY 10115. (212) 870-3300. FAX: (212) 870-2132. Director: Dr. Elizabeth G. Ferris.

Responds ecumenically, as part of the National Council of Churches, to the plight of refugees, migrants, displaced persons, immigrants, and persons seeking asylum and safe haven. Resettles refugees and assists immigrants through its network of 38 affiliate offices in cooperation with participating denominations. Provides first asylum services in the U.S. Supports and participates in the development of national and international policies and programs advocating protection for the uprooted. Works with ecumenical organizations worldwide, including the World Council of Churches.

Cultural Survival, Inc., 215 First Street, Cambridge, MA 02142. (617) 621-3818. FAX: (617) 621-3814. Executive Director: Alexander H. See.

Advocates for the rights of indigenous peoples and ethnic minorities. Supports programs on five continents, as well as direct assistance projects designed and run by indigenous peoples; conducts research and produces publications dealing with the vital issues confronting these populations; and advocates on their behalf along with outreach to inform the general public.

Direct Relief International, 27 S. La Patera Lane, P.O. Box 30820, Santa Barbara, CA 93130. (805) 964-4767. President: Ann W. Carlos.

Receives and donates contributions of pharmaceuticals, medical supplies, and equipment to assist refugees, other victims of natural disaster and civil strife, and needy health facilities in medically less developed areas of the world.

Documentation Exchange, Refugee Legal Support Service, Box 2327, Austin, TX 78768. (512) 476-9841. FAX: (512) 476-0130. Director: Jill McRae.

Established in 1983, provides political asylum documentation for refugees worldwide. Information is obtained from an extensive human rights database of computer-indexed U.S., Central American, and international human rights reports, news clipping services, and church and government reports. Referrals are made to direct service organizations and to attorneys with comparable cases.

*Episcopal Migration Ministries, 815 Second Avenue, New York, NY 10017. (212) 922-5198. Executive Director: Diane Porter.

Official channel through which the Episcopal Church responds to relief and development needs of refugees, migrants, displaced persons, and asylum seekers globally. Resettles refugees and assists immigrants and asylum seekers globally. Resettles refugees and assists immigrants and asylum seekers in the U.S. through 98 Episcopal dioceses. Assists refugees worldwide in concert with the Anglican Communion and partner agencies, in cooperation with the Presiding Bishop's Fund for World Relief. Advocates for legislation to respond to the protection and resettlement needs of refugees and displaced persons.

Eritrean Relief Committee, Inc., 1325 15th Street, NW, Suite 112, Washington, DC 2005. (202) 387-5001. FAX: (202) 287-5006. Executive Director: Dr. Amdetsion Kidane.

Founded in 1976, aids Eritreans affected by war, drought, and famine, including people displaced internally and refugees in the Sudan. U.S. partner agency of the indigenous Eritrean Relief and Rehabilitation Association (ERRA), which focuses on self-help and grassroots initiatives. Emergency assistance includes food, medicine, shelter, and pest control. Development support includes an agricultural rehabilitation program, rural health care facilities, and vocational and academic education projects.

*Ethiopian Community Development Council, Inc. (ECDC), 1038 S. Highland Street, Arlington, VA 22204. (703) 685-0510. FAX: (703) 685-0529. Director: Tsehaye Teferra.

Established in 1983, a nonprofit agency providing cultural, educational, and socio-economic development programs in the immigrant and refugee community. Locally, provides social and support services designed to help newcomers build economically independent lives. Nationally, carries out public education programs to expand awareness of the needs of African refugees, enhances networking among African refugee organizations, and assists them in organizational and community development. Also resettles refugees from around the world through its network of affiliates nationwide.

Exodus World Service, P.O. Box 620, Itasca, IL 60143-0620. (708) 775-1500 or (312) REFUGEE. FAX: (78) 775-1505. Executive Director: Heidi Moll Schoedel.

Humanitarian agency that focuses on engaging the private sector in service to refugees. Exodus produces educational materials for individuals, churches, and community groups that heighten awareness of and sensitivity to refugees; designs and implements innovative programs that recruit material and volunteer assistance for refugees; and provides training to refugee service agencies on volunteer recruitment and training.

*Hebrew Immigrant Aid Society, Inc. (HIAS), 333 Seventh Avenue, New York, NY 10001-5004. Executive Vice President: Martin A. Wenick.

The refugee and migration agency of the organized American Jewish community. Assists Jewish refugees and migrants from the former U.S.S.R., Eastern Europe, the Near East, North Africa, and elsewhere; in the last decade alone, HIAS has helped more than 200,000 Soviet Jewish refugees immigrate to the U.S. Also assists Indochinese, Ethiopian, Afghan, and other non-Jewish refugees through programs in cooperation with the U.S. government. Global network of offices, country representatives, and affiliated organizations in 45 countries on six continents.

Human Rights Internet, c/o Human Rights Centre, University of Ottawa, 57 Louis Pasteur, Ottowa, Ontario, K1N 6N5, Canada. (613) 564-3492. FAX: (613) 564-4054. Executive Director: Laurie S. Wiseberg.

An international communications network and clearinghouse serving the information needs of the human rights community. Publishes *Human Rights Internet Reporter,* a comprehensive reference work on humanitarian activity worldwide, and the *Human*

Rights Tribune, a quarterly magazine focusing on current human rights issues. Publishes directories describing the work of human rights organizations worldwide and a biennial "MASTERLIST" with the addresses, telephone, and fax numbers of more than 4,000 organizations concerned with human rights.

Human Rights Watch, 485 5th Avenue, New York, NY 10017. (212) 972-8400. FAX: (212) 972-0905. Executive Director: Kenneth Roth. Washington, DC office: 1522 K Street, NW, Washington, DC, 20005. Director: Holly Burkhalter. (202) 371-6592.

Human Rights Watch and its Africa, Americas, Asia, Helsinki, and Middle East divisions monitor and promote human rights in more than 70 countries worldwide. Documents arbitrary imprisonment, censorship, disappearances, due process of law, murder, prison conditions, torture, violations of laws of war, and other abuses of internationally recognized human rights.

*Immigration and Refugee Services of America (IRSA), (formerly American Council for Nationalities Service), 1717 Massachusetts Avenue, NW, Suite 701, Washington, DC 20036. (202) 797-2105. FAX: (202) 797-2363. Executive Director: Roger P. Winter.

Nonsectarian organization with 74-year history of service to refugees, immigrants, and others in migration. Forty community-based affiliates located throughout the U.S. provide refugee resettlement, immigration counseling, and other supportive services meant to ease the burden of transition both for the newcomers and the communities receiving them. Agencies provide asylum representation and advocate on behalf of the rights of immigrants and refugees. International Social Services/American Branch, providing intercountry casework services to families and children around the world, is a program of IRSA. The U.S. Committee for Refugees (USCR) is the public information arm of IRSA.

Institute for Education and Advocacy, 1403 Harmon Place, Minneapolis, MN 55403. (612) 341-8082. St. Paul office: 1550 Summit Avenue, St. Paul, MN 55105. (612) 698-8509.

Builds the capacity of refugees and immigrants to participate actively in the social, economic, and political life of Minnesota. Operates network of education and self-reliance programs under the auspices of the Episcopal Diocese of Minnesota.

InterAction (American Council for Voluntary International Action), 1717 Massachusetts Avenue, NW, 8th Floor, Washington, DC 20036. (202) 667-8227. President and CEO: Julia Taft. Program Officer, Refugee Affairs: Timothy M. McCully.

A broadly based membership association of 120 private and voluntary U.S. organizations working in international development; humanitarian and emergency relief; refugee relief, assistance, and resettlement; public policy and federal relations; and development education. Member agencies participate in any or all of six working committees: Development Assistance, Migration and Refugee Affairs, Disaster Response and Resources, Public Policy, Development Education, and Private Funding.

*International Rescue Committee, 122 E. 42nd Street, 12th floor, New York, NY 10168-1289. (212) 551-3000. President: Robert P. DeVecchi.

Founded 60 years ago at the request of Albert Einstein, IRC is a nonsectarian voluntary private agency that assists refugees worldwide. Assists refugees who are victims of racial, religious, and ethnic persecution and oppression, as well as people uprooted by war and violence. Also assists internally displaced populations within their own countries, refugees during repatriation, and refugees being resettled in third countries. Responds rapidly to refugee emergencies, delivering medical services, food, public health, and sanitation assistance essential to saving lives. When crisis has stabilized, establishes training programs and education, income-generating, and self-reliance projects that enable refugees to cope with life in exile. Programs operate in 24 countries. Also resettles 12,000 refugees annually in the United States through a domestic resettlement network of 15 offices as well as overseas refugee processing offices in Bangkok, Zagreb, Rome, Vienna, and Madrid.

Jesuit Refugee Services (JRS), 1424 16th Street, NW, Suite 300, Washington, DC 20036. (202) 462-5200. Director: Rev. Robert W. McChesney, S.J.

The central coordinating office in the United States of the international JRS, founded in 1981 under the auspices of the Society of Jesus. Regionally organized, operates programs for refugees and internally displaced persons in over 35 countries in Asia, Africa, Central and North America, Europe, and Australia. Major program foci include pastoral care,

legal assistance, health, education, research, and advocacy on refugee and human rights issues.

Lawyers Committee for Human Rights (LCHR), 330 Seventh Avenue, 10th Floor, New York, NY 10001. (212) 629-6170. Executive Director: Michael Posner. Director, Asylum Representation Program: Stephanie Marks. Washington, DC office: 100 Maryland Avenue, NE, Room 502, Washington, DC 20002. (202) 547-5692. Staff Attorney: Elisa Massimino.

Public interest law center in the fields of International human rights and refugee law. Monitors human rights in countries around the world, including those receiving U.S. foreign aid. Works to ensure that persons seeking refuge in the U.S. receive the protections they are guaranteed under the U.S. Constitution and international law. Legal representation is provided by volunteer attorneys for individual asylum applicants who cannot afford counsel.

*Lutheran Immigration and Refugee Service, 390 Park Avenue, South, New York NY 10016-8803. (212) 532-6350. Executive Director: Ralston Deffenbaugh, Jr.

National agency of Lutheran churches in the U.S. for ministry with refugees, asylum seekers, undocumented persons, and immigrants. Founded in 1939 to resettle World War II refugees, the agency now serves in advocacy for protection and humane treatment for uprooted people worldwide as well as in immigration services and resettlement. Works through 26 regional affiliate social service agency offices that support the direct assistance of church and community volunteers; 19 partner agencies that help unaccompanied minor children; more than 40 ecumenical community-based projects that help asylum seekers; and immigration training that assists service providers.

Lutheran World Relief, 390 Park Avenue, South, New York, NY 10016. (212) 532-6350. Executive Director: Kathryn F. Wolford.

Serves as the overseas development and relief agency on behalf of most U.S. Lutherans to assist with longterm and emergency help for people, especially in Asia, Africa, and Latin America. Refugee assistance is often channeled through programs of the Lutheran World Federation.

Mennonite Central Committee, 21 South 12th Street, Akron PA 17501. (717) 859-1151. Canadian Office: 134 Plaza Drive, Winnipeg, Manitoba R3T 5K9. (204) 261-6381. Executive Secretary: John A Lapp.

Cooperative relief and service agency for Mennonites and Brethren in Christ in North America. Provides material aid and development assistance to refugees from human and natural disasters. Current work includes assistance to refugees in East, Central, and Southern Africa; the Middle East; Central America; and South/Southeast Asia. Supports resettlement programs for refugees in Canada and the U.S.

Minority Rights Group (International), 379 Brixton Road, London SW9 7DE, U.K. (44-71) 978-9498. FAX: (44-71) 738-6265.

An independent, international organization that undertakes research, provides information, and develops education programs on minorities. Publishes reports on minority groups worldwide and on thematic issues concerning minority rights. Convenes conferences of scholars and practitioners, and advocates minority rights at the UN and other international forums. Has affiliates in twenty countries.

National Coalition for Haitian Refugees (NCHR), 16 East 42nd Street, 3rd floor, New York, NY 10017. (212) 867-0020. FAX: (212) 867-1668. Executive Director: Mr. Jocelyn McCalla.

Established in 1982, NCHR is an alliance of nearly 40 prominent U.S. civil rights, labor, human rights, religious, and immigrants' rights organizations. NCHR acts in accord with both U.S. and international law to uphold the rights of refugees fleeing repression in Haiti for new lives in the United States. NCHR further advocates for Haitian refugees by facilitating cooperation among various agencies providing humanitarian service and by promoting democratic institution-building in Haiti.

National Immigration Forum, 220 I Street, NE, Suite 220, Washington, DC 20002. (202) 544-0004. Director: Frank Sharry.

A national, multi-institutional, and multi-ethnic coalition dedicated to extending and defending the rights and opportunities of the United States' newcomers, as well as to helping the communities that receive them. Advocates for policies and programs that ensure safe haven for those fleeing persecution and civil strife, reunification of families, and availability of services for newcomers integrating into our society.

Operation USA, 8320 Melrose Avenue, #200, Los Angeles, CA 90069. (213) 658-8876. FAX: (213) 653-7846. President: Richard Walden.

A nonprofit organization founded in 1979 that provides disaster relief, development assistance, and disaster preparedness training. Distributes medical, nutritional, and shelter supplies to children, refugees, and disaster victims in Africa, Asia, Latin America, the Caribbean, Eastern Europe, and the United States.

Oxfam America, 26 West Street, Boston, MA 02111-1206. (617) 482-1211. Executive Director: Dr. John Hammock.

A nonprofit international agency that funds self-help development and disaster relief projects in poor countries in Africa, Asia, Latin America, and the Caribbean. Also produces and distributes educational materials for people in the United States on issues of hunger and development. One of seven autonomous Oxfams worldwide. Oxfam America was founded in 1970.

Rav Tov, Inc., International Jewish Rescue Organization, 500 Bedford Avenue, Brooklyn, NY 11211. (718) 963-1991. Executive Director: David Niederman.

Through its network of overseas offices, provides care and maintenance, medical assistance, visa documentation and pre-migration planning to refugees while in transit. In countries of resettlement, provides a full range of services including reception, housing, medical care, language training, education, employment counseling, and maintenance assistance.

Refugee Policy Group (RPG), 1424 16th Street, NW, Suite 401, Washington, DC 20036. (202) 387-3015. Executive Director: Dennis Gallagher.

Serves as an independent center of policy analysis and research on domestic and international refugee issues. Houses a refugee resource library and provides auspices for policy analysts, researchers, and program developers to meet and conduct their work.

Refugee Studies Programme, Oxford University, Queen Elizabeth House, 21 St. Giles, Oxford OX1 3LA. (44-865) 270-722. FAX: (44-865) 270-721. E-mail: RSP@VAX.OXFORD.AC.UK Director: Dr. Barbara Harrell-Bond.

Center for multi-disciplinary research, public education, and teaching. Offers courses for researchers and professionals including a four-week summer school for senior administrators in the field of forced migration. Computerized library of some 17,000 documents. Publishes the *Journal of Refugee Studies*, a journal on forced migration; the *Refugee Participation Network*, a newsletter for practitioners; and other works.

Refugee Voices Inc., 3041 Fourth Street, NE, Washington DC 20017-1102. (202) 832-0020. FAX: (202) 832-5616 or (800) 688-REFUGEE. FAX: (202) 832-5616. Director: Frank Moan, S.J.

A nonprofit agency that publicizes the stories of refugees regardless of race, religion, or politics. Refugee Voices brings uprooted people to the attention of U.S. citizens through a free quarterly newsletter, forums, and radio productions aired nationally on approximately 300 radio stations. Refugee Voices links U.S. citizens as volunteers with refugees in the United States.

Refugee Women in Development (RefWID), Inc., 810 First St., NE, Suite 300, Washington, DC 20002. (202) 289-1104. FAX: (202) 887-0812. Executive Director: Sima Wali.

Addresses the needs and concerns of refugee women resettled in the U.S. and overseas. Programs include leadership development, human rights protection, and international representation. Priorities include conducting training in domestic violence prevention and intervention; developing practical program models for leadership development and coalition building, and institutional development; and carrying out education and advocacy with refugee and mainstream organizations, policy makers, and the general public.

Refugees International, 21 Dupont Circle, NW, Washington, DC 20036. (202) 828-0110. Executive Director: Lionel Rosenblatt.

Monitors refugee situations worldwide to ensure that refugees' basic needs for protection and care are met. Provides information to policy makers and the public. Advocates for fair refugee policy at home and abroad.

The Salvation Army World Service Office (SAWSO), 615 Slaters Lane, Third Floor, Alexandria, VA 22314. (703) 684-5500. Executive Director: Dean B. Seiler.

Provides technical assistance and support through indigenous Salvation Army affiliates in developing countries. Supports self-help initiatives that address the underlying causes of poverty, including programs for community development, leadership development and training, health, employment, and disaster relief/reconstruction. With the aim to assist victims to return to a more normal existence as quickly as possible, disaster relief and reconstruction aid are critical elements in promoting self-help development. Assistance is available in the 99 countries and territories in which the Salvation Army operates.

Save the Children Federation, Inc., 54 Wilton Road, Westport, CT 06880. (203) 221-4000. President: Charles F. MacCormack.

Founded in 1932, serves children through community development in 35 countries including the U.S. Provides assistance to help refugees become self-sufficient and to provide a base for long-term development. Program components include agriculture, nutrition, health care, mental health of refugee children, education, and small-scale enterprise in Somalia, Sudan, Pakistan, and Zimbabwe; training in literacy, cultural orientation, vocational skills, and secondary and primary education in Thailand and Indonesia; repatriation programs, economic development, and food security in Vietnam and Laos; and in Croatia, educational and psychosocial assistance to refugee children from Bosnia.

Southeast Asia Resource Action Center (SEARAC), 1628 16th Street, NW, 3rd floor, Washington, DC 20009. (202) 667-4690. FAX: (202) 667-6449. Executive Director: Le Xuan Khoa.

A national nonprofit, formed in 1979 to educate the general public about the refugee situation in Southeast Asia and to assist public and private agencies in assisting refugees from Cambodia, Laos, and Vietnam. A leading advocate, a source for technical assistance and training, and an information clearinghouse for Southeast Asian groups in the U.S. Major program areas include: public education and advocacy, leadership development and community empowerment, and international development and reconstruction.

*Tolstoy Foundation, Inc., 200 Park Ave., South, Suite 1612, New York, NY 10003. (212) 677-7770. Executive Director: Alexis Troubetzkoy.

Founded in 1939 to assist Russian refugees. Scope broadened to provide services to refugees from Eastern Europe, the Near East, Southeast Asia, and Africa. Also assists oppressed minorities such as Tibetans, Circassians, Armenians, and Bosnians. European offices in Munich, Paris, and Brussels; South American headquarters in Buenos Aires. Six regional offices in the U.S. provide resettlement services. Provides continuing services, including housing and access to nursing homes for elderly emigres.

United States Association for UNHCR, Suite 500, 2012 Massachusetts Ave., NW, Washington, DC 20036. (202) 296-1115. FAX: (202) 296-1081.

A public awareness, education, and fundraising program in support of refugees and the protection and assistance mandate of the U.N. High Commissioner for Refugees. Works with media, educational, governmental and nongovernmental organizations, refugee communities, and concerned Americans to keep refugee protection concerns before the public and to nurture generous U.S. policies and contributions to humanitarian assistance programs of UNHCR and others.

*United States Catholic Conference/Migration and Refugee Services (USCC/MRS), 3211 4th Street, NE, Washington, DC 20017-1194. (202) 541-3315. FAX: (202) 541-3245. Executive Director: Rev. Richard Ryscavage, S.J.

A public policy and social action agency of the U.S. Catholic Conference, carries out Church policy on migration, refugee, and immigration issues. Provides program support and regional coordination for a network of more than 140 diocesan refugee resettlement offices. Office for the Pastoral Care of Migrants and Refugees provides the pastoral foundation for all MRS programs and assists the Bishops in encouraging the integration of immigrants, migrants, and refugees into the life and mission of the local Church. The Catholic Legal Immigration Network, Inc. (CLINIC) ensures that all newcomers have access to affordable immigration related services.

U.S. Committee for Refugees, 1717 Massachusetts Avenue, NW, Suite 701, Washington, DC 20036. (202) 347-3507. FAX: (202) 347-3418. Director: Roger P. Winter.

Public information program of Immigration and Refugee Services of America. Goes to the scene of refugee emergencies, determines what steps are necessary to improve protection and assistance, and then works to construct a plan of action. USCR testifies before Congress, briefs government officials, communicates concerns directly to foreign governments, provides firsthand assessments to the media, and conducts an educational outreach program in U.S. schools. Advocates for fair U.S. asylum and refugee policy, as well as U.S. support for humanitarian efforts overseas. Publishes the *World Refugee Survey; Refugee Reports*, a monthly news service on refugee issues; and issue papers.

U.S. Committee for UNICEF, 333 East 38th Street, New York, NY 10016. (212) 686-5522. Executive Vice President: Tsugiko Y. Scullion.

Established in 1947, the oldest and largest of 32 national committees for UNICEF. Informs Americans about UNICEF's efforts to assist the developing world's children and their mothers. Raises funds for UNICEF.

Washington Lawyers' Committee for Civil Rights and Urban Affairs/Asylum and Refugee Rights Law Project, 1400 "Eye" Street, NW, Suite 450, Washington, DC 20005. (202) 682-5900. FAX: (202) 842-2171. Director: Deborah Sanders.

Begun in 1978 by the Washington Lawyers' Committee for Civil Rights Under Law, provides legal assistance to newcomers, focusing on asylum and refugee issues as well as those cases where aliens suffer employment or housing discrimination because of immigration status.

Women's Commission for Refugee Women and Children, c/o International Rescue Committee, 122 E. 42nd Street, 12th floor, New York, NY 10168-1289. (212) 551-3000. Director: Mary Diaz.

Founded in 1989 under the auspices of the International Rescue Committee. Speaks on behalf of the 16 million women and children around the world who have been forced to flee from their homes because of war, civil strife, famine, or persecution. Dispatches fact-finding delegations of distinguished women to refugee areas all over the world, testifies before Congress, and presents findings to the U.S. State Department, U.N. officials, and other governments.

World Concern International, P.O. Box 33000, 19303 Fremont Avenue, North, Seattle, WA 98133. (206) 546-7201. Executive Director: Fred Gregory.

Provides emergency relief, but focuses primarily on long-term development to refugees and non-refugee populations in Asia, Africa, and the Americas. Assistance is usually provided through indigenous agencies in the form of technical assistance, grants, and commodities.

World Learning Inc., Southeast Asia Programs, Box 676, Brattleboro, VT 05302. (802) 258-3124. Vice President: Claude De L. Pepin.

As the "Consortium" (with Save the Children/US and World Education), operates education and training programs in Phanat Nikhom, Thailand, for refugees en route to resettlement. The Consortium also administers repatriation programs in Laos, a credit program with a focus on assisting returnees in Vietnam, and participates with UNICEF in a cluster schools project in Cambodia.

*World Relief of the National Association of Evangelicals, 201 Rt. 9W North, Congers, NY 10920. (914) 268-4135. Director of United States Ministries: Donald N. Hammond.

Overseas, provides relief and development assistance in countries of first asylum. Domestically, provided refugee resettlement services to more than 10,000 individuals in FY 93. Also provides orientation and training to sponsoring churches, community groups, families, and individuals to assist the evangelical community to meet the needs of refugees. World Relief has a national network of 28 offices throughout the U.S.

World Vision, Inc., 919 West Huntington Drive, Monrovia, CA 91016. (818) 305-7836. President: Dr. Robert A. Seiple. Director, Refugee Programs: Rev. "Duke" Duc X. Nguyen.

Established in 1950, an international Christian child-care, relief, and development agency that supports more than 6,000 projects in 94 countries worldwide. U.S. programs work with at-risk children, Amerasians, and urban poor. Through emergency disaster relief, child sponsorship, primary health care, agricultural development, and community leadership training projects, benefits approximately 17 million people, including more than one million sponsored children.

UNIVERSAL DECLARATION OF HUMAN RIGHTS

Adopted by the United Nations General Assembly, December 10, 1948

Whereas recognition of the inherent dignity and of the equal and inalienable rights of all members of the human family is the foundation of freedom, justice and peace in the world,

Whereas disregard and contempt for human rights have resulted in barbarous acts which have outraged the conscience of mankind, and the advent of a world in which human beings shall enjoy freedom of speech and belief and freedom from fear and want has been proclaimed as the highest aspiration of the common people,

Whereas it is essential, if man is not to be compelled to have recourse, as a last resort, to rebellion against tyranny and oppression, that human rights should be protected by the rule of law,

Whereas it is essential to promote the development of friendly relations between nations

Whereas the peoples of the United Nations have in the Charter reaffirmed their faith in fundamental human rights, in the dignity and worth of the human person and in the equal rights of men and women and have determined to promote social progress and better standards of life in larger freedom,

hereas Member States have pledged themselves to achieve, in cooperation with the United Nations, the promotion of universal respect for and observance of human rights and fundamental freedoms,

Whereas a common understanding of these rights and freedoms is of the greatest importance for the full realization of this pledge,

Now, therefore, **the General Assembly** *proclaims* **this Universal Declaration of Human Rights** as a common standard of achievement for all peoples and all nations, to the end that every individual and every organ of society, keeping this Declaration constantly in mind, shall strive by teaching and education to promote respect for these rights and freedoms and by progressive measures, national and international, to secure their universal and effective recognition and observance, both among the peoples of Member States themselves and among the peoples of territories under their jurisdiction.

Article 1. All human beings are born free and equal in dignity and rights. They are endowed with reason and conscience and should act towards one another in a spirit of brotherhood.

Article 2. Everyone is entitled to all the rights and freedoms set forth in this Declaration, without distinction of any kind, such as race, colour, sex, language, religion, political or other opinion, national or social origin, property, birth or other status. Furthermore, no distinction shall be made on the basis of the political, jurisdictional or international status of the country or territory to which a person belongs, whether it be independent, trust, non-self-governing or under any other limitation of sovereignty.

Article 3. Everyone has the right to life, liberty and security of person.

Article 4. No one shall be held in slavery or servitude; slavery and the slave trade shall be prohibited in all their forms.

Article 5. No one shall be subjected to torture or to cruel, inhuman or degrading treatment or punishment.

Article 6. Everyone has the right to recognition everywhere as a person before the law.

Article 7. All are equal before the law and are entitled without any discrimination to equal protection of the law. All are entitled to equal protection against any discrimination in violation of this Declaration and against any incitement to such discrimination.

Article 8. Everyone has the right to an effective remedy by the competent national tribunals for acts violating the fundamental rights granted him by the constitution or by law.

Article 9. No one shall be subjected to arbitrary arrest, detention or exile.

Article 10. Everyone is entitled in full equality to a fair and public hearing by an independent and impartial tribunal, in the determination of his rights and obligations and of any criminal charge against him.

Article 11. *1.* Everyone charged with a penal offence has the right to be presumed innocent until proved guilty according to law in a public trial at which he has had all the guarantees necessary for his defense. *2.* No one shall be held guilty of any penal offense on account of any act or omission which did not constitute a penal offense, under national or international law, at the time when it was committed. Nor shall a heavier penalty be imposed than the one that was applicable at the time the penal offense was committed.

Article 12. No one shall be subjected to arbitrary interference with his privacy, family, home or correspondence, nor to attacks upon his honour and reputation. Everyone has the right to the protection of the law against such interference or attacks.

Article 13. *1.* Ev 1eryone has the right to freedom of movem 1ent and residence within the borders of each State. *2.* Everyone has the right to leave any country, including his own, and to return to his country.

Article 14. *1.* Everyone has the right to seek and to enjoy in other countries asylum from persecution. *2.* This right may not be invoked in the case of prosecution genuinely arising from non-political crimes or from acts contrary to the purposes and principles of the United Nations.

Article 15. *1.* Everyone has the right to a nationality. *2.* No one shall be arbitrarily deprived of his nationality nor denied the right to change his nationality.

Article 16. *1.* Men and women of full age, without any limitation due to race, nationality or religion, have the right to marry and to found a family. They are entitled to equal rights as to marriage, during marriage and at its dissolution. *2.* Marriage shall be entered into only with the free and full consent of the intending spouses. *3.* The family is the natural and fundamental group unit of society and is entitled to protection by society and the State.

Article 17. *1.* Everyone has the right to own property alone as well as in association with others. *2.* No one shall be arbitrarily deprived of his property.

Article 18. Everyone has the right to freedom of thought, conscience and religion; this right includes freedom to change his religion or belief, and freedom, either alone or in community with others and in public or private, to manifest his religion or belief in teaching, practice, worship and observance.

Article 19. Everyone has the right to freedom of opinion and expression; this right includes freedom to hold opinions without interference and to seek, receive and impart information and ideas through any media and regardless of frontiers.

Article 20. *1.* Everyone has the right to freedom of peaceful assembly and association. *2.* No one may be compelled to belong to an association.

Article 21. *1.* Everyone has the right to take part in the government of his country, directly or through freely chosen representatives. *2.* Everyone has the right of equal access to public service in his country. *3.* The will of the people shall be the basis of the authority of government; this will shall be expressed in periodic and genuine elections which shall be by universal and equal suffrage and shall be held by secret vote or by equivalent free voting procedures.

Article 22. Everyone, as a member of society, has the right to social security and is entitled to realization, through national effort and international co-operation and in accordance with the organization and resources of each State, of the economic, social and cultural rights indispensable for his dignity and the free development of his personality.

Article 23. *1.* Everyone has the right to work, to free choice of employment, to just and favourable conditions of work and to protection against unemployment. *2.* Everyone, without any discrimination, has the right to equal pay for equal work. *3.* Everyone who works has the right to just and favourable remuneration ensuring for himself and his family an existence worthy of human dignity, and supplemented, if necessary, by other means of social protection. *4.* Everyone has the right to form and to join trade unions for the protection of his interests.

Article 24. Everyone has the right to rest and leisure, including reasonable limitation or working hours and periodic holidays with pay.

Article 25. *1.* Everyone has the right to a standard of living adequate for the health and well-being of himself and of his family, including food, clothing, housing and medical care and necessary social services, and the right to security in the event of unemployment, sickness, disability, widowhood, old age or other lack of livelihood in circumstances beyond his control. *2.* Motherhood and childhood are entitled to special care and assistance. All children, whether born in or out of wedlock, shall enjoy the same social protection.

Article 26. *1.* Everyone has the right to education. Education shall be free, at least in the elementary and fundamental stages. Elementary education shall be compulsory. Technical and professional education shall be made generally available and higher education shall be equally accessible to all on the basis of merit. *2.* Education shall be directed to the full development of the human personality and to the strengthening of respect for human rights and fundamental freedoms. It shall promote understanding, tolerance and friendship among all nations, racial or religious groups, and shall further the activities of the United Nations for the maintenance of peace. *3.* Parents have a prior right to choose the kind of education that shall be given to their children.

Article 27. *1.* Everyone has the right freely to participate in the cultural life of the community, to enjoy the arts and to share in scientific advancement and its benefits. *2.* Everyone has the right to the protection of the moral and material interests resulting from any scientific, literary or artistic production of which he is the author.

Article 28. Everyone is entitled to a social and international order in which the rights and freedoms set forth in this Declaration can be fully realized.

Article 29. Everyone has duties to the community in which alone the free and full development of his personality is possible. *2.* In the exercise of his rights and freedoms, everyone shall be subject only to such limitations as are determined by law solely for the purpose of securing due recognition and respect for the rights and freedoms of others and of meeting the just requirements of morality, public order and the general welfare in a democratic society. *3.* These rights and freedoms may in no case be exercised contrary to the purposes and principles of the United Nations.

Article 30. Nothing in this Declaration may be interpreted as implying for any State, group or person any right to engage in any activity or to perform any act aimed at the destruction of any of the rights and freedoms set forth herein.

UNIVERSAL DECLARATION OF HUMAN RIGHTS
Colloquial Version

By Little House Alternative School, Dorchester, Massachusetts

Article 1. All human beings are born free and equal. You are worth the same, and have the same rights as anyone else. You are born with the ability to think and to know right from wrong, and should act toward others in a spirit of friendliness.

Article 2. Everyone should have all the rights and freedoms in this statement, no matter what race, sex, or color he or she may be. It shouldn't matter where you were born, what language you speak, what religion you are, what political opinions you have, or whether you're rich or poor. Everyone should have all of the rights in this statement.

Article 3. Everyone has the right to live, to be free, and to feel safe.

Article 4. No one should be held in slavery for any reason. The buying and selling of human beings should be prevented at all times.

Article 5. No one shall be put through torture, or any other treatment or punishment that is cruel, or makes him or her feel less than human.

Article 6. Everyone has the right to be accepted everywhere as a person, according to law.

Article 7. You have the right to be treated equally by the law, and to have the same protection under the law as anyone else. Everyone should have protection from being treated in ways that go against this document, and from having anyone cause others to go against the rights in this document.

Article 8. If your rights under the law are violated, you should have the right to fair and skillful judges who will see that justice is done.

Article 9. No one shall be arrested, held in jail, or thrown and kept out of her or his own country for no good reason.

Article 10. You have the same right as anyone else to a fair and public hearing by courts that will be open-minded and free to make their own decisions if you are ever accused of breaking the law, or if you have to go to court for some other reason.

Article 11. *1.* If you are blamed for a crime, you have the right to be thought of as innocent until you are proved guilty, according to the law, in a fair and public trial where you have the basic things you need to defend yourself. *2.* No one shall be punished for anything that was not illegal when it happened. Nor can anyone be given a greater punishment than the one that applied when the crime was committed.

Article 12. No one has the right to butt into your privacy, home, or mail, or attack your honesty and self-respect for no good reason. Everyone has the right to have the law protect him or her against all such meddling or attacks.

Article 13. *1.* Within any country you have the right to go and live where you want. *2.* You have the right to leave any country including your own, and return to it when you want.

Article 14. *1.* Everyone has the right to seek shelter from harassment in another country. *2.* This right does not apply in cases where the person has done something against the law that has nothing to do with politics, or when she or he has done something that is against what the United Nations is all about.

Article 15. *1.* You have a right to a country where you're from. *2.* No one should be able to take you away from, or stop you from changing your country for no good reason.

Article 16. *1.* Grown men and women have the right to marry and start a family, without anyone trying to stop them or make it hard because of their race, country, or religion. Both partners have equal rights in getting married, during the marriage, and if and when they decide to end it. *2.* A marriage shall take place only with the agreement of the couple. *3.* The family is the basic part of society, and should be protected by it.

Article 17. *1.* Everyone has the right to have belongings that they can keep alone, or share with other people. *2.* No one has the right to take your things away from you for no good reason.

Article 18. You have the right to believe the things you want to believe, to have ideas about right and wrong, and to believe in any religion you want. This includes the right to change your religion if you want, and to practice it without anybody interfering.

Article 19. You have the right to tell people how you feel about things without being told that you have to keep quiet. You have the right to read the newspaper of listen to the radio without someone trying to stop you, no matter where you live. Finally, you have the right to print your opinions in a newspaper or magazine, and send them anywhere without having someone try to stop you.

Article 20. *1.* You have the right to gather peacefully with people, and to be with anyone you want. *2.* No one can force you to join or belong to any group.

Article 21. *1.* You have the right to be part of your government by being in it, or choosing the people who are in fair elections. *2.* Everyone has the right to serve her or his country in some way. *3.* The first job of any government is to do what its people want it to do. This means you have the right to have elections every so often, where each person's vote counts the same, and where everyone's vote is his or her own business.

Article 22. Everyone, as a person on this planet, has the right to have her or his basic needs met, and should have whatever it takes to live with pride, and become the person he or she wants to be. Every country or group of countries should do everything they possibly can to make this happen.

Article 23. *1.* You have the right to work and to choose your job, to have fair and safe working conditions, and to be protected against not having to work. *2.* You have the right to the same pay as anyone else who does the same work, without anyone playing favorites. *3.* You have the right to decent pay so that you and your family can get by with pride. That means that if you don't get paid enough to do that, you should get other kinds of help. *4.* You have the right to form or be part of a union that will serve and protect your interests.

Article 24. Everyone has the right to rest and relaxation, which includes limiting the number of hours he or she has to work, and allowing for holidays with pay once in a while.

Article 25. You have the right to have what you need to live a decent life, including food, clothes, a home, and medical care for you and your family. You have the right to get help from society if you're sick or unable to work, or if you're older or a widow, or if you're in any other kind of situation that keeps you from working through no fault of your own.

Article 26. *1.* Everyone has the right to an education. It should be free of charge, and should be required for all, at least in the early years. Later education for jobs and college has to be there for anyone who wants it and is able to do it. *2.* The idea of education is to help people become the best they can be. It should teach them to respect and understand each other, and to be kind to everyone, no matter who they are or where they are from. Education should help to promote the activities of the United Nations in an effort to create a peaceful world.

Article 27. *1.* You have the right to join in and be part of the world of art, music, and books. You have the right to enjoy the arts, and to share in the advantages that come from new discoveries in the sciences. *2.* You have the right to get the credit and any profit that comes from something that you have written, made, or discovered.

Article 28. Everyone has the right to the kind of world where their rights and freedoms, such as the ones in this statement, are respected and made to happen.

Article 29. *1.* You have a responsibility to the place you live and the people around you—we all do. Only by watching out for each other can we each become our individual best. *2.* In order to be free, there have to be laws and limits that respect everyone's rights, meet our sense of right and wrong, and keep the peace in a world where we all play an active part. *3.* Nobody should use her or his freedom to go against what the United Nations is all about.

Article 30. There is nothing in this statement that says that anybody has the right to do anything that would weaken or take away these rights.

INDEX